# ELITE WEAPONS FOR LEGO FANATICS

Skyhorse Publishing books may be purchased in bulk at special discounts for sales promotion, corporate gifts, fund-raising, or educational purposes. Special editions can also be created to specifications. For details, contact the Special Sales Department, Skyhorse Publishing, 307 West 36th Street, 11th Floor, New York, NY 10018 or info@skyhorsepublishing.com.

Skyhorse® and Skyhorse Publishing® are registered trademarks of Skyhorse Publishing, Inc.®, a Delaware corporation.

Visit our website at www.skyhorsepublishing.com.

10 9 8 7 6 5 4 3 2 1

Library of Congress Cataloging-in-Publication Data is available on file.

Print ISBN: 978-1-63220-506-3
Ebook ISBN: 978-1-63220-885-9

Printed in the United States of America

Thanks to Birgit Fischer, Mona Schütze, Katharina Mahrt, Dorothea Mahrt, Moritz Herda, Chris Bothge, Olli Wesnigk, Ulrik Pilegaard, Nathanael Kuipers, and to my supporting fans!

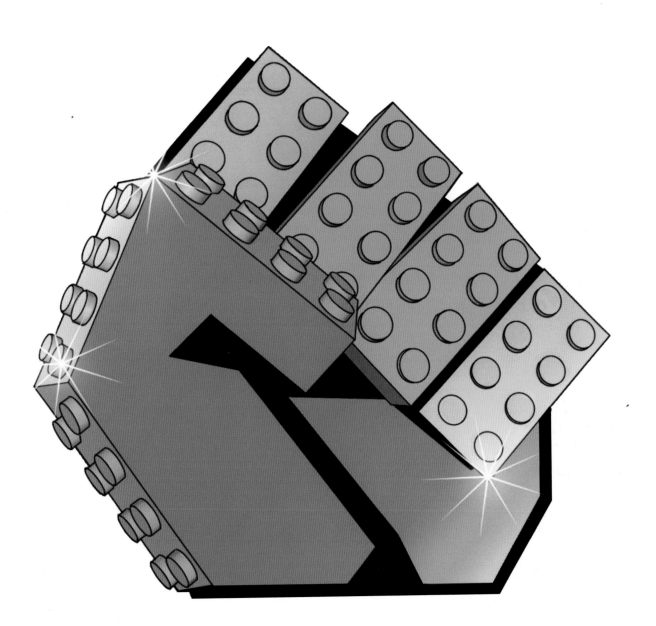

# ELITE WEAPONS FOR LEGO FANATICS

## Build Working Handcuffs, Body Armor, Batons, Sunglasses, and the World's Hardest Hitting Brick Guns

Martin Hüdepohl

**Photography: Rike Gössel**
**Photo Model: Roxanna Maurer**

Skyhorse Publishing

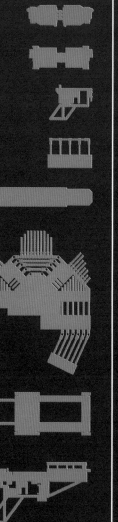

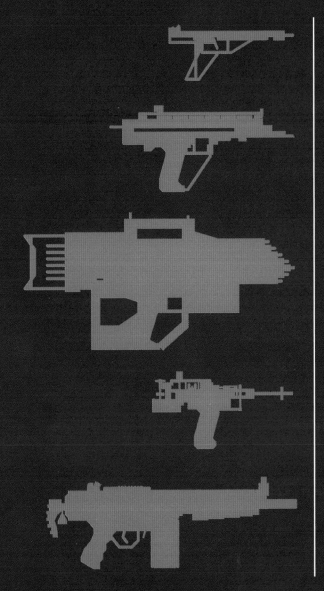

# CONTENTS

# PREFACE

# The World of Weapons

A wise man once said: "The most powerful weapon on earth is the human soul on fire."

Well, that might be the case—on earth. On the LEGO planets, in the infamous sectors of the Milky Way, other rules prevail. The human soul does not need to be on fire there in order to win the war—just the enemy. For this, of course, you need the right tools. But the quote is also mistaken when it postulates "the most powerful weapon." There is no such thing. How powerful a weapon is always depends on the situation. You know, a fusion bomb in your backpack is pretty useless when a pesky alien already has its slimy claw on your throat. That's the reason why galactic scouts like me are equipped with the book you're currently holding in your hands, *Elite Weapons for LEGO Fanatics*. It contains all the weapons you need in all situations you can think of.

While the HITMAN gives you an edge in hand-to-hand fights, the HAMMERHEAD crossbows are perfect for long-distance exterminations. While the NICE-1, a pocket-size pistol, is the choice for covert operations, the gigantic DINOSAUR SUPERIOR is the right machine for mass destruction. Sometimes, it's the better choice to take an enemy prisoner rather than to take him down. Even for this, the book has its respective model: the LOVELOCK.

Throughout the following pages you'll learn how to build the most sophisticated, most powerful weapons in the LEGO universe, and will learn how they once saved my hide . . . back in the days of my mission on Pyrodoom-5.

Another wise man, Nelson Mandela, once said, "Education is the most powerful weapon, which you can use to change the world." This opinion I share—if you use this book for education!

# PART 1

UNIX TIME 3509568000
CMDR. Doublegood Alpha

Here it finally is. Pyrodoom-5. A big junk pile of a dreary hillbilly moon in maybe the most frustrating sector of the Milky Way. And at the same time: my home and my destiny for the next 7 pentades.

Eye protectors SPECTOR
—available in two sizes. Obviously the
perfect eyewear for this kind of radiation
exposure.

# SPECTOR

## ⊹ SPECS

| NAME | SPECTOR |
|---|---|
| TYPE | Sunglasses |
| PARTS | 70 |
| SIZE | 6.7" x 6.6" x 2.0" |
| SKILL LEVEL | Novice |

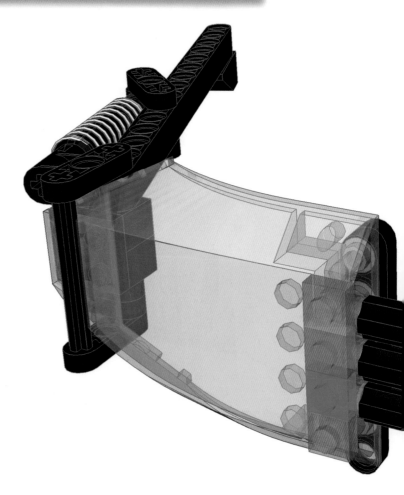

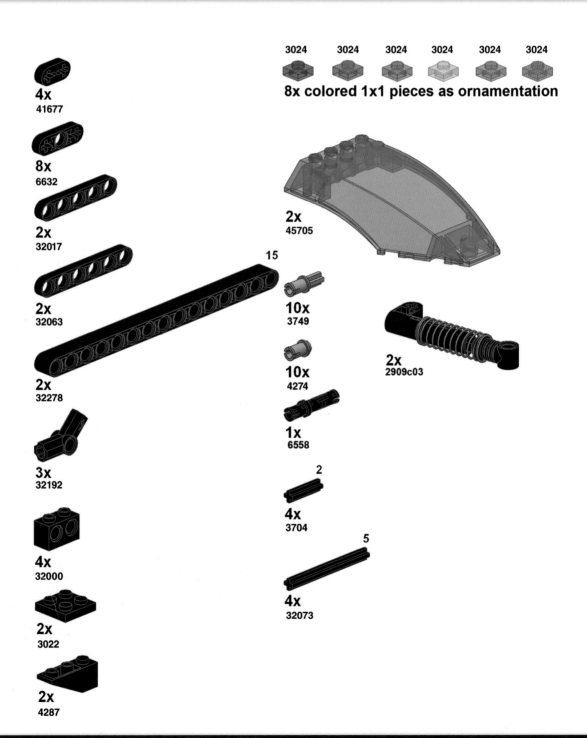

3024 3024 3024 3024 3024 3024

**8x colored 1x1 pieces as ornamentation**

**4x**
41677

**8x**
6632

**2x**
32017

**2x**
32063

**2x**
32278

15

**2x**
45705

**3x**
32192

**10x**
3749

**10x**
4274

**2x**
2909c03

**1x**
6558

**4x**
32000

2

**4x**
3704

5

**2x**
3022

**4x**
32073

**2x**
4287

**1**

 1x 3x 6x

**2**

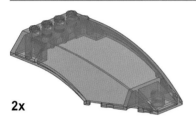 2x

**3**

 10x 2x

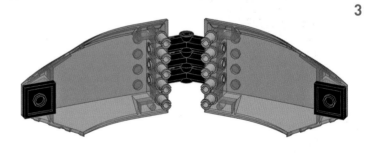

**4**

 4x 2x 2x 4x

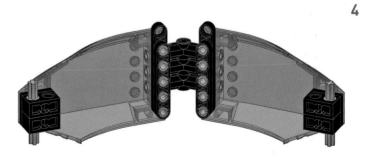

15

5

4x

4x

2x

4x

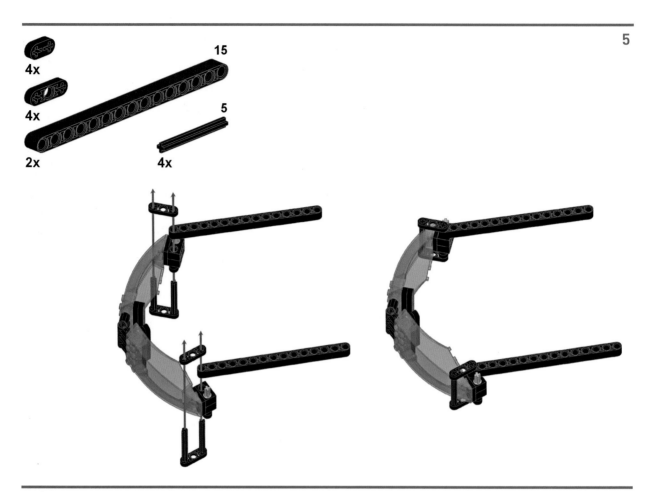

2

4x

4x

2x

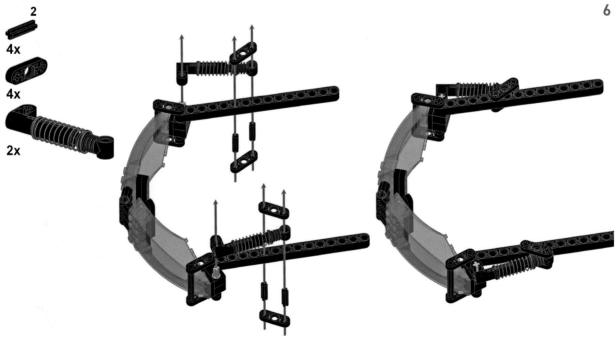

2x

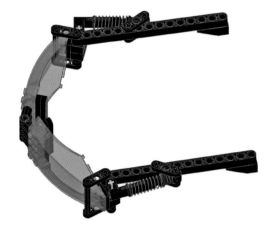

2x  2x  3x  1x

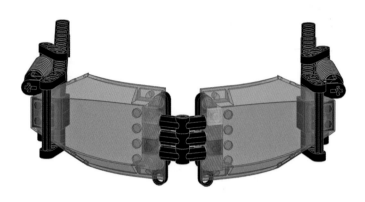

# SPECTOR JR

✛ SPECS

| NAME | SPECTOR Junior |
|---|---|
| TYPE | Sunglasses for kids |
| PARTS | 60 |
| SIZE | 5.5" x 6.3" x 2.2" |
| SKILL LEVEL | Novice |

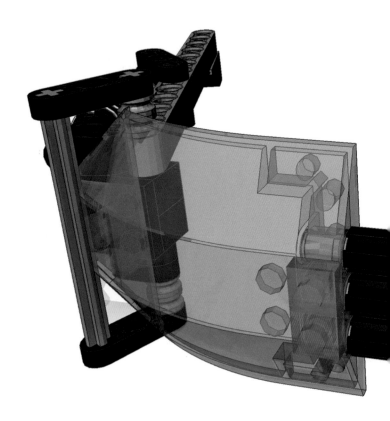

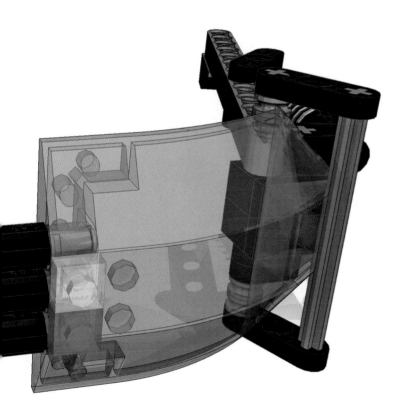

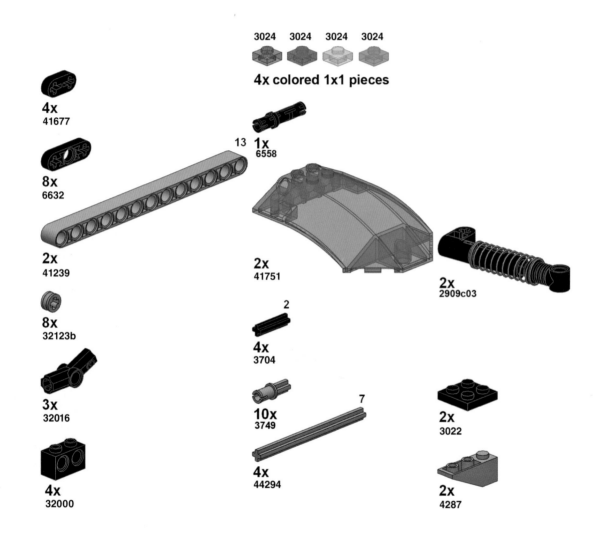

3024 3024 3024 3024

**4x colored 1x1 pieces**

**4x**
41677

**8x**
6632

13

**1x**
6558

**2x**
41239

**2x**
41751

**2x**
2909c03

**8x**
32123b

2

**4x**
3704

**3x**
32016

**10x**
3749

7

**2x**
3022

**4x**
32000

**4x**
44294

**2x**
4287

# BUILDING INSTRUCTIONS

**1**

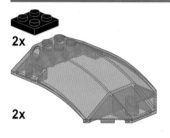 3x 1x 6x

**2**

 2x

2x

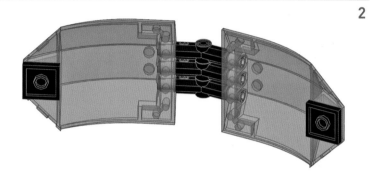

**3**

 4x

4x

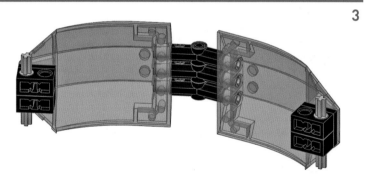

**4**

4x

7

2x

4x 4x

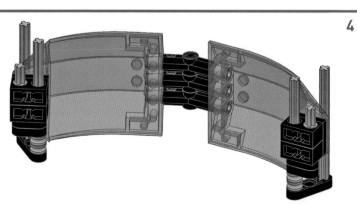

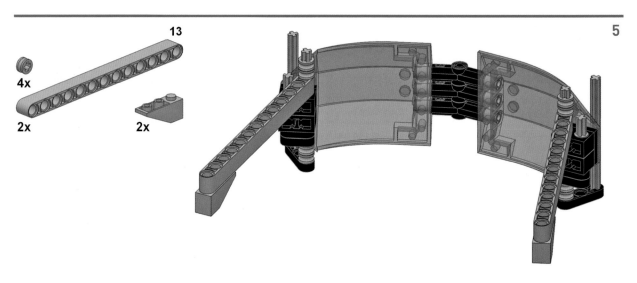

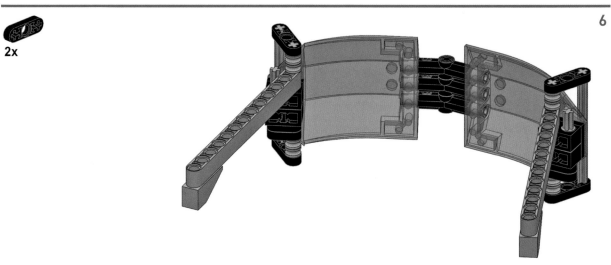

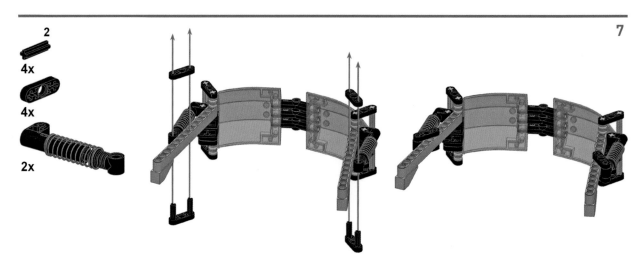

1x   1x   2x

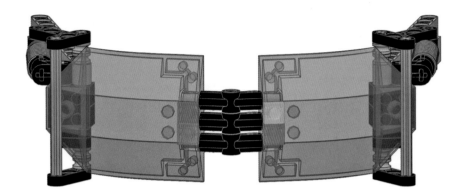

# PART 2

# NICE-1

| ⌖SPECS | |
|---|---|
| **NAME** | NICE-1 |
| **TYPE** | Single shot micro pistol |
| **PARTS** | 99 |
| **SIZE** | 4.3" x 1.1" x 3.4" |
| **SKILL LEVEL** | Novice |

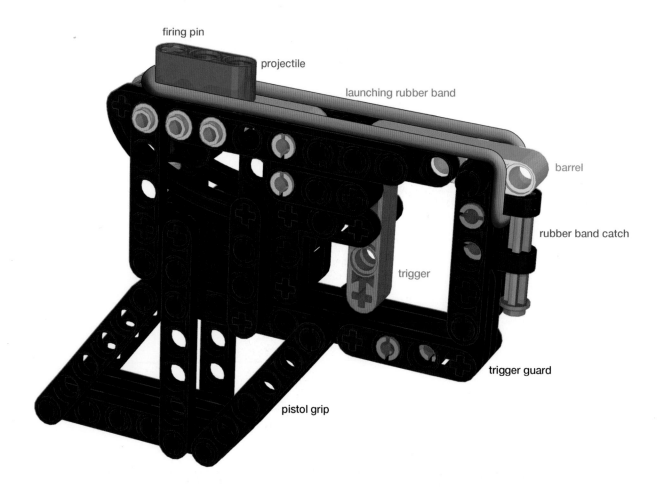

firing pin

projectile

launching rubber band

barrel

rubber band catch

trigger

trigger guard

pistol grip

**The Nice-1 is extremely compact . . .**

**. . . and it can also launch nearly any projectile.**

# HOW IT WORKS

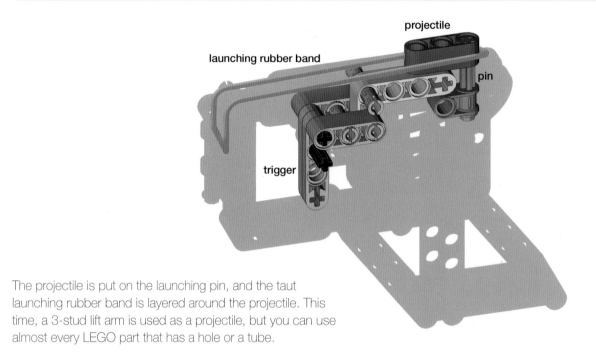

The projectile is put on the launching pin, and the taut launching rubber band is layered around the projectile. This time, a 3-stud lift arm is used as a projectile, but you can use almost every LEGO part that has a hole or a tube.

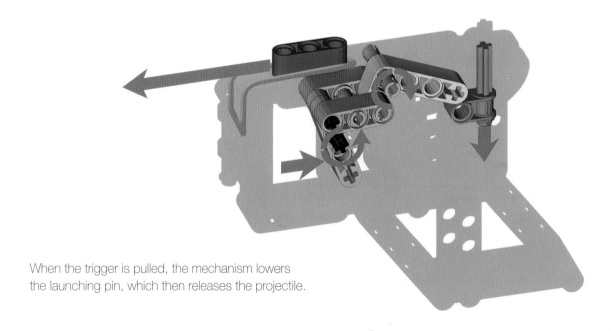

When the trigger is pulled, the mechanism lowers the launching pin, which then releases the projectile.

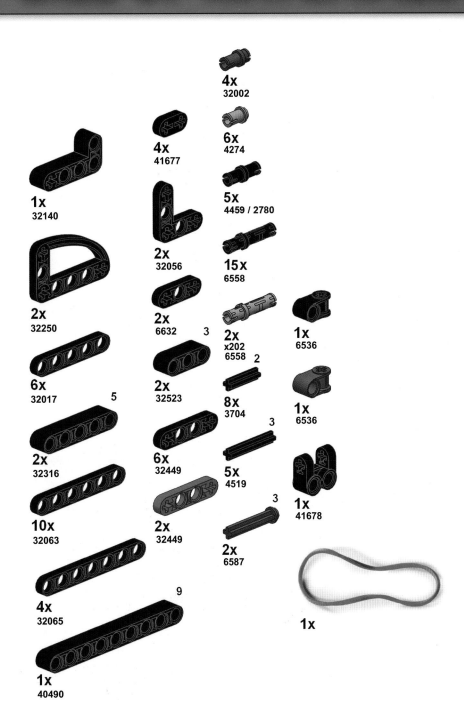

**4x**
32002

**6x**
4274

**4x**
41677

**5x**
4459 / 2780

**1x**
32140

**2x**
32056

**15x**
6558

**2x**
32250

**2x**
6632

3

**2x**
x202
6558

**1x**
6536

**6x**
32017

5

**2x**
32523

2

**8x**
3704

**1x**
6536

**2x**
32316

**6x**
32449

3

**5x**
4519

**1x**
41678

**10x**
32063

**2x**
32449

3

**2x**
6587

**4x**
32065

9

**1x**

**1x**
40490

**1**

1x
1x
3x
3x
2x
1x

**2**

3
2
1x 1x 1x 1x

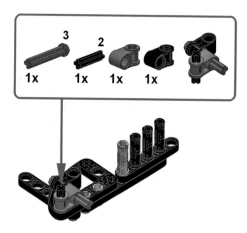

**3**

1x 3
3x
4x
2x
1x

4x 2
3x
5
2x

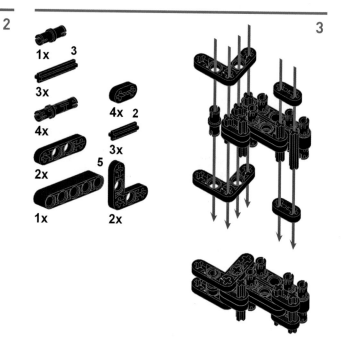

**4**

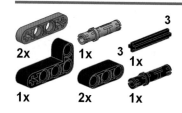

2x
1x
1x
3
3
1x
2x
1x

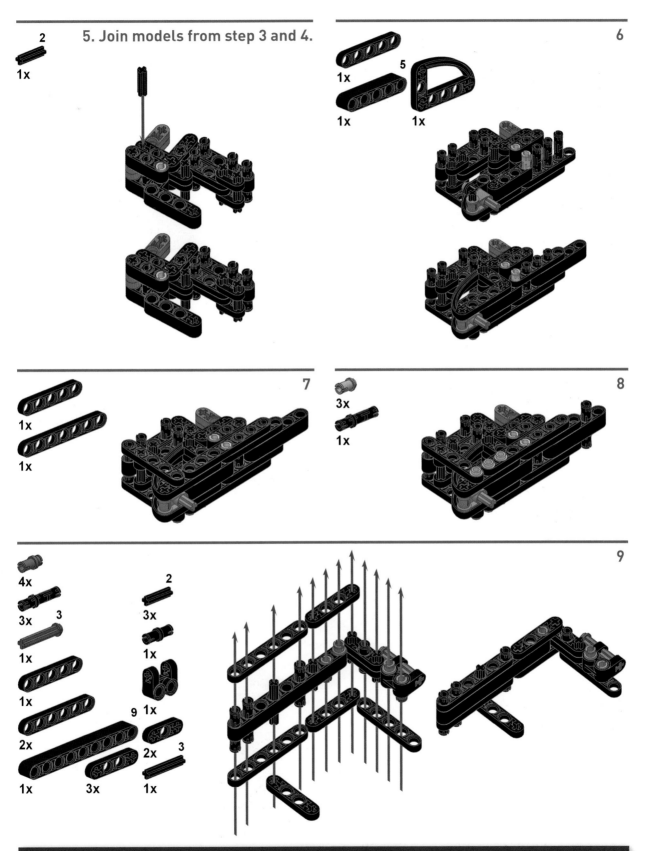

**5. Join models from step 3 and 4.**

2
1x

6
1x
1x
5
1x

7
1x
1x

8
3x
1x

9
4x
3x 3
1x
1x
2x
1x
3x
2
3x
1x
1x
9 1x
2x 3
1x

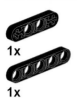
1x

1x

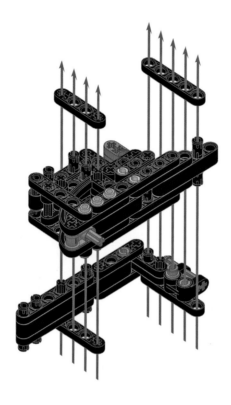

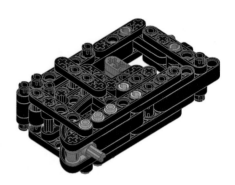

4x

3x

3x

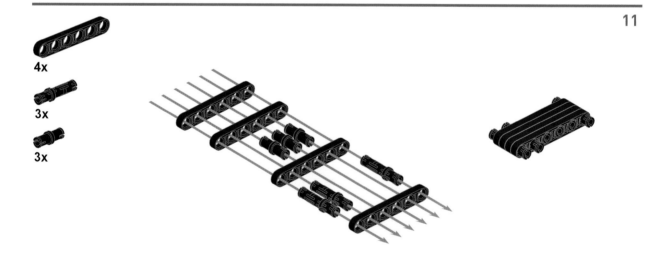

4x

2x

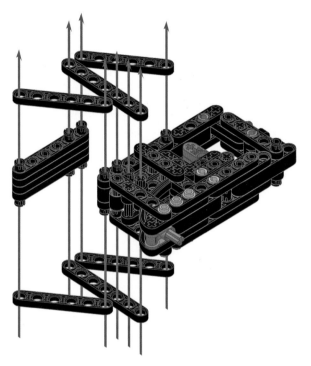

# HOW IT'S LOADED

Hook the rubber band into the rubber band catch and close it.

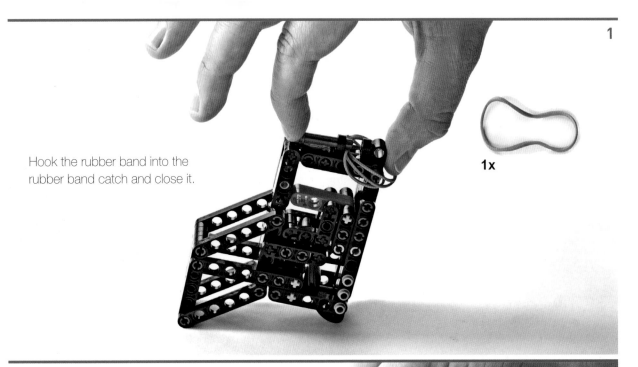

1x

Push up the launching pin and position the projectile on it.

Pull the rubber band back and
hook it around the projectile.

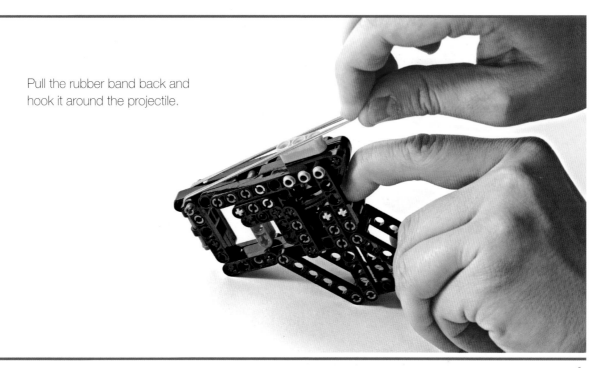

# The NICE-1 is ready to fire!

# PART 3

# HITMAN

| ⊹ SPECS | |
|---|---|
| NAME | HITMAN |
| TYPE | Plastic knuckles |
| PARTS | 40 |
| SIZE | 2.8" x 4.4" x 0.8" |
| SKILL LEVEL | Beginner |

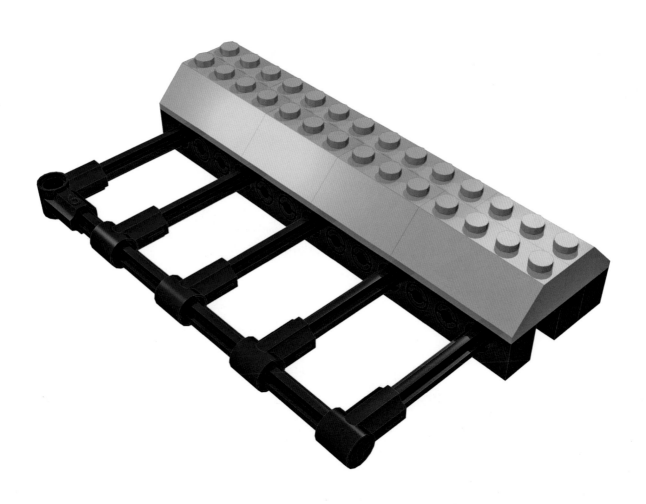

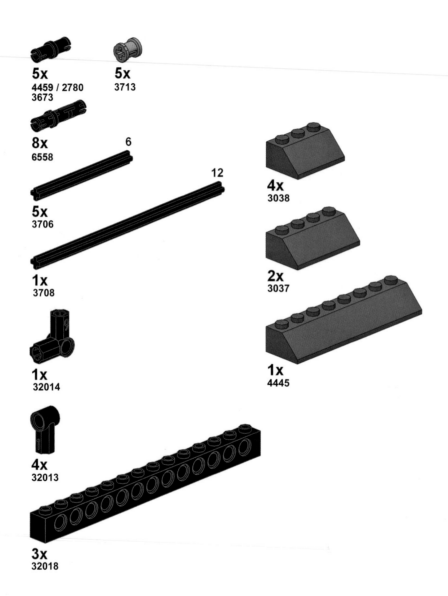

**5x**
4459 / 2780
3673

**5x**
3713

**8x**
6558

6

**5x**
3706

12

**4x**
3038

**1x**
3708

**2x**
3037

**1x**
32014

**1x**
4445

**4x**
32013

**3x**
32018

# BUILDING INSTRUCTIONS

### 1

5x

1x

8x

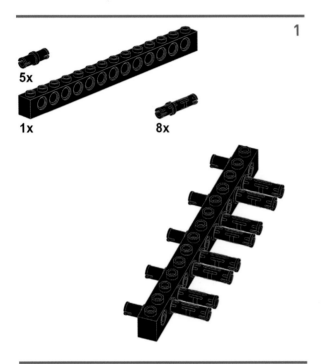

### 2

4x

1x

6

5x

5x

12

1x

1x

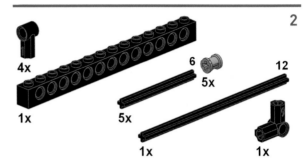

### 3. Combine models from steps 1 and 2.

1x

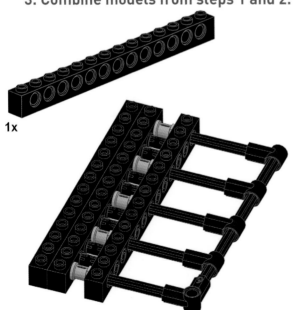

### 4

4x

2x

1x

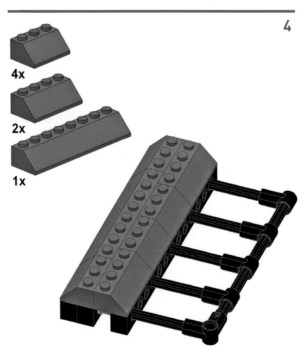

# PART 4

Feels solid and seems to pack a lot of punch! But this time I better not rely on the small version. Let's see what else the manual has to offer ...

# KLOPSTOCK

| ✛ SPECS | |
|---|---|
| NAME | KLOPSTOCK |
| TYPE | Baton |
| PARTS | 206 |
| SIZE | 28.0" x 1.6" |
| SKILL LEVEL | Novice |

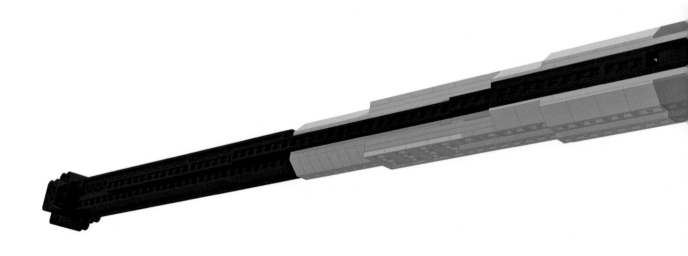

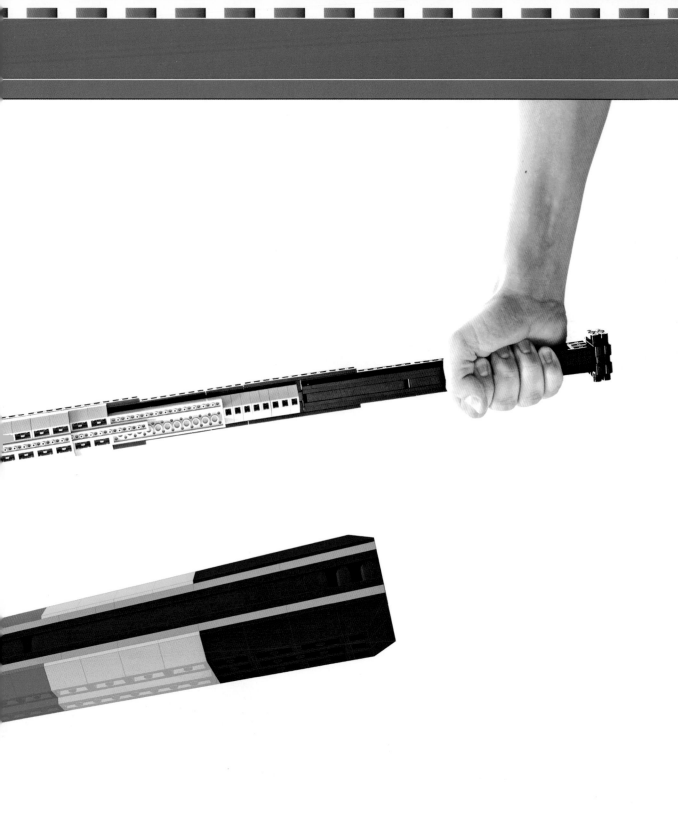

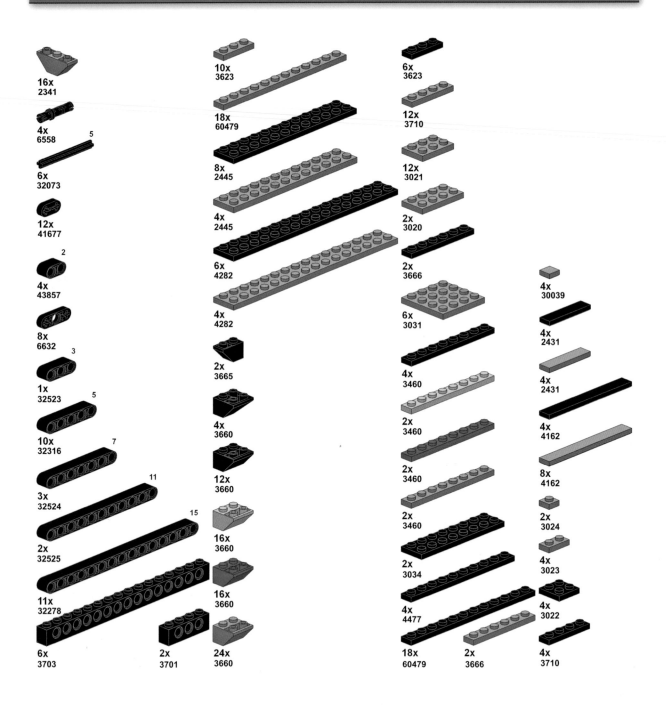

16x
2341

4x
6558

5

6x
32073

12x
41677

2

4x
43857

3

8x
6632

1x
32523

5

10x
32316

7

3x
32524

11

2x
32525

15

11x
32278

6x
3703

2x
3701

10x
3623

18x
60479

8x
2445

4x
2445

6x
4282

4x
4282

2x
3665

4x
3660

12x
3660

16x
3660

16x
3660

24x
3660

6x
3623

12x
3710

12x
3021

2x
3020

2x
3666

6x
3031

4x
3460

2x
3460

2x
3460

2x
3460

2x
3034

4x
4477

18x
60479

2x
3666

4x
30039

4x
2431

4x
2431

4x
4162

8x
4162

2x
3024

4x
3023

4x
3022

4x
3710

# BUILDING INSTRUCTIONS

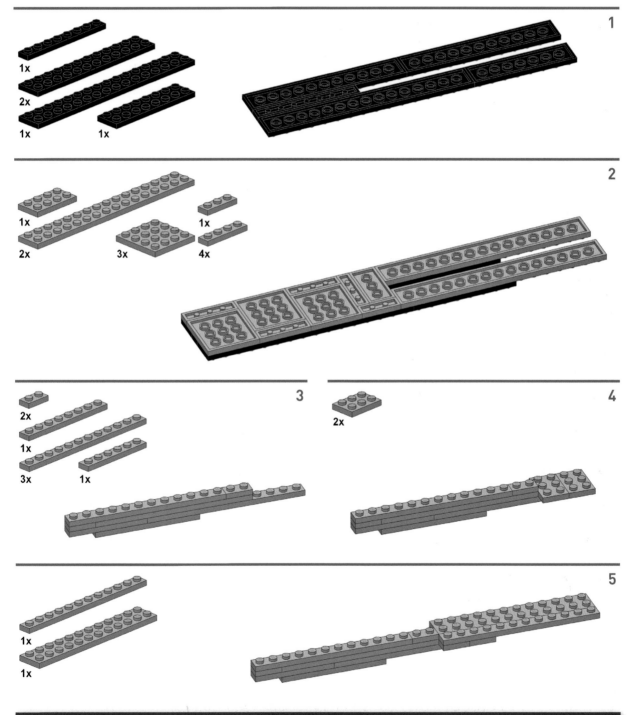

1

1x
2x
1x
1x

2

1x
2x
3x
1x
4x

3

2x
1x
3x
1x

4

2x

5

1x
1x

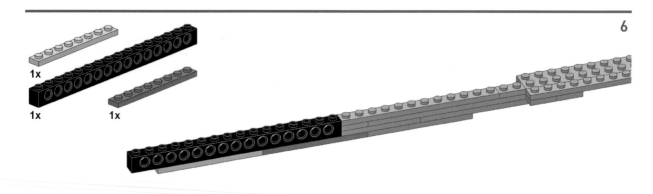

**1x**
**1x**
**1x**

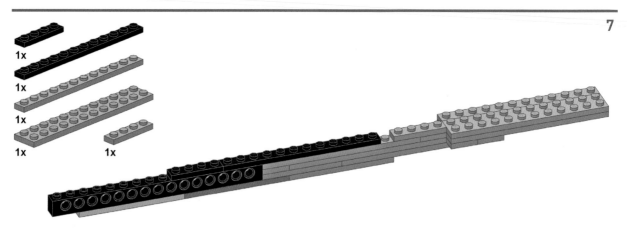

**1x**
**1x**
**1x**
**1x**
**1x**

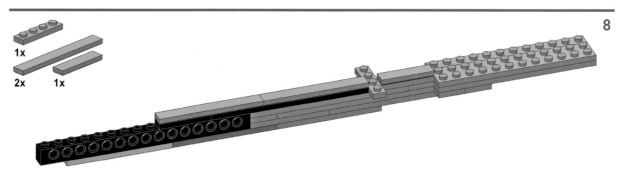

**1x**
**2x** **1x**

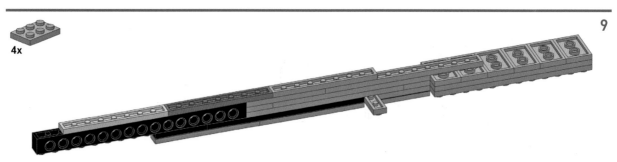

**4x**

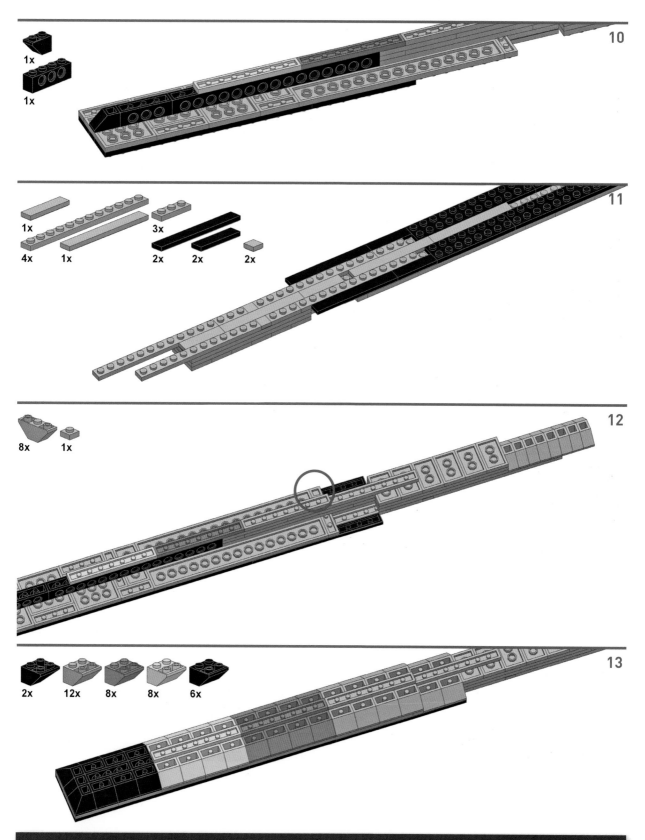

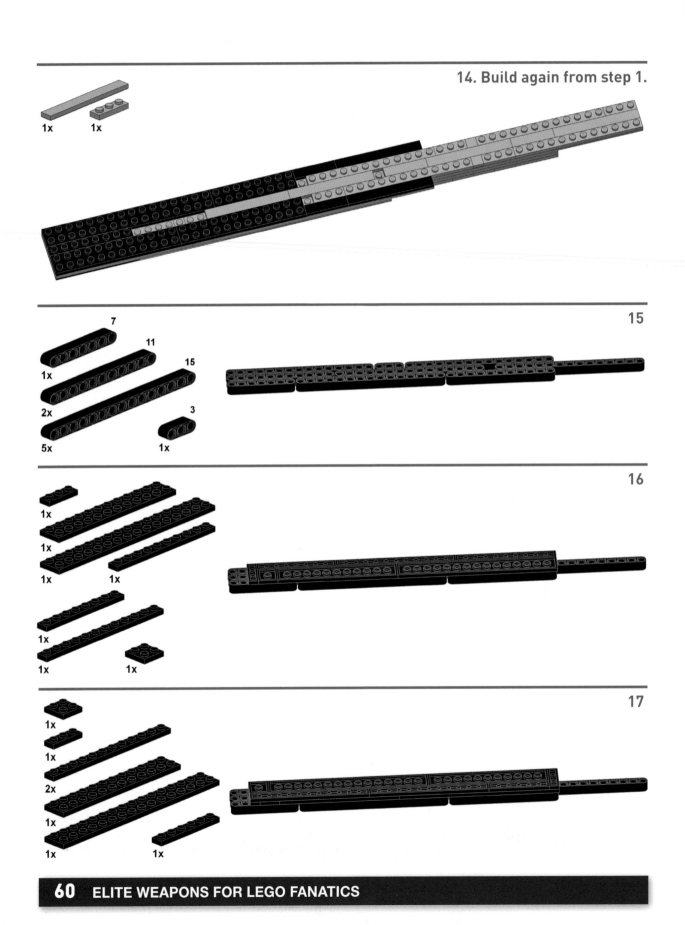

1x   1x

15

7
1x
11
2x
15
5x
3
1x

16

1x
1x
1x   1x
1x
1x   1x

17

1x
1x
2x
1x
1x   1x

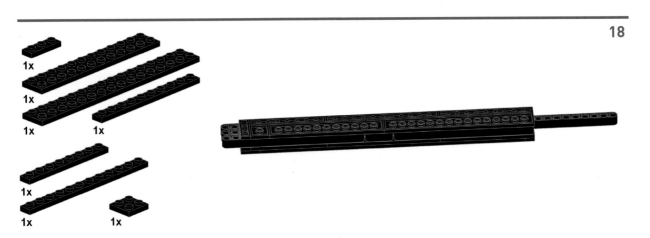

1x
1x
1x  1x
1x
1x  1x

6x  2
2x
4x
4x  5
6x  5
4x

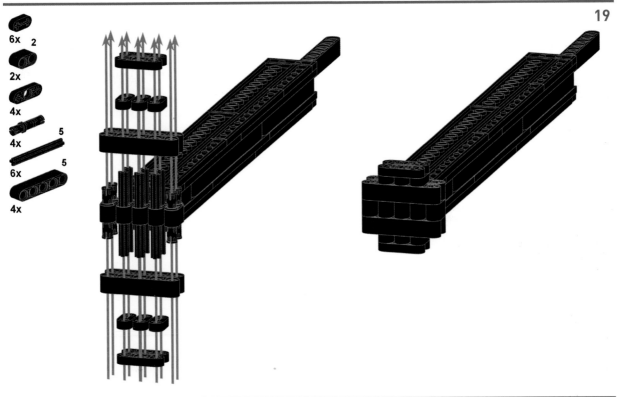

15
2x
4x

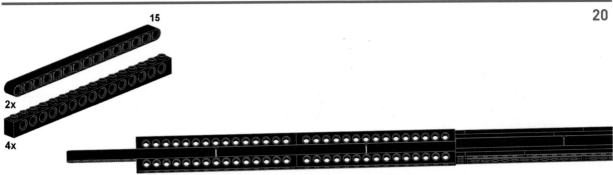

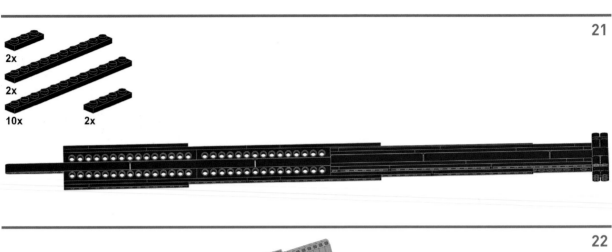

2x
2x
10x
2x

1x

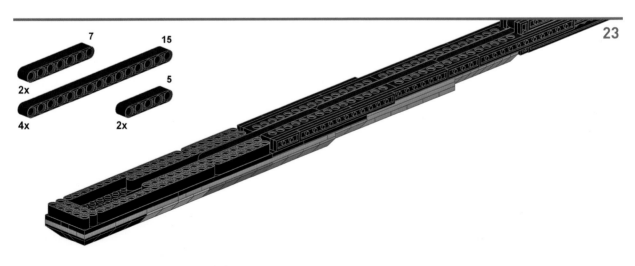

7
15
2x
4x
5
2x

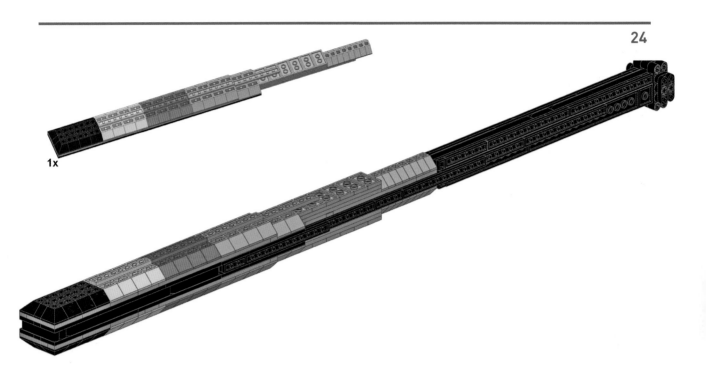

1x

# PART 5

It's perfectly balanced
and easy to wield.
The cold, hard plastic in my fist
gives me the feeling of unlimited power!
Time to do what galactic scouts always do
with dangerous species: knock them out
and take them prisoner. Let's see what
the KLOPSTOCK can do!

Finally, it pays off that I was the batter of our academy's spaceball team!

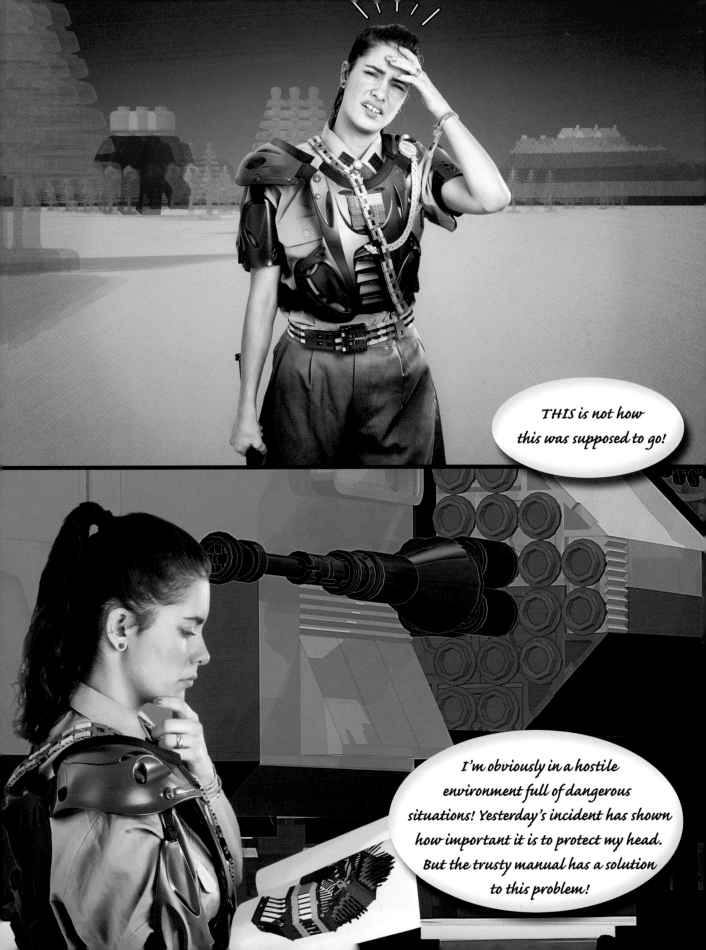

# PANZER POD

| SPECS | |
|---|---|
| **NAME** | **PANZER POD** |
| **TYPE** | **Combat Helmet** |
| **PARTS** | **908** |
| **SIZE** | **10.4" x 7.8" x 12.9"** |
| **SKILL LEVEL** | **Expert** |

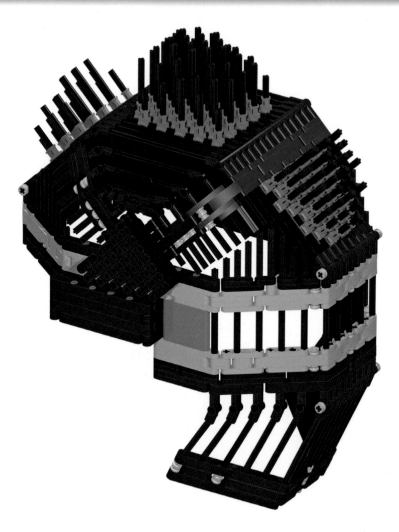

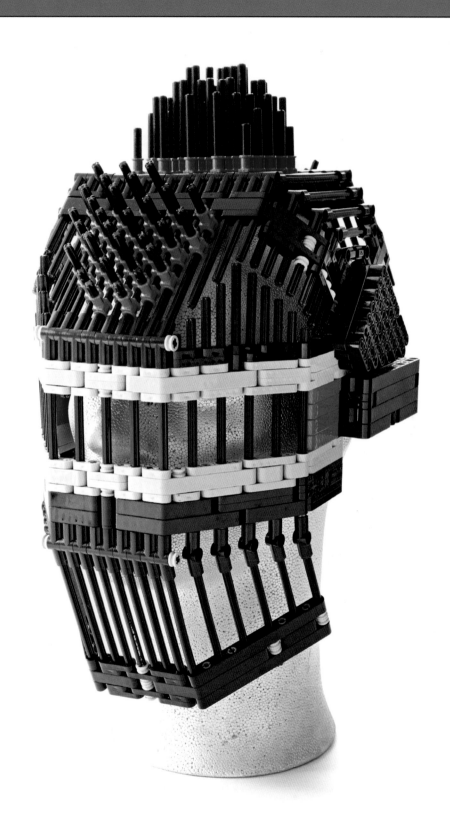

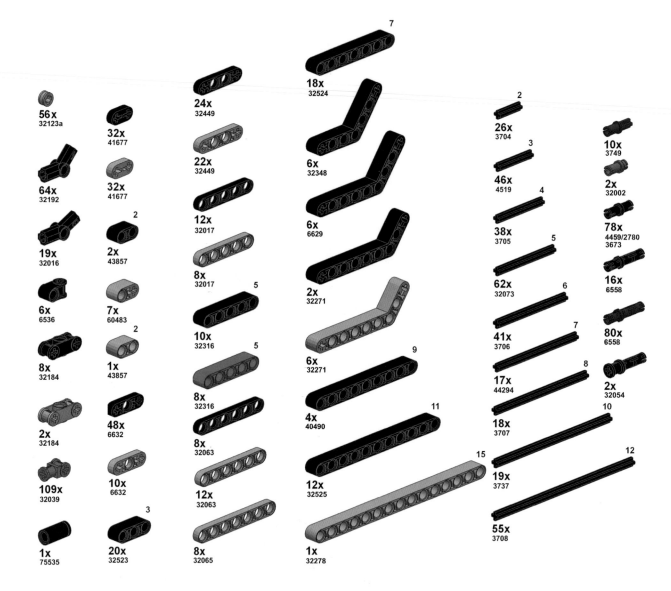

56x
32123a

32x
41677

64x
32192

32x
41677

19x
32016

2x
43857

6x
6536

7x
60483

8x
32184

1x
43857

2x
32184

48x
6632

109x
32039

10x
6632

1x
75535

20x
32523

24x
32449

22x
32449

12x
32017

8x
32017

10x
32316

8x
32316

8x
32063

12x
32063

8x
32065

18x
32524

6x
32348

6x
6629

2x
32271

6x
32271

4x
40490

12x
32525

1x
32278

26x
3704

46x
4519

38x
3705

62x
32073

41x
3706

17x
44294

18x
3707

19x
3737

55x
3708

10x
3749

2x
32002

78x
4459/2780
3673

16x
6558

80x
6558

2x
32054

**1**

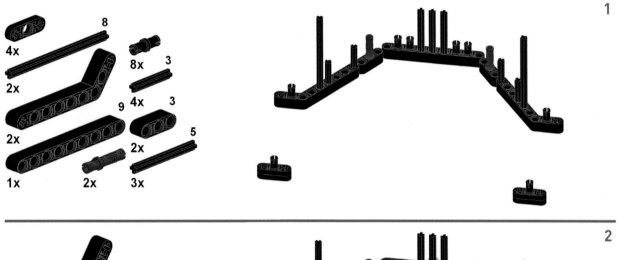

**2**

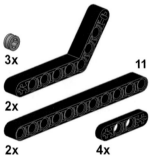

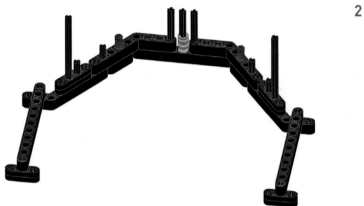

**3**

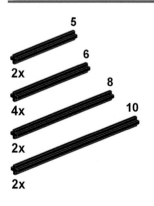

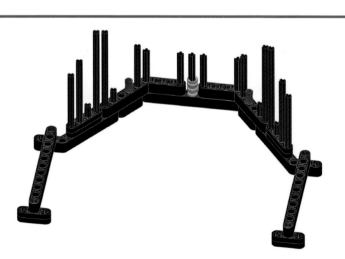

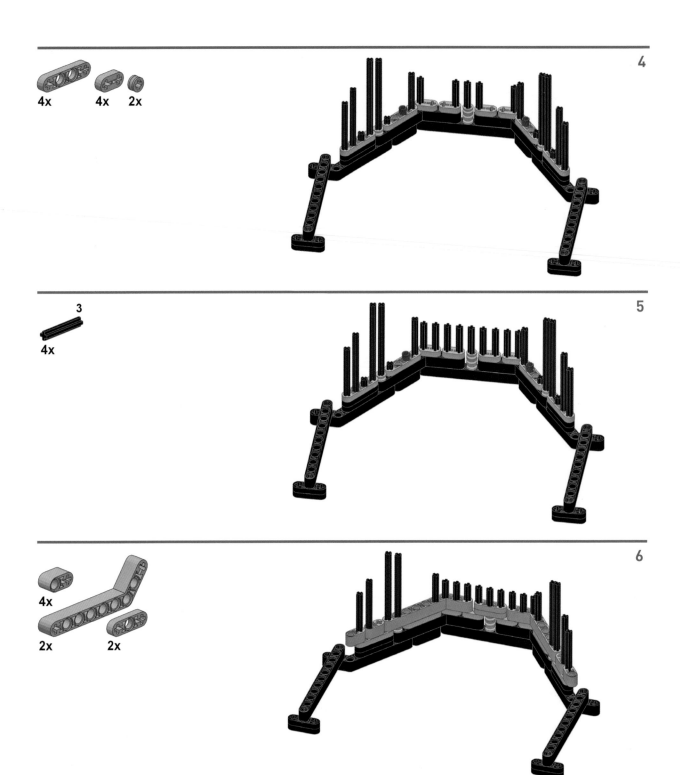

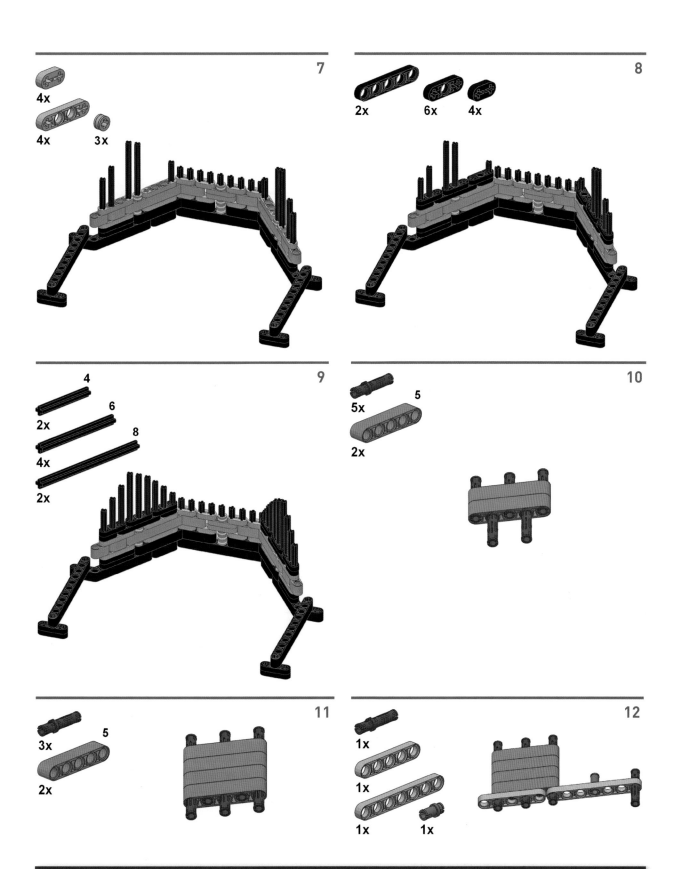

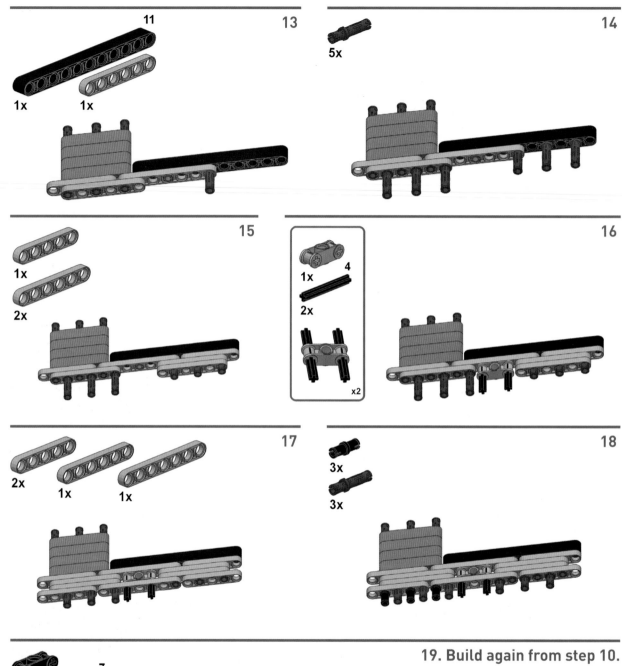

**13**

11
1x    1x

**14**

5x

**15**

1x
2x

**16**

1x    4
2x
x2

**17**

2x
1x    1x

**18**

3x
3x

7
1x
2x

## 19. Build again from step 10.

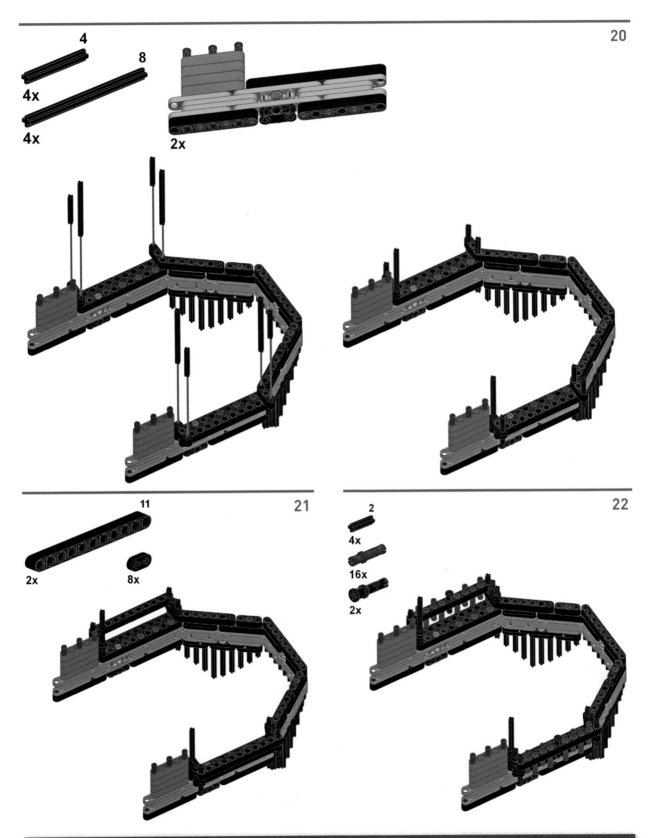

20

4
4x

8
4x

2x

21

11
2x

8x

22

2
4x

16x

2x

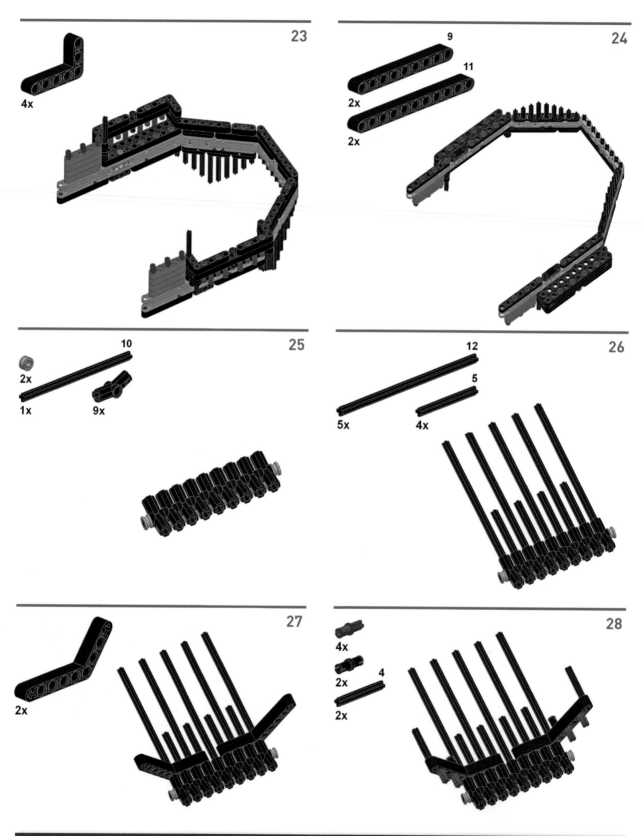

23

4x

24

9
2x

11
2x

25

2x
1x

10

9x

26

12
5x

5
4x

27

2x

28

4x

2x

4
2x

4x

2x

4

2x

2x

4x

2x

2x

5

2x

4x

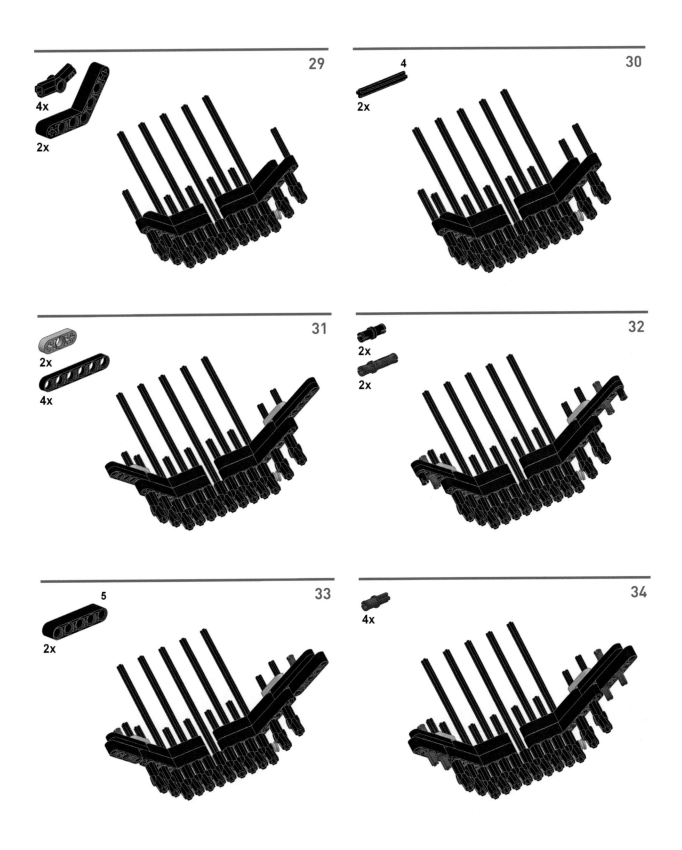

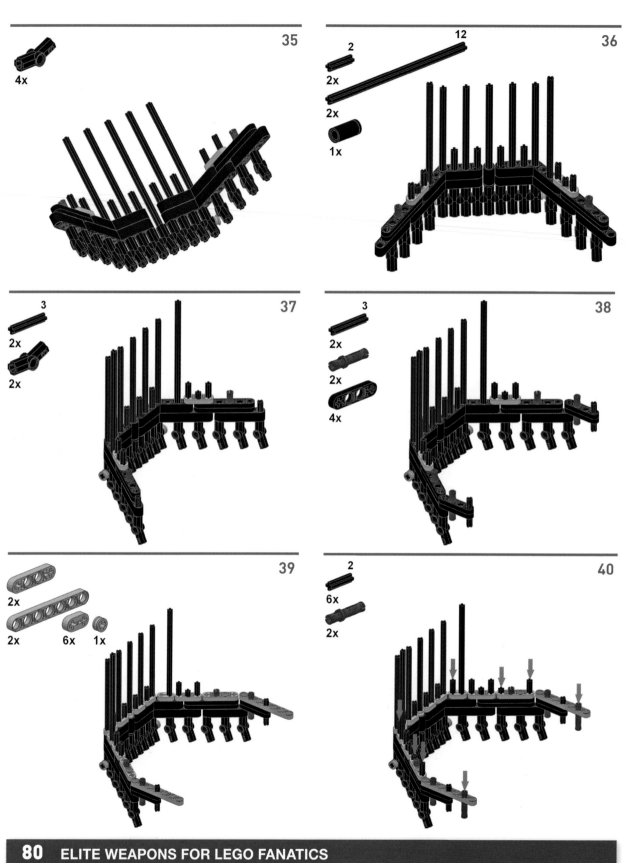

35

2x

4x

12

2

2x

2x

1x

36

3

2x

2x

37

3

2x

2x

4x

38

2x

2x

6x

1x

39

2

6x

2x

40

**41**

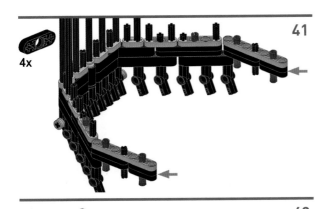

4x

**42**

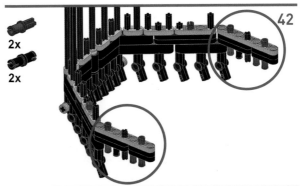

2x

2x

**43**

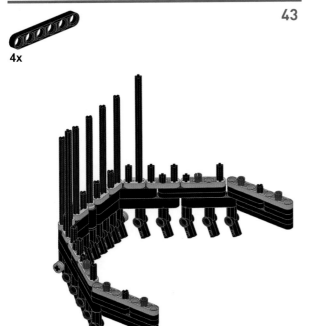

4x

**44**

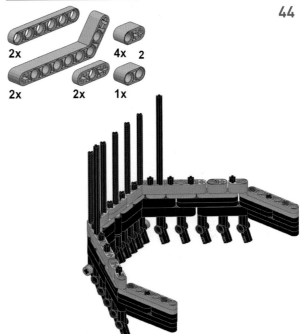

2x

2x

4x

2x

2

1x

**45**

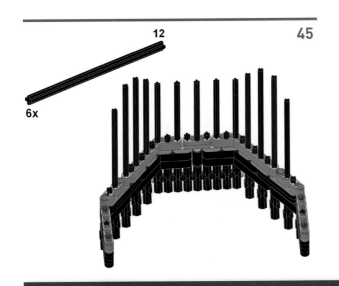

12

6x

**46**

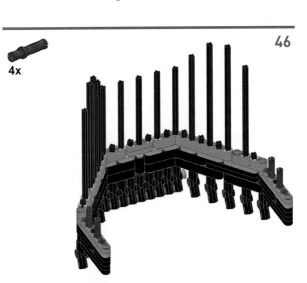

4x

**47**

2x
2x

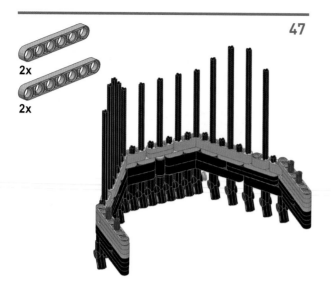

**48**

4x
4x
2x
1x

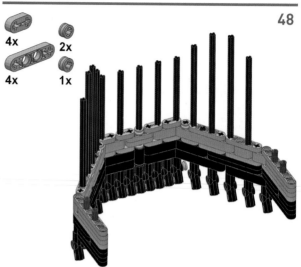

**49**

2x
2x
1x
6x

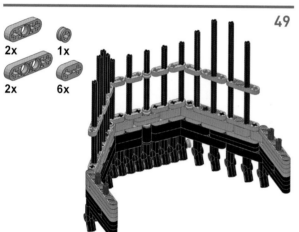

**50**

4x
2x
2x

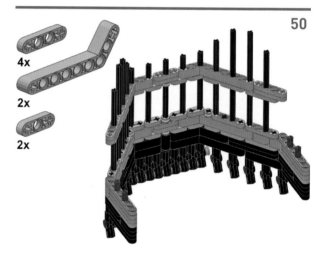

**51**

3
4x
4
2x
5
2x
6
4x
7
2x

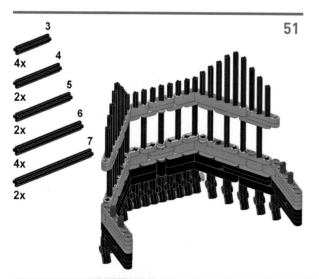

**52**

2x
8x
1x

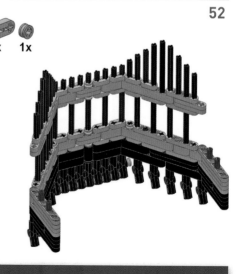

**53**

**4x**

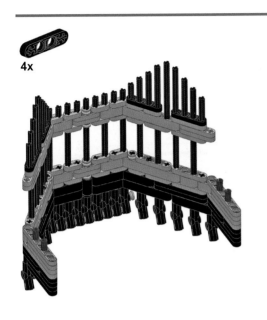

**54**

**15**

**1x**

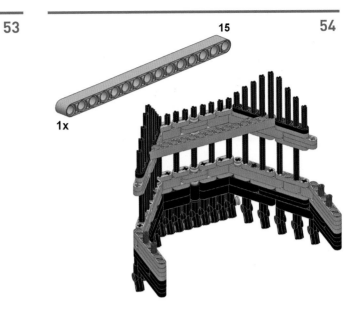

**55**

**2x**    **6x**

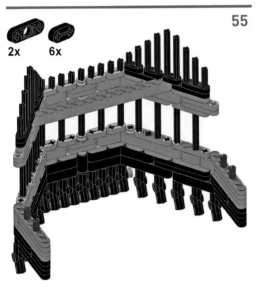

**56**

**8**

**10**

**12**

**4x**

**6x**

**9x**

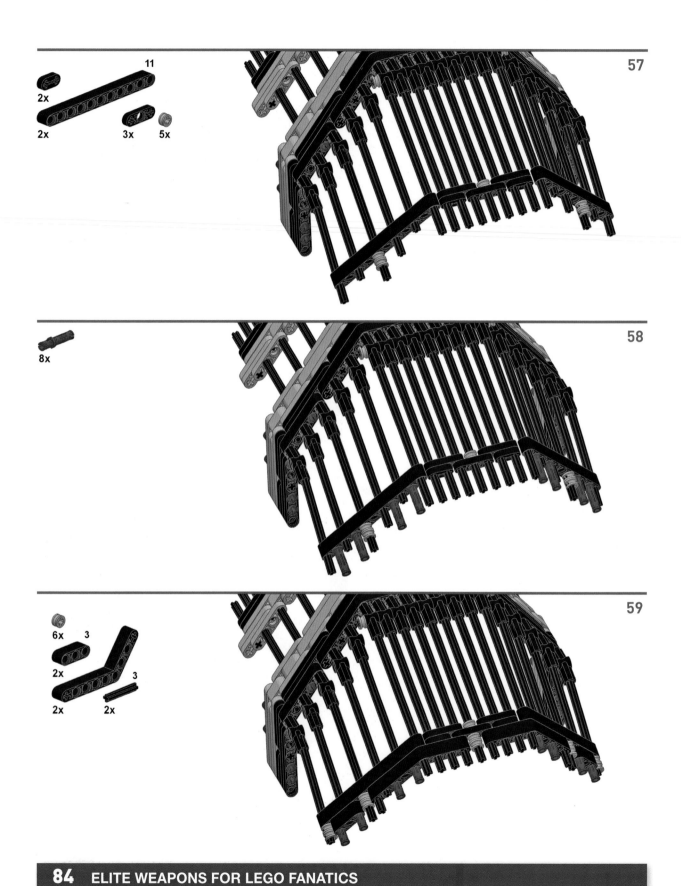

**11**

2x

2x    3x    1x

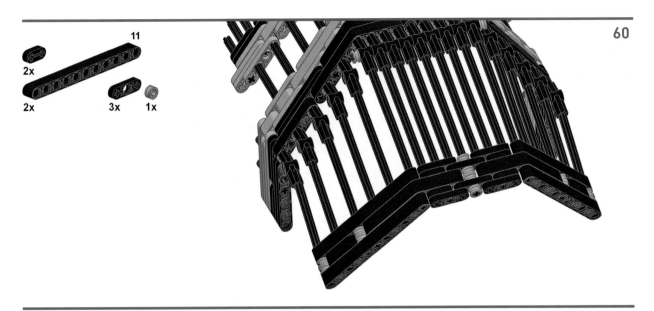

**10**

2x

1x

1x

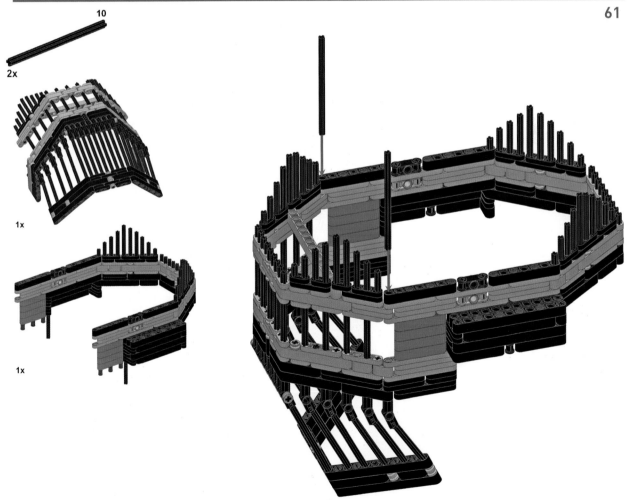

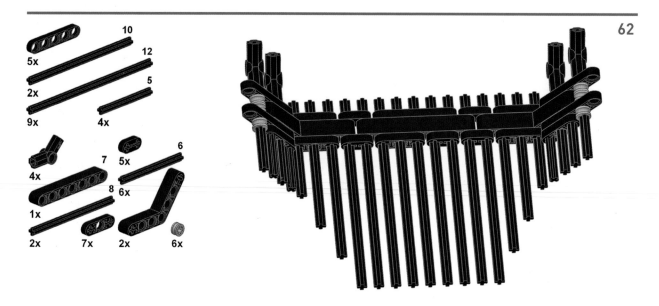

5x 10
2x 12
9x 5
4x

4x
7 5x 6
1x 8 6x
2x 7x 2x 6x

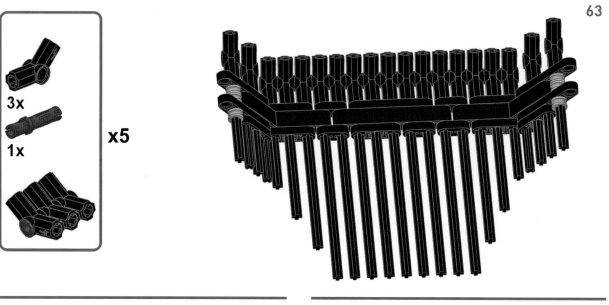

3x
1x
x5

1x 6
1x 2x 2
2x 7
1x 5
1x 3x 2x 2x

1x 6
2x 1x
2x 7
1x 5
2x 3
1x 3x 2x 1x

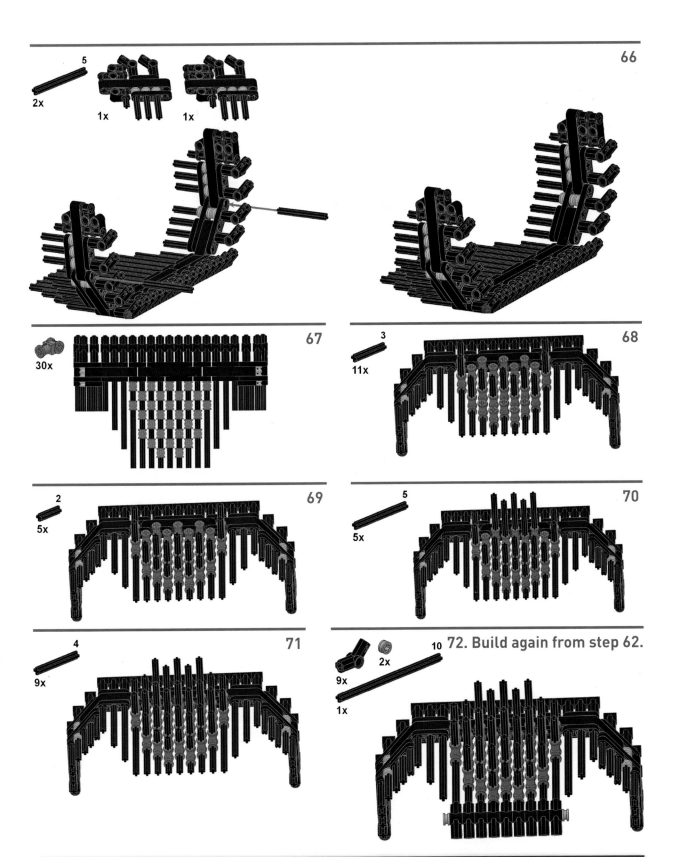

66

5
2x

1x     1x

67

30x

68

3
11x

69

2
5x

70

5
5x

71

4
9x

72. Build again from step 62.

10

2x

9x

1x

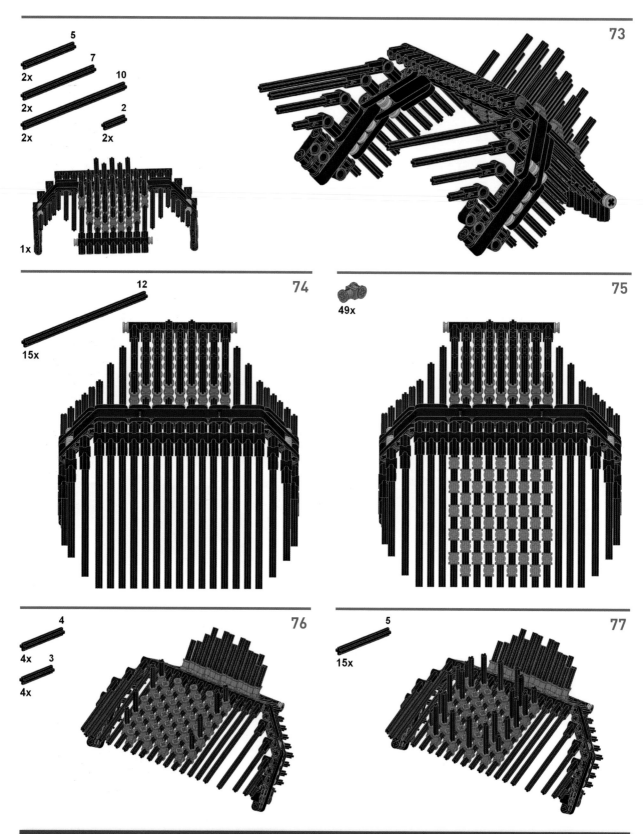

73

5
2x

7
2x

10
2x

2
2x

1x

74
12
15x

75
49x

76
4
4x

3
4x

77
5
15x

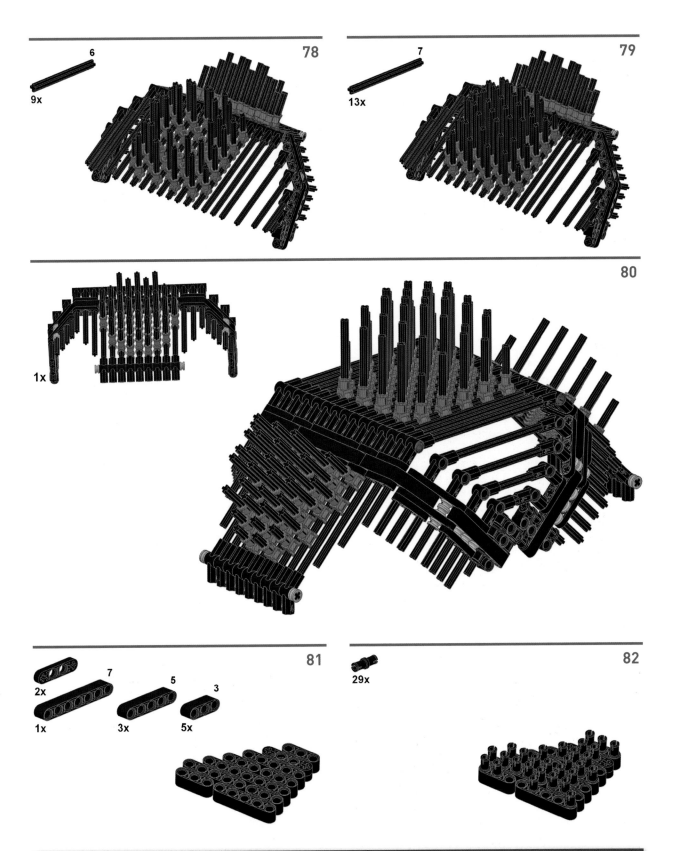

**78**

6
9x

**79**

7
13x

**80**

1x

**81**

7
2x
1x

5
3x

3
5x

**82**

29x

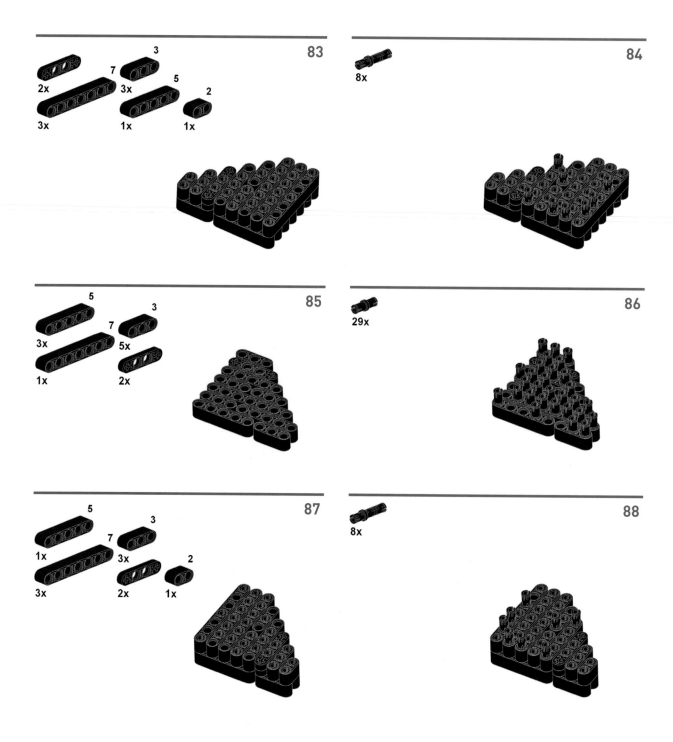

**83**

3
7
2x
3x
5
3x
1x
2
1x

**84**

8x

**85**

5
3x
7
1x
5x
3
2x

**86**

29x

**87**

5
1x
7
3x
3x
3
2x
2
1x

**88**

8x

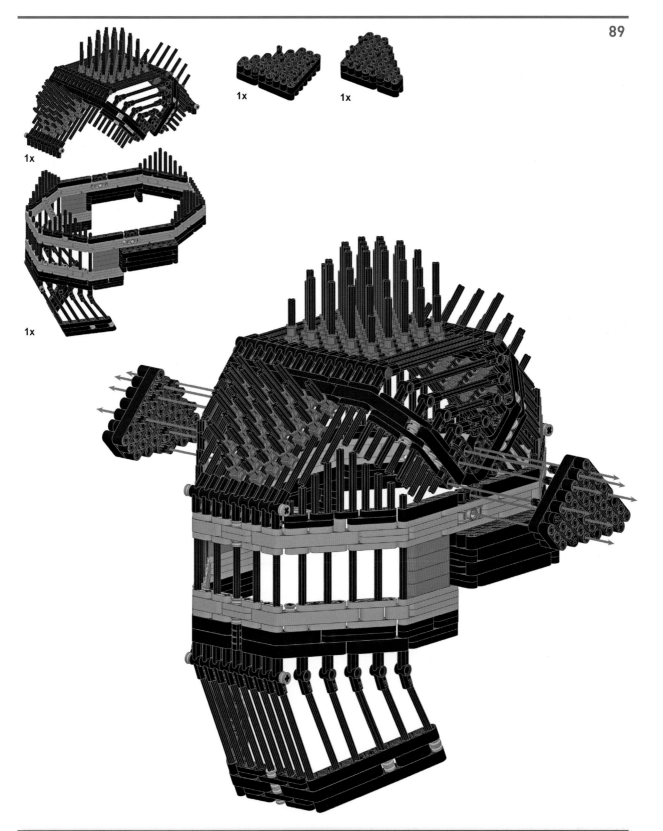

1x

1x

1x

1x

# PART 6

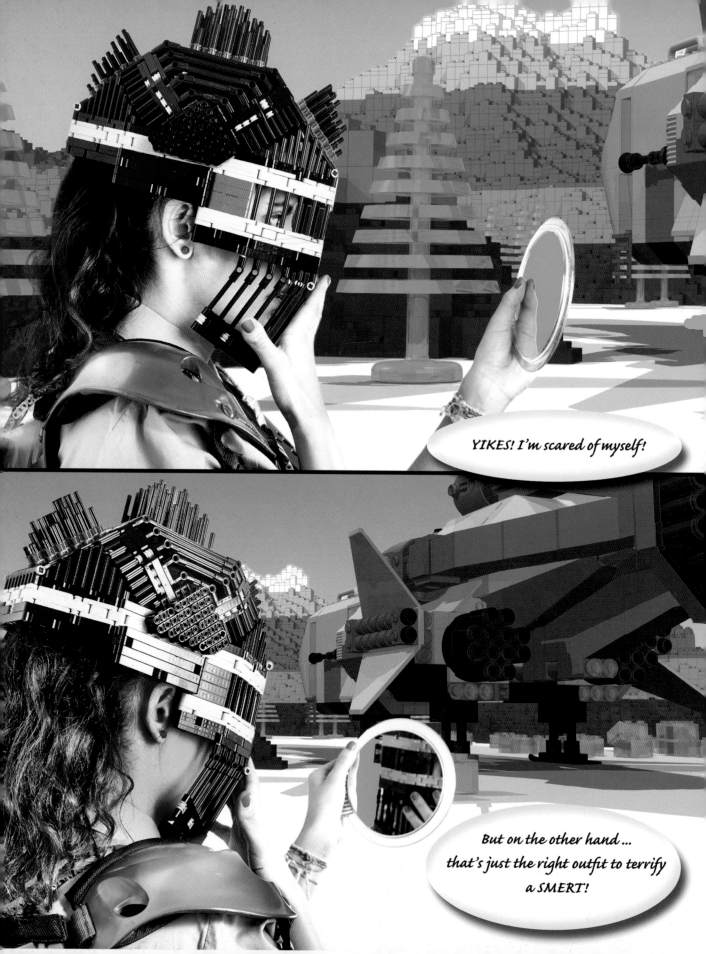

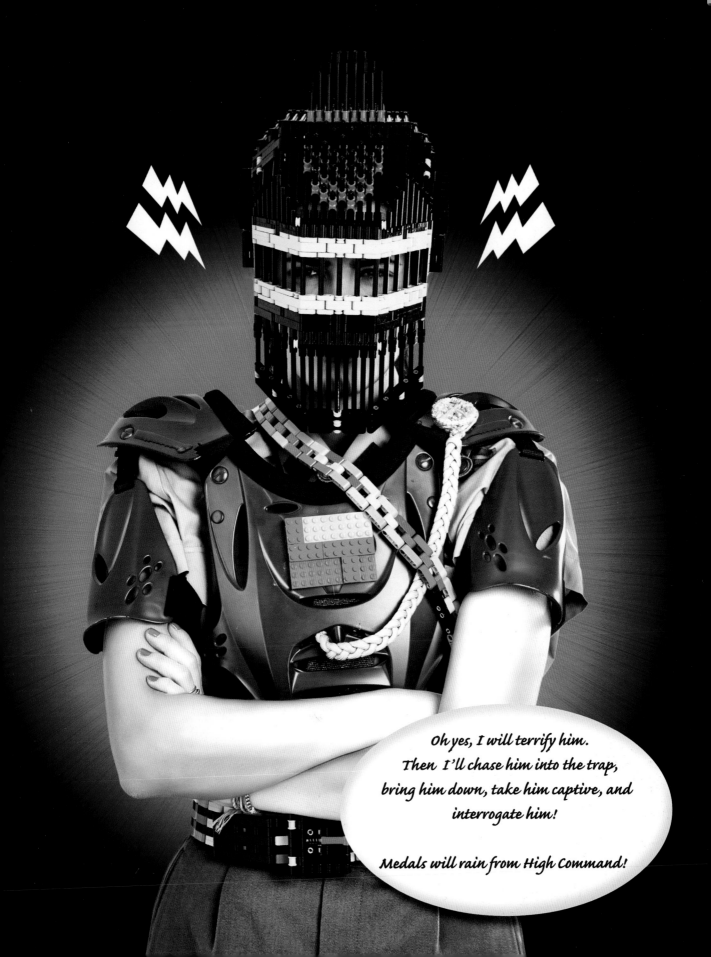

# LOVELOCK

| | SPECS |
|---|---|
| **NAME** | **LOVELOCK** |
| **TYPE** | **Handcuffs** |
| **PARTS** | **334** |
| **SIZE** | **12.3" x 2.1" x 5.9"** |
| **SKILL LEVEL** | **Expert** |

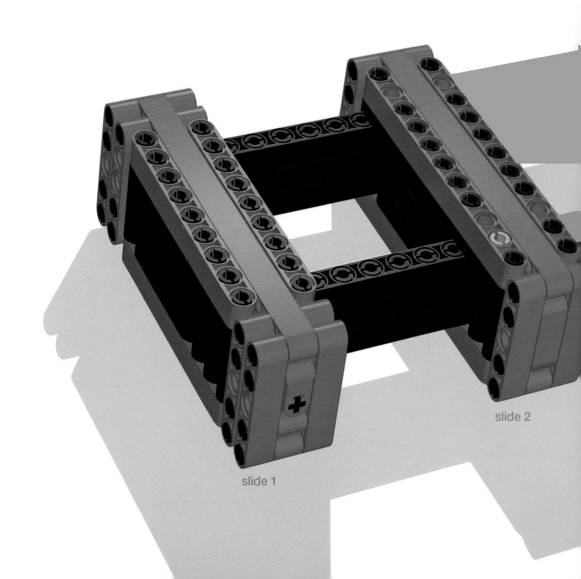

slide 1

slide 2

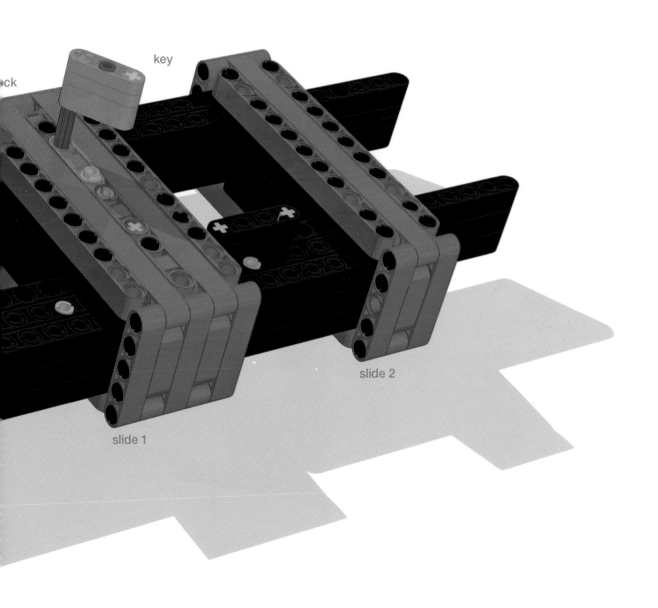

ck

key

slide 2

slide 1

# HOW IT WORKS

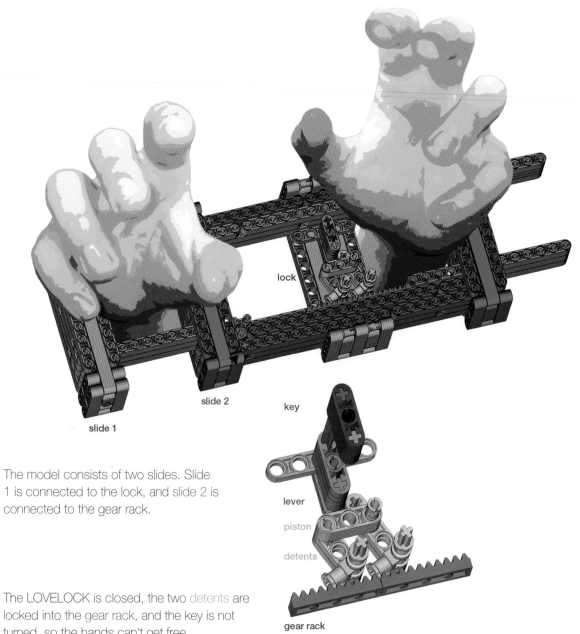

lock

slide 2

slide 1

key

lever

piston

detents

gear rack

The model consists of two slides. Slide 1 is connected to the lock, and slide 2 is connected to the gear rack.

The LOVELOCK is closed, the two detents are locked into the gear rack, and the key is not turned, so the hands can't get free.

The key turns the lever, which then pushes the detents, which then raise from the gear rack. The two slides aren't locked together anymore. The LOVELOCK can be opened.

key

lever

piston

detents

gear rack

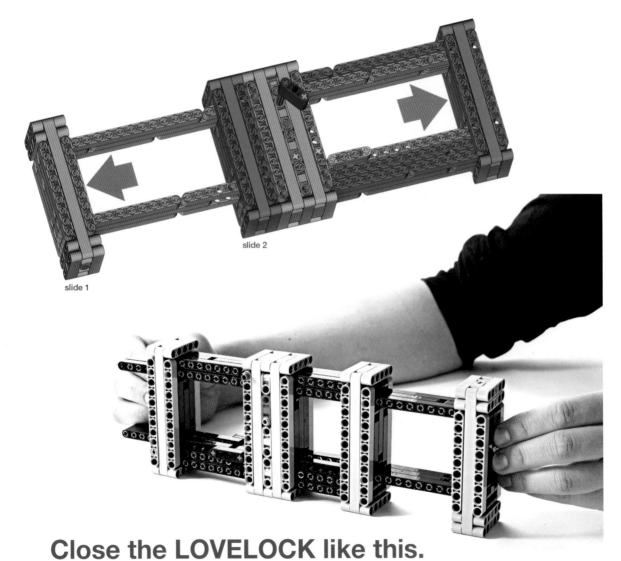

slide 1

slide 2

# Close the LOVELOCK like this.

# BILL OF MATERIALS

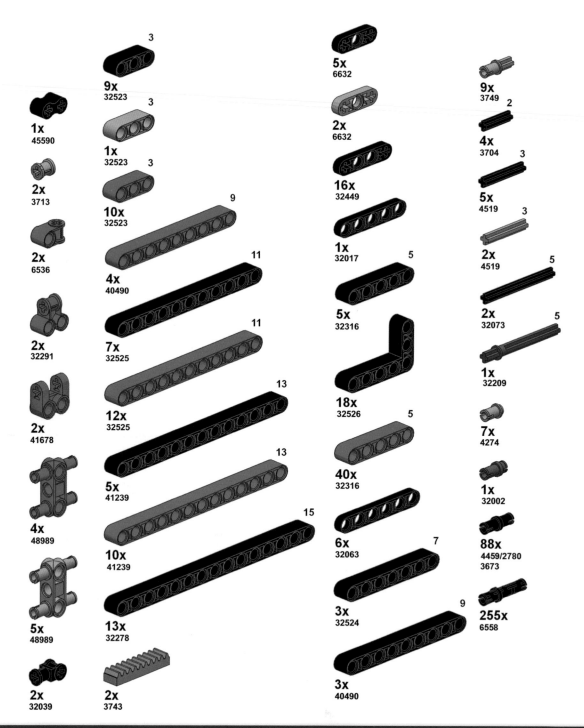

**1x**
45590

**2x**
3713

**2x**
6536

**2x**
32291

**2x**
41678

**4x**
48989

**5x**
48989

**2x**
32039

**9x**
32523
3

**1x**
32523
3

**10x**
32523
3

**4x**
40490
9

**7x**
32525
11

**12x**
32525
11

**5x**
41239
13

**10x**
41239
13

**13x**
32278
15

**2x**
3743

**5x**
6632

**2x**
6632

**16x**
32449

**1x**
32017

**5x**
32316
5

**18x**
32526

**40x**
32316
5

**6x**
32063

**3x**
32524
5

**3x**
40490
7

**9x**
3749

**4x**
3704
2

**5x**
4519
3

**2x**
4519
3

**2x**
32073
5

**1x**
32209
5

**7x**
4274

**1x**
32002

**88x**
4459/2780
3673

**255x**
6558
9

# BUILDING INSTRUCTIONS

## 1

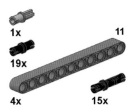

1x
19x
4x

11
15x

## 2

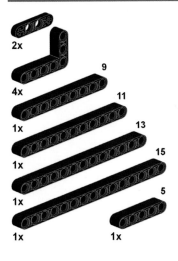

2x
4x — 9
1x — 11
1x — 13
1x — 15
1x
1x — 5

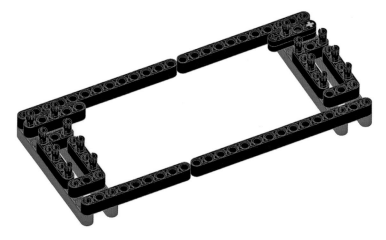

## 3

3
3x
46x

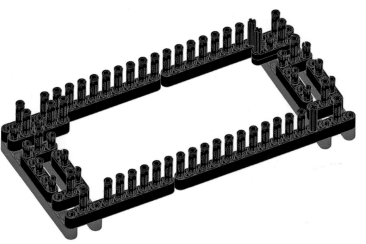

7

15

2x

5 4x

2x

2x

2x

4x

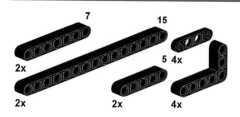

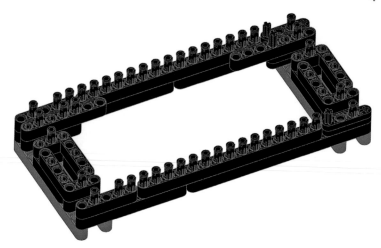

3

1x

19x

5x

9x

1x

15

3x

2x

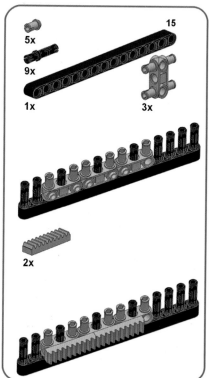

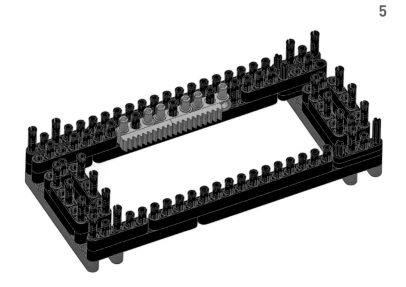

**6**

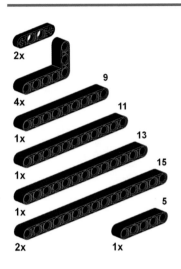
2x

9
4x

11
1x

13
1x

15
1x

5
2x · 1x

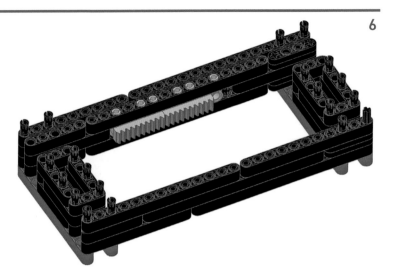

---

**7**

1x

15x

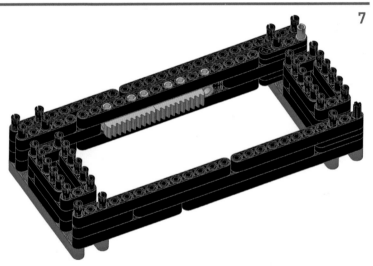

---

**8**

11
4x

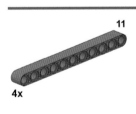

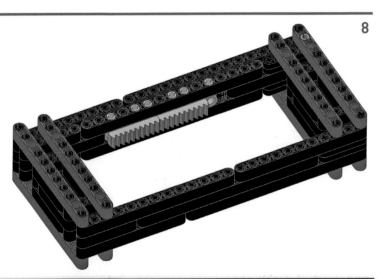

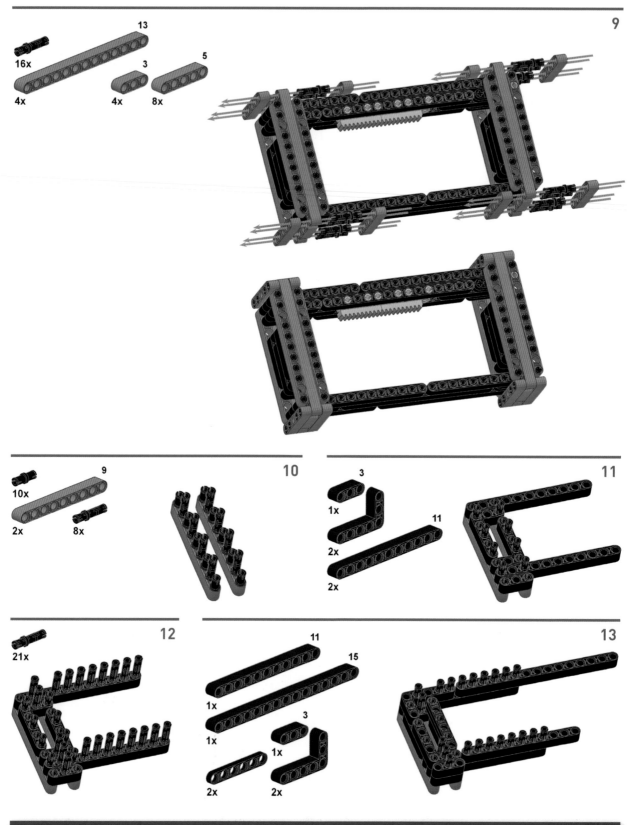

**14**

21x

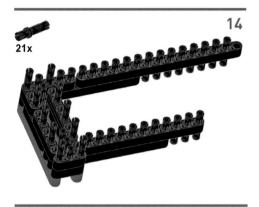

**15**

11
2x

15
1x

1x

3
1x

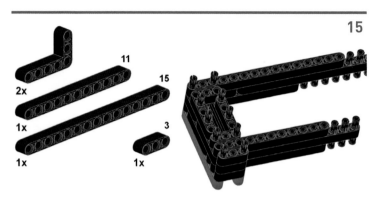

**16**

8x

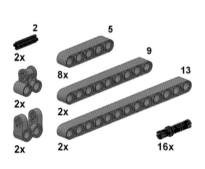

**17**

2
2x

5
8x

9
2x

13
2x

16x

2x

2x

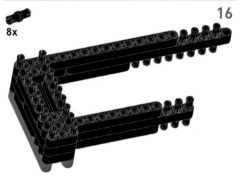

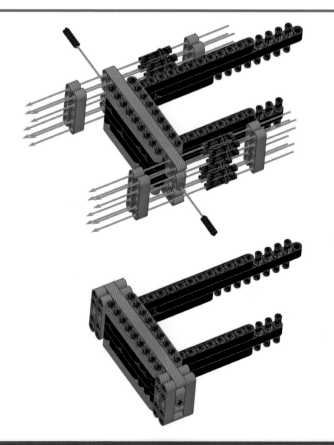

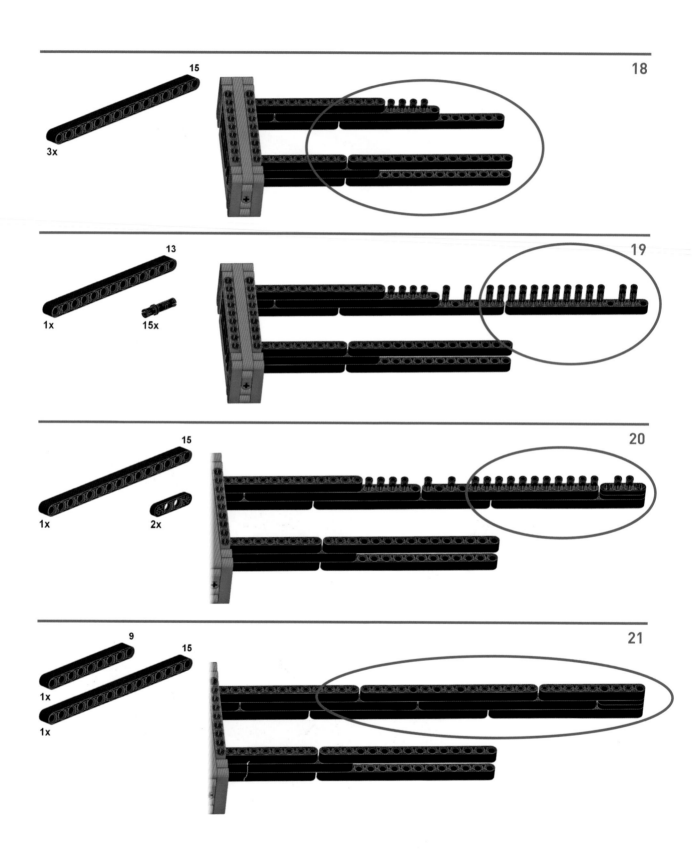

18

15
3x

19

13
1x

15x

20

15
1x

2x

21

9
1x

15
1x

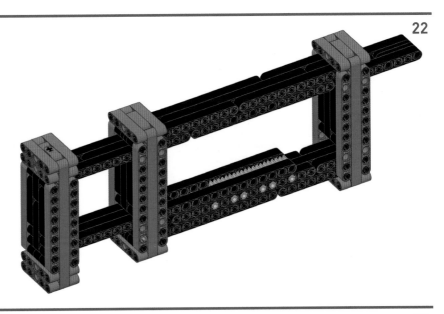

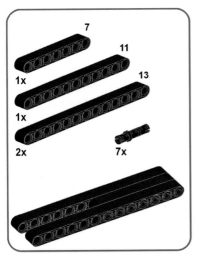

7
11
1x
13
1x
2x
7x

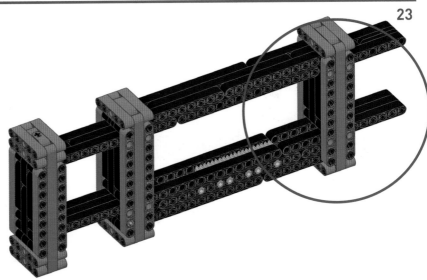

4x
4x
4x

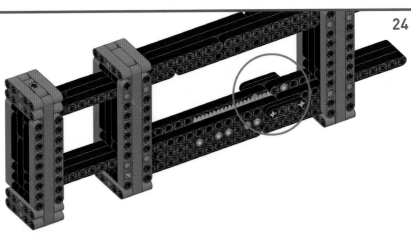

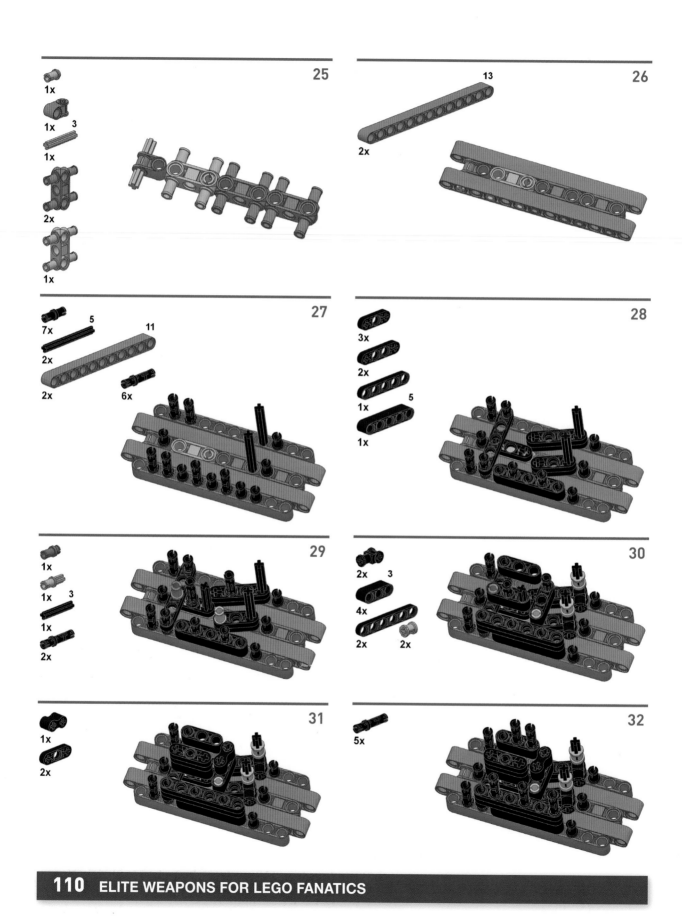

**33**

3

2x

2x

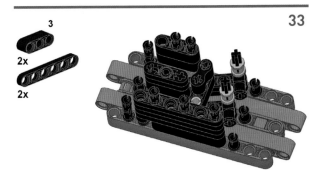

**34**

1x

4x

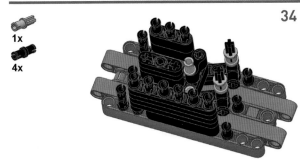

**35**

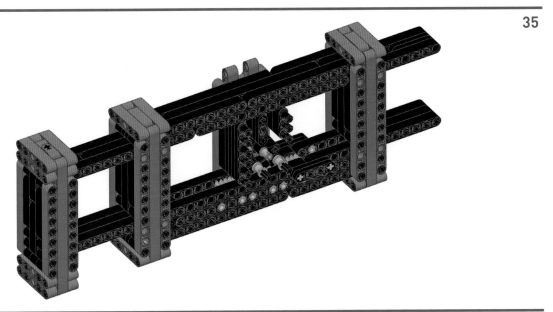

**36**

11

5x

2x    2x

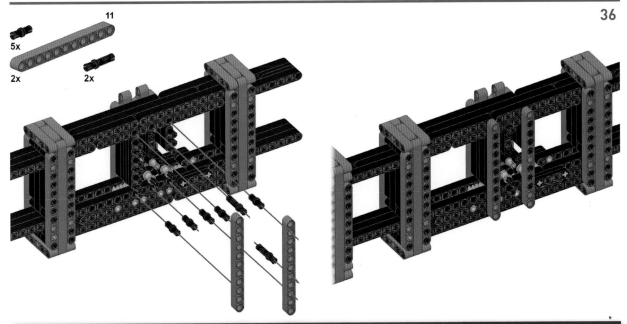

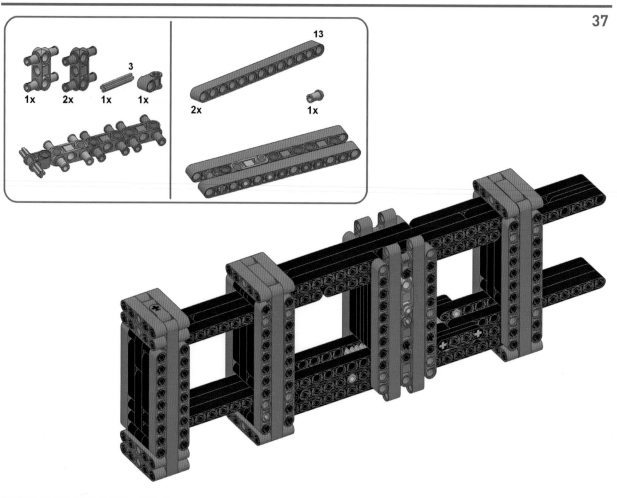

**5** **3**

3x 2x 5x 5x

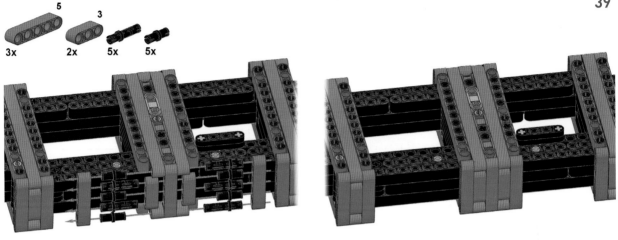

**5** **3**

1x 1x 2x 1x 1x

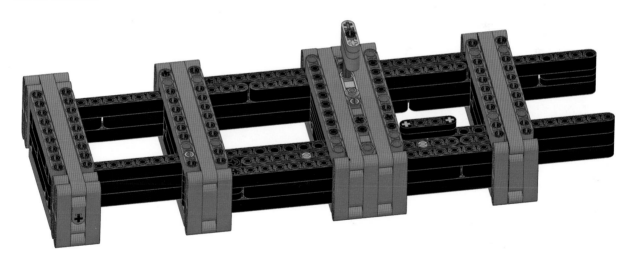

# TIPS

Tie your victims behind the back.
Makes it more difficult to pick the lock.

# CHINAHOOK

| ⊹ SPECS | |
|---|---|
| **NAME** | **CHINAHOOK** |
| **TYPE** | **Grappling Gun** |
| **PARTS** | **334** |
| **SIZE** | **12.3" x 2.1" x 5.9"** |
| **SKILL LEVEL** | **Expert** |

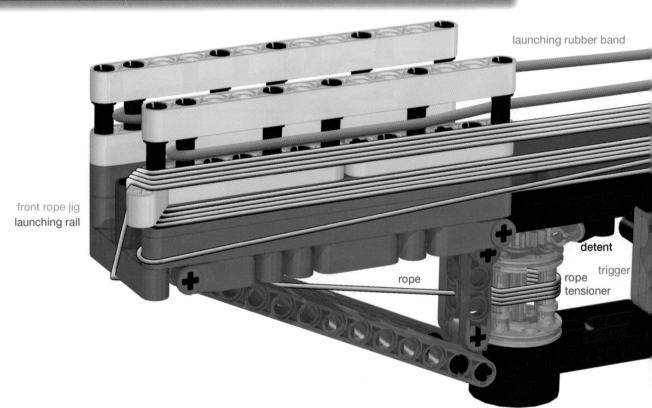

launching rubber band

front rope jig
launching rail

detent

trigger

rope

rope
tensioner

tensioning wheel

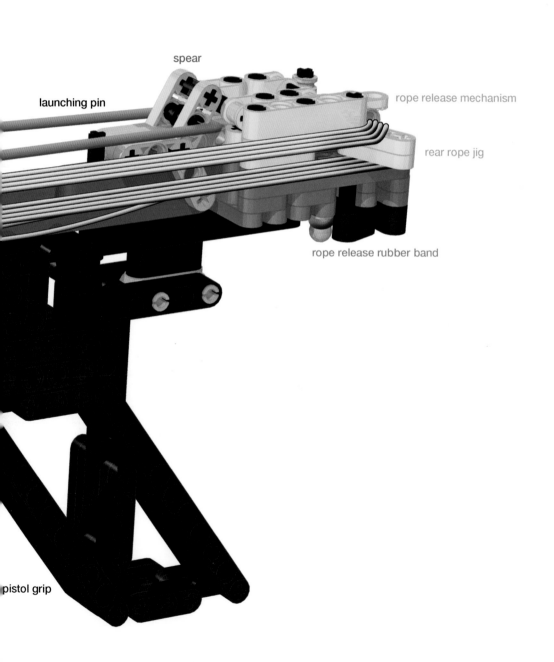

spear

launching pin

rope release mechanism

rear rope jig

rope release rubber band

pistol grip

# HOW IT WORKS

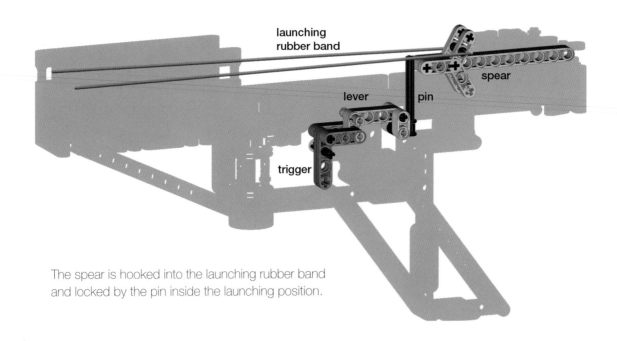

launching
rubber band

spear

lever    pin

trigger

The spear is hooked into the launching rubber band
and locked by the pin inside the launching position.

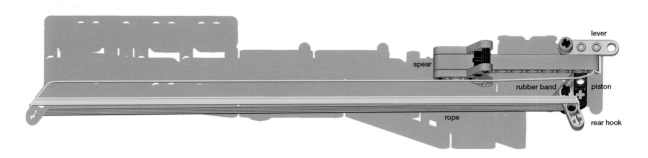

lever

spear

rubber band    piston

rope

rear hook

The rope is wound around the front and rear hook.
The spear being in launching position prevents the
lever from getting turned inwards by the rubber
band. The CHINAHOOK is ready to fire.

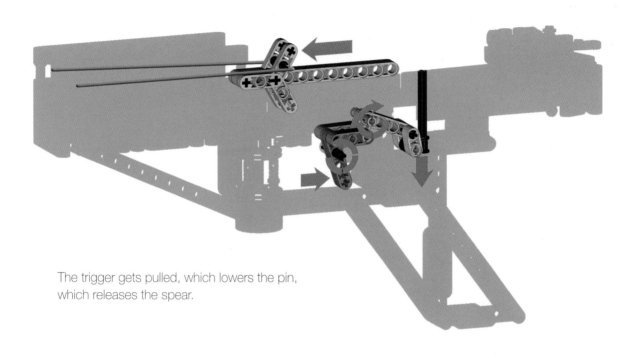

The trigger gets pulled, which lowers the pin,
which releases the spear.

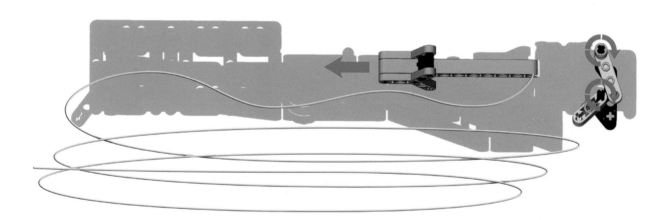

The spear gets catapulted forward and releases the lever, which gets instantly turned inside by the
rubber band. Because the rear hook is connected to the lever through the piston, it also turns and
releases the rope immediately. When the spear leaves the gun, the rope is in free fall. And that's the cool
thing about the CHINAHOOK: the rope doesn't need to be uncoiled from somewhere, which would
slow down the spear dramatically, but rather, it is already in the air as soon as the spear moves forward.

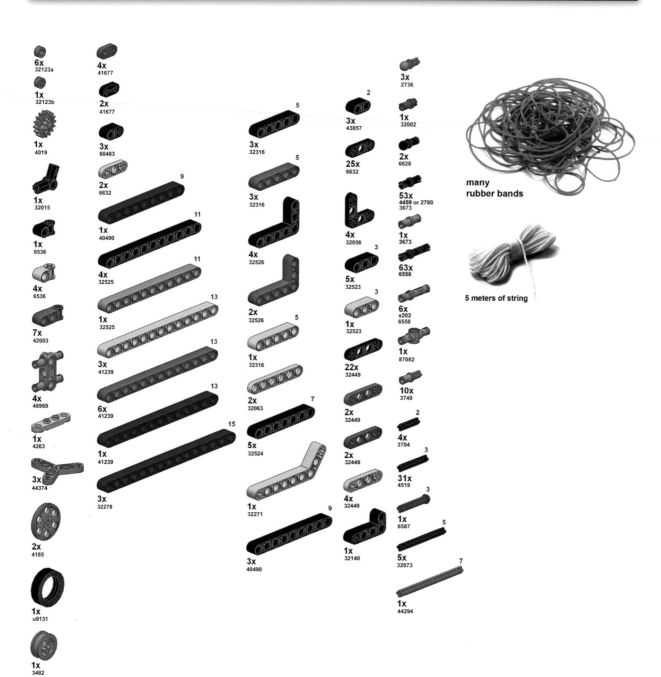

**6x** 32123a

**1x** 32123b

**1x** 4019

**1x** 32015

**1x** 6536

**4x** 6536

**7x** 42003

**4x** 48989

**1x** 4263

**3x** 44374

**2x** 4185

**1x** u9131

**1x** 3482

**4x** 41677

**2x** 41677

**3x** 60483

**2x** 6632

5

**1x** 40490

9

**4x** 32525

11

**1x** 32525

11

**3x** 41239

13

**6x** 41239

13

**1x** 41239

13

**3x** 32278

15

5

**3x** 32316

5

**3x** 32316

**4x** 32526

**2x** 32526

5

**1x** 32316

**2x** 32063

**5x** 32524

**1x** 32271

7

**3x** 40490

9

2

**3x** 43857

**25x** 6632

**3x** 32316

**4x** 32056

**5x** 32523

3

**1x** 32523

**22x** 32449

**2x** 32449

**2x** 32449

**4x** 32449

3

**1x** 32140

**3x** 2736

**1x** 32002

**2x** 6628

**53x** 4459 or 2780 3673

**1x** 3673

**63x** 6558

**6x** x202 6558

**1x** 87082

**10x** 3749

2

**4x** 3704

3

**31x** 4519

3

**1x** 6587

5

**5x** 32073

7

**1x** 44294

many rubber bands

5 meters of string

# BUILDING INSTRUCTIONS

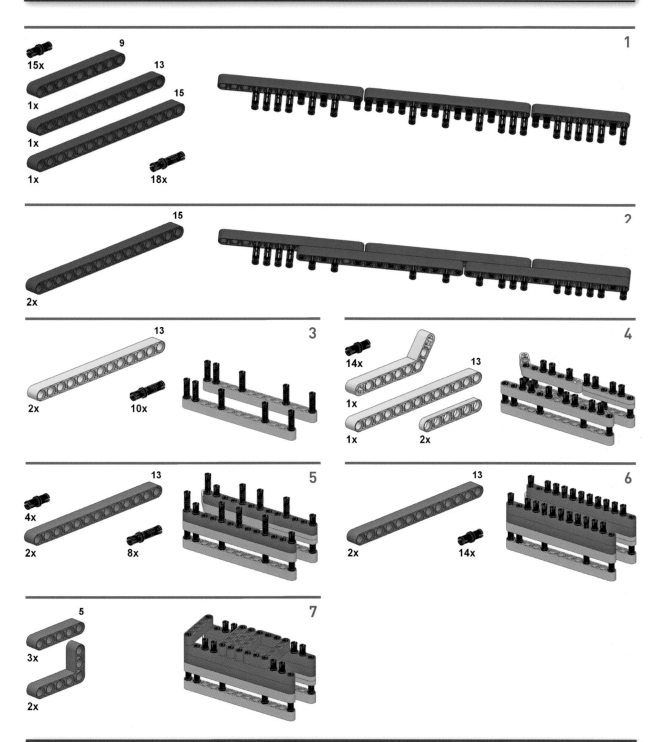

## 8

4x 2

1x

4x 3

2x

2x

5

1x 3x

13

1x

2x 1x 3x

5

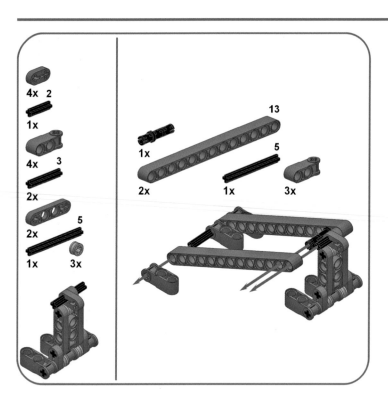

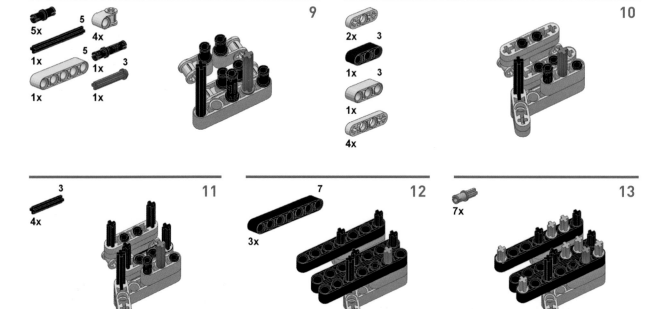

5x 5

4x

1x 5

1x 3

1x 1x

2x 3

1x 3

1x

4x

3

4x

7

3x

7x

**14**

6x 4x 2x

**15**

2x
2x

**16**

2x
1x
5

**17**

2x 1x
2x 2x

**18**

1x

**19**

1x 1x 2x

**20**

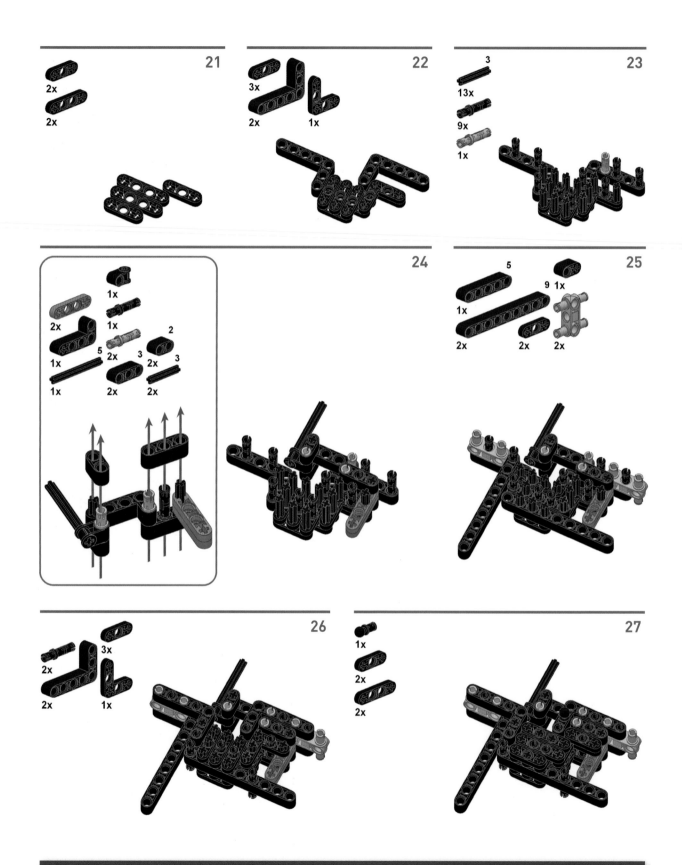

21

2x
2x

22

3x
2x
1x

23

3
13x
9x
1x

24

1x
2x
1x
1x
1x
5
1x
2x
2
3
2x
3
2x

25

5
9 1x
1x
2x
2x
2x

26

2x
2x
3x
1x

27

1x
2x
2x

**28**

1x

1x

1x

2x

5

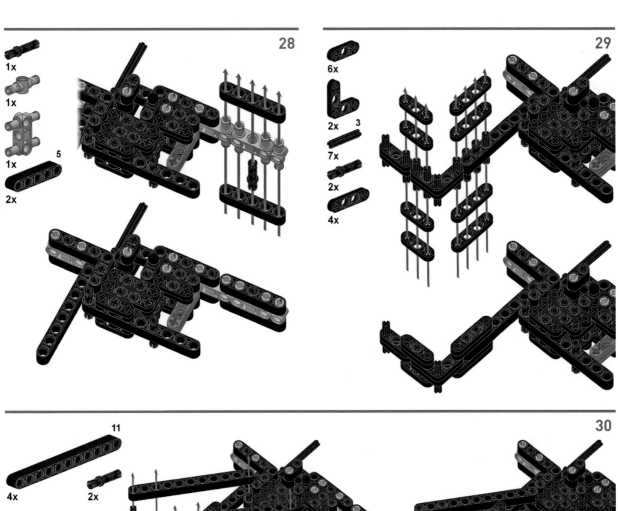

**29**

6x

2x  3

7x

2x

4x

**30**

11

4x  2x

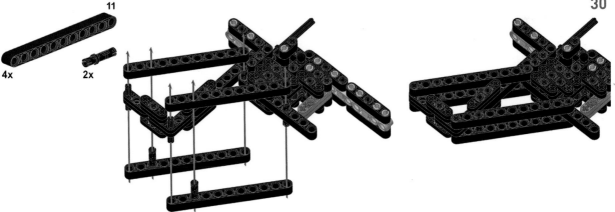

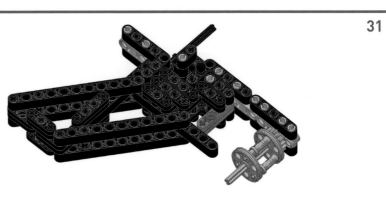

**31**

1x  7

1x  3x  2x

32

4x

7

1x

1x

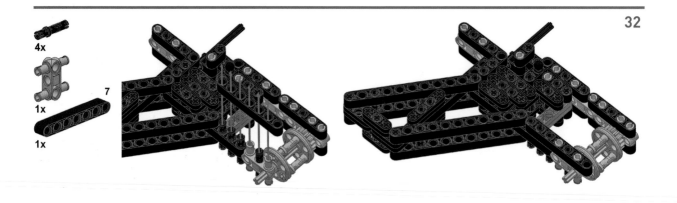

33

1x     1x

1x     1x

34

1x

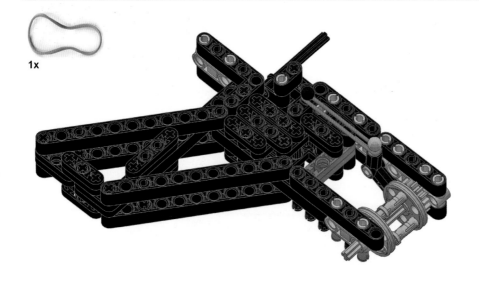

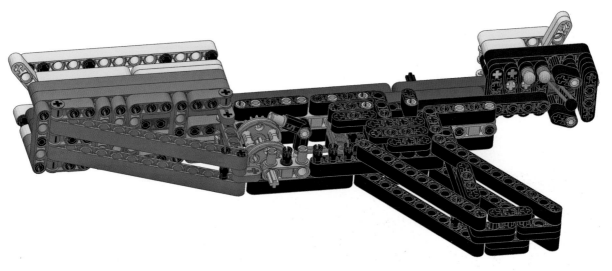

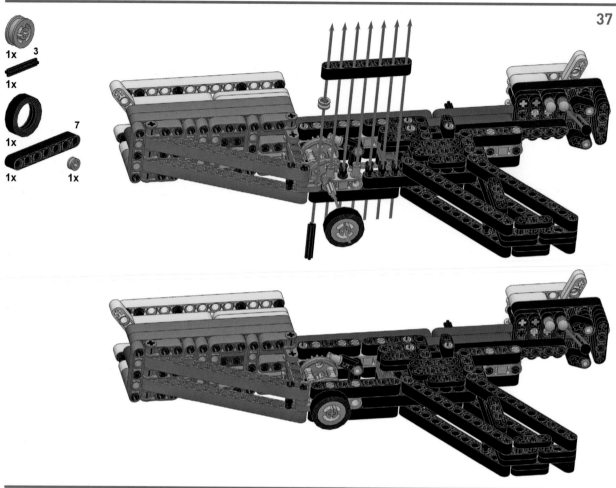

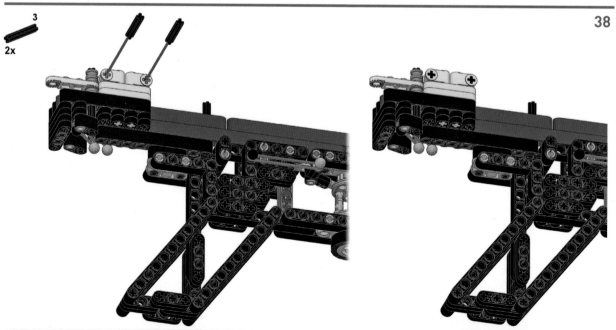

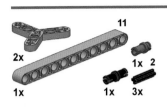

**11**

**2x**

**1x**

**1x 2**

**1x**

**3x**

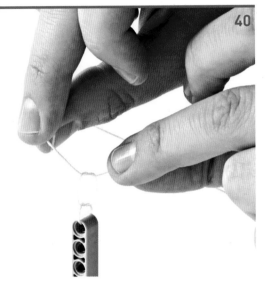

40

Tie one end of the rope to the spear . . .

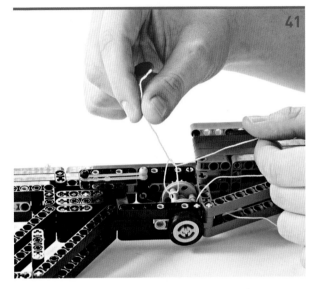

41

. . . and the other end to the rope tensioner.

# HOW IT'S LOADED

Insert the spear from the front.

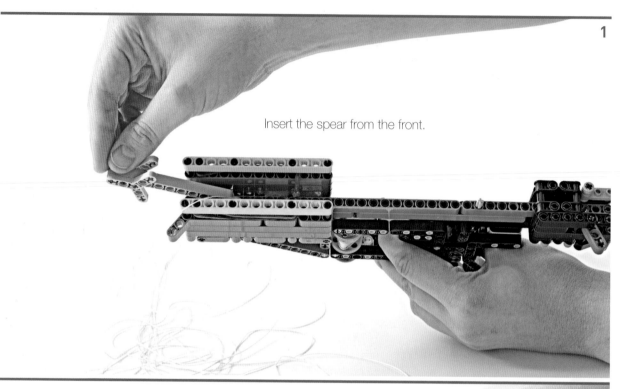

Hook it into the launching rubber band.

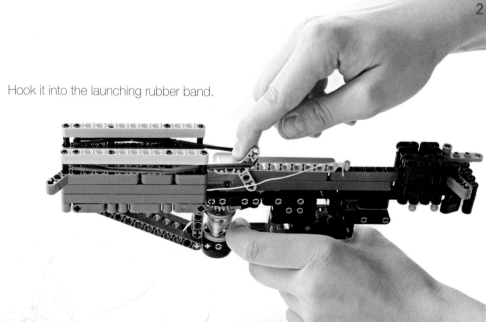

Pull the spear all the way back.

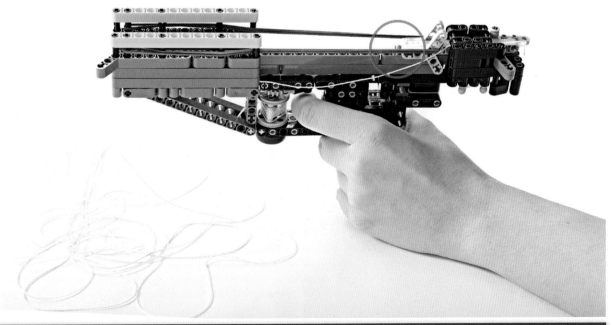

The spear is now locked behind the launching pin.

Wrap the rope first around the rear jig and then around the front jig.

Repeat this until there is almost no loose rope left.

Turn the tension wheel counterclockwise until the rope is taut.

# The **CHINAHOOK** is ready to fire its rope!

# TIPS

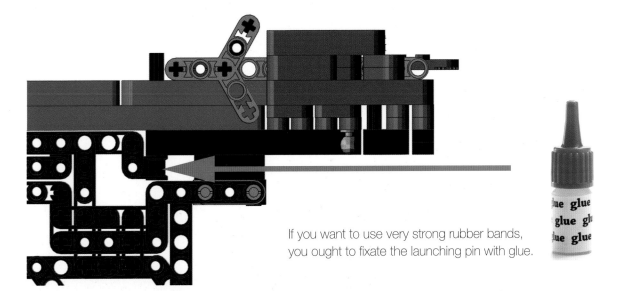

If you want to use very strong rubber bands, you ought to fixate the launching pin with glue.

# PART 7

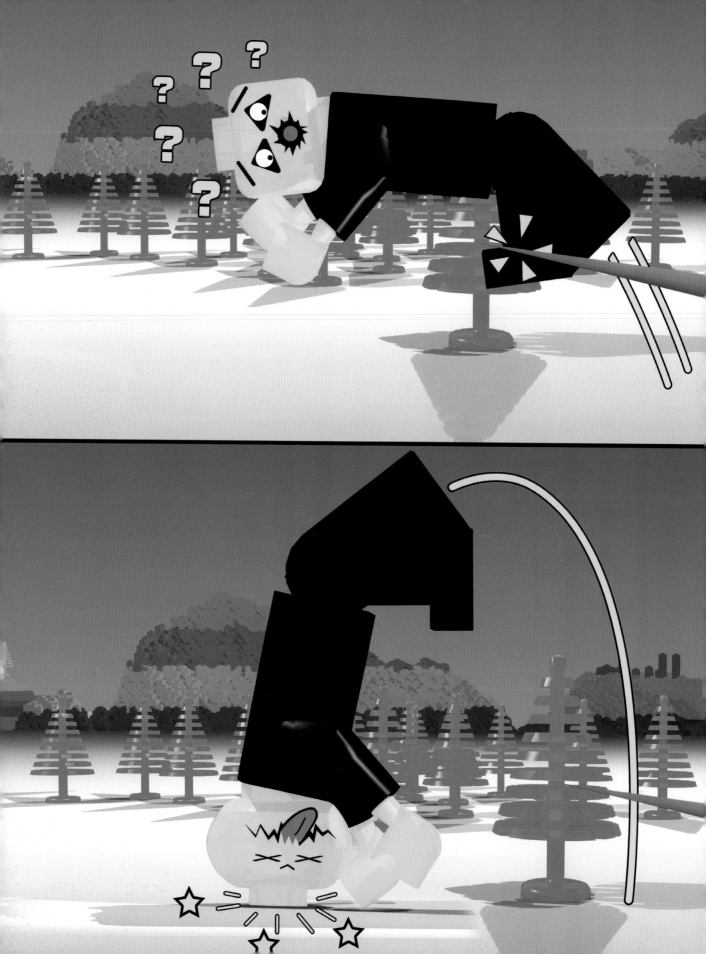

# HAMMERHEAD JR

| ✛ SPECS | |
|---|---|
| **NAME** | **HAMMERHEAD JUNIOR** |
| **TYPE** | **Single Shot Crossbow Pistol** |
| **PARTS** | **203** |
| **SIZE** | **12.2" x 7.7" x 5.3"** |
| **SKILL LEVEL** | **Amateur** |

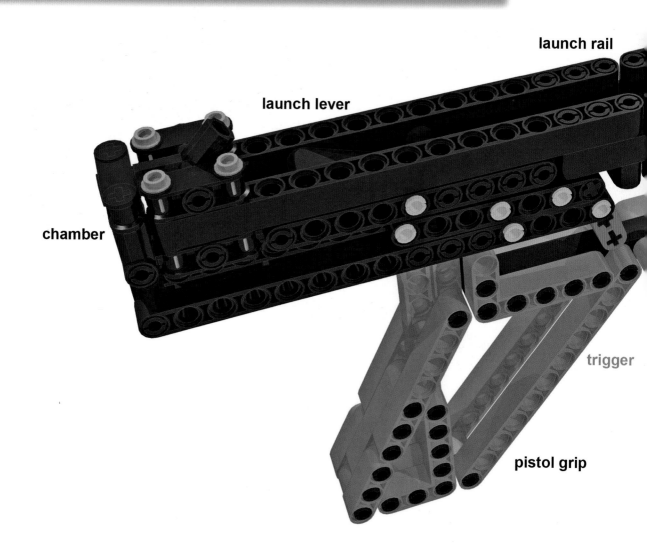

launch rail

launch lever

chamber

trigger

pistol grip

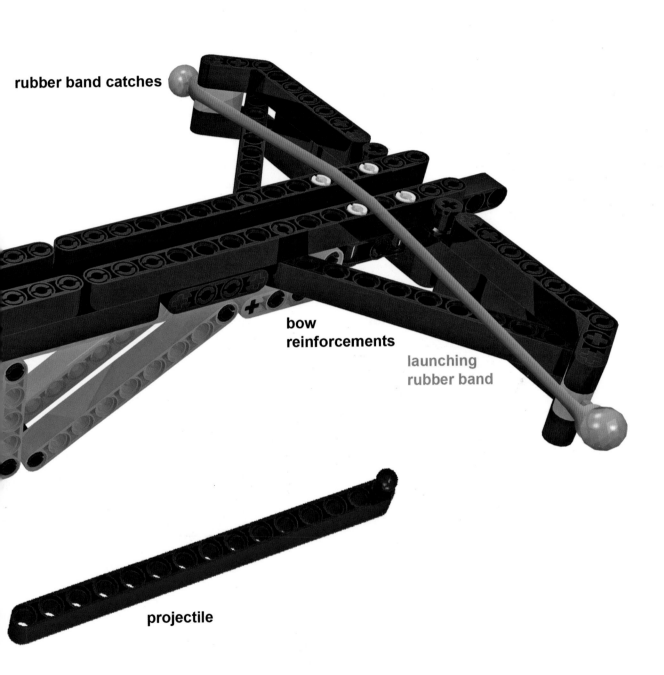

rubber band catches

bow
reinforcements

launching
rubber band

projectile

# HOW IT WORKS

The HAMMERHEAD JUNIOR in its ready-to-fire state. The projectile is in the chamber and under tension by the launching rubber band. It can't get free, because the launching lever is raised and therefore locks it in place. The trigger mechanism works in the same way as that of the HAMMERHEAD SENIOR.

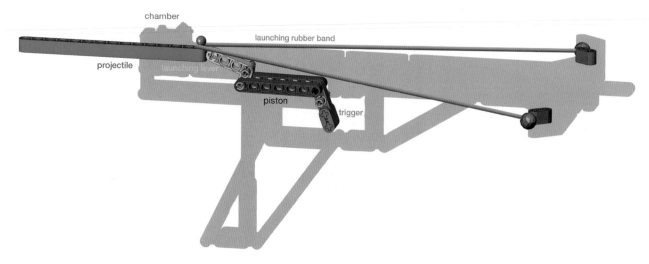

When the trigger gets pulled, the force gets through the piston transferred to the launching lever, which then turns out of the running rail and unleashes the projectile, which then gets catapulted forward by the rubber band.

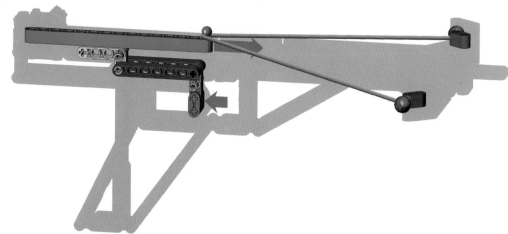

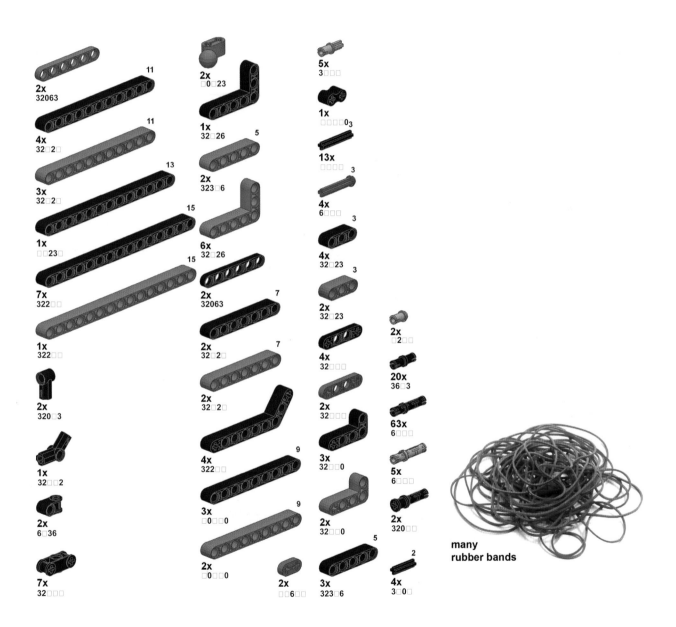

**2x**
32063

**4x**
32□2□
11

**3x**
32□2□
11

**1x**
□□23□
13

**7x**
322□□
15

**1x**
322□□
15

**2x**
320□3

**1x**
32□□2

**2x**
6□36

**7x**
32□□□

**2x**
□0□23

**1x**
32□26

**2x**
323□6
5

**6x**
32□26

**2x**
32063
15

**2x**
32□2□
7

**2x**
32□2□
7

**4x**
322□□
9

**3x**
□0□□0
9

**2x**
□0□□0

**2x**
□□6□□

**5x**
3□□□

**1x**
□□□□0₃

**13x**
□□□□
3

**4x**
6□□□
3

**4x**
32□23
3

**2x**
32□23
3

**4x**
32□□□

**2x**
32□□□

**3x**
32□□0

**2x**
32□□0

**3x**
323□6
5

**2x**
□2□□

**20x**
36□3

**63x**
6□□□

**5x**
6□□□

**2x**
320□□

**4x**
3□0□
2

many
rubber bands

# BUILDING INSTRUCTIONS

**1**

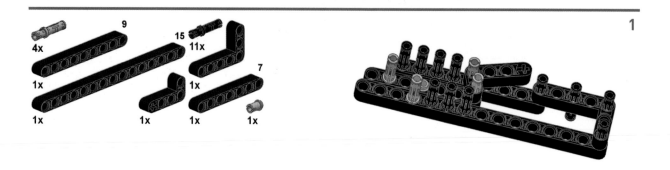

**2**

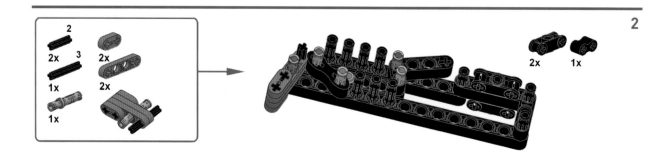

**3**

**4**

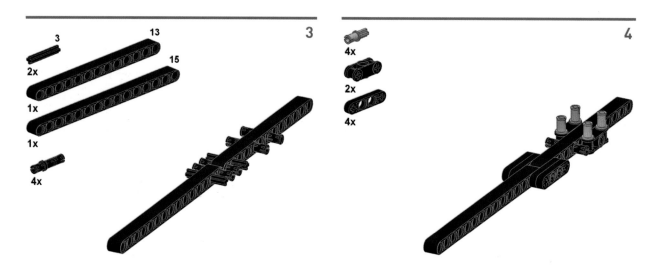

**5**

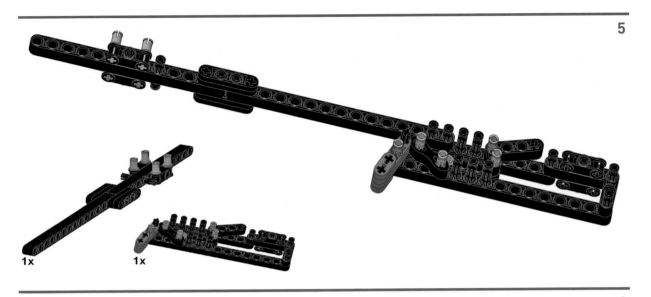

1x

1x

**6**

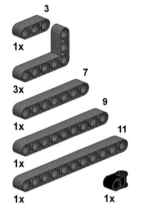

3
1x

7
3x

9
1x

11
1x

1x

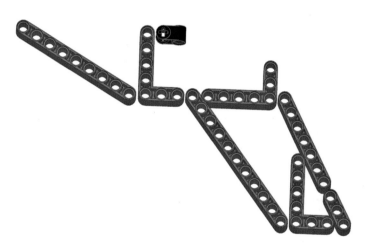

**7**

3
1x

28x

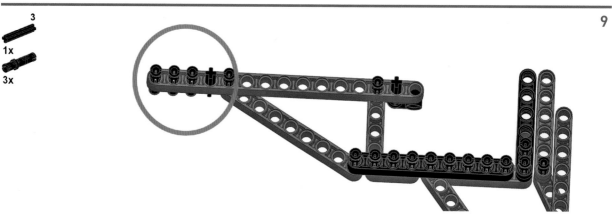

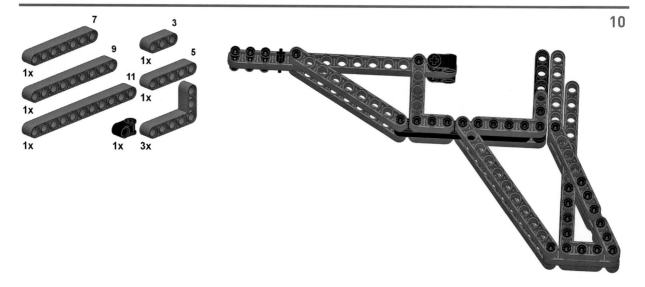

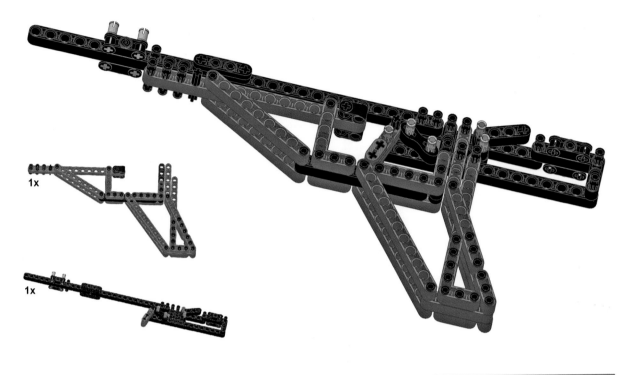

1x

1x

9

15

1x

1x

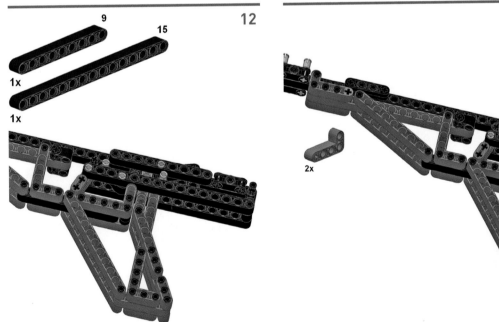

7

1x

1x

2x

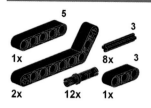

1x
5

2x

8x

12x

3

3

1x

2x

2x

11

2x

2x

3

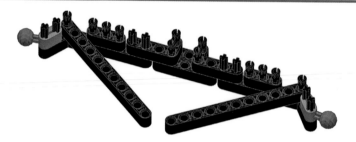

2x

2x

2x

2x

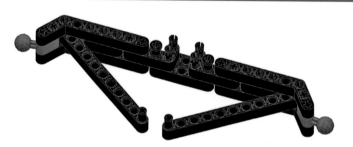

1x

1x

**18x**

**15**

**4x**

**5**

**4x**

**2x**

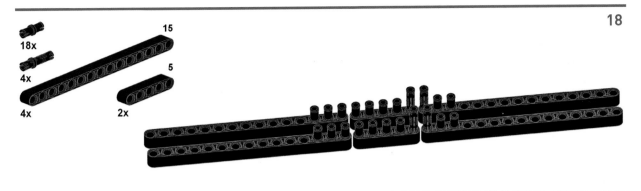

**11**

**2x**

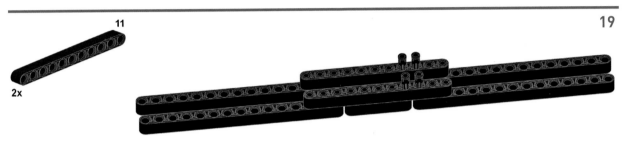

**1x**

**1x**

**2x**

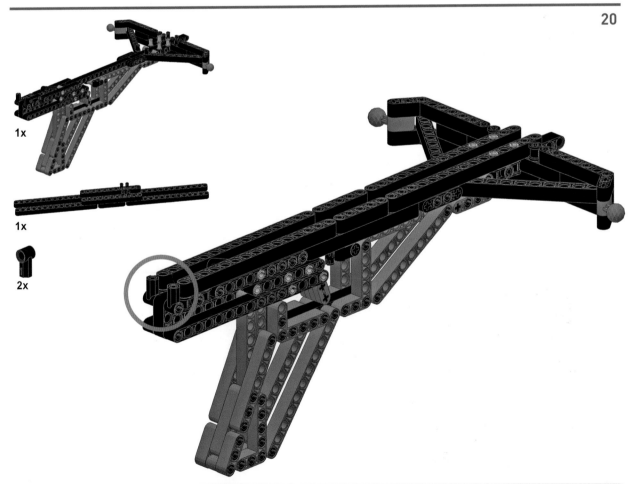

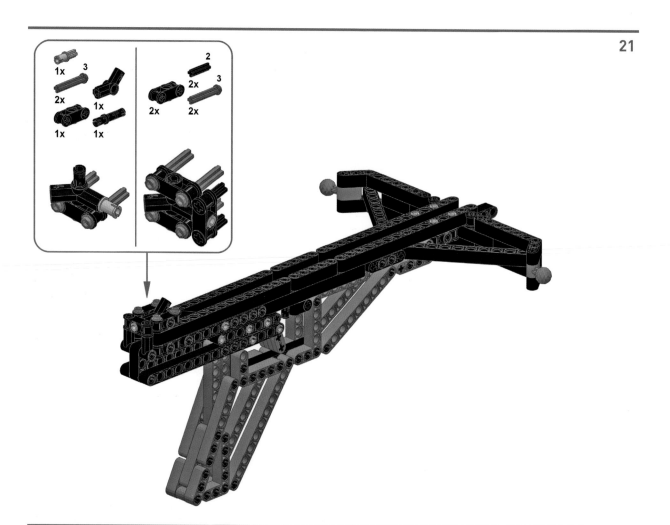

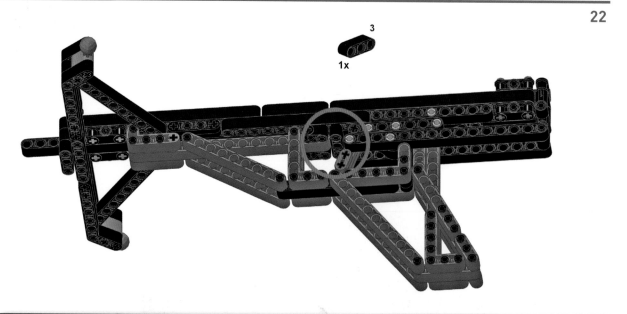

**1.**

**1x**

**2. Twist.**

**3. Connect it to the other hook.**

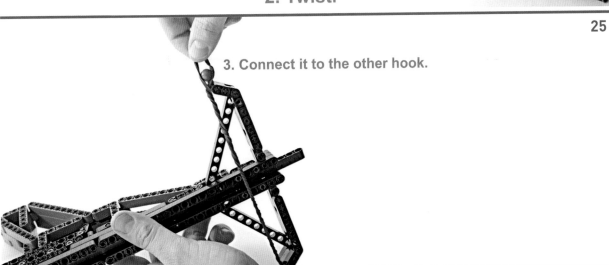

# HOW IT'S LOADED

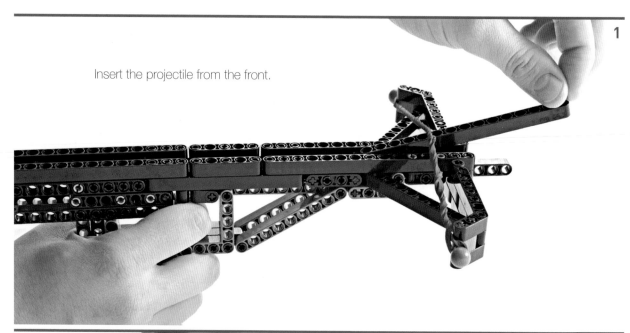

1

Insert the projectile from the front.

2

Pull it back into the chamber, until it gets caught by the launching lever.

# The **HAMMERHEAD JUNIOR** is ready to fire!

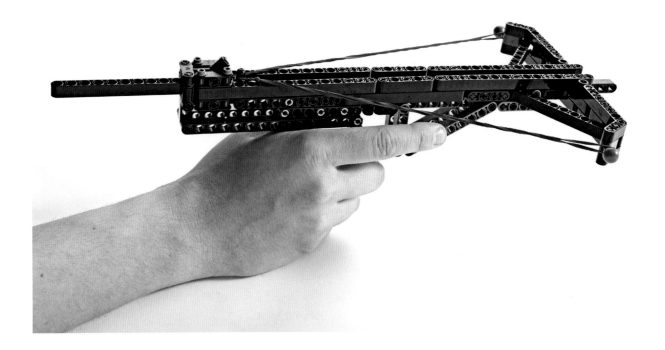

# HAMMERHEAD SR

## ⊹SPECS

| NAME | HAMMERHEAD SENIOR |
|---|---|
| TYPE | Heavy Duty Slide Action Crossbow Pistol (7 shots) |
| PARTS | 734 |
| SIZE | 18.1" x 10.8" x 8.1" |
| SKILL LEVEL | Expert |

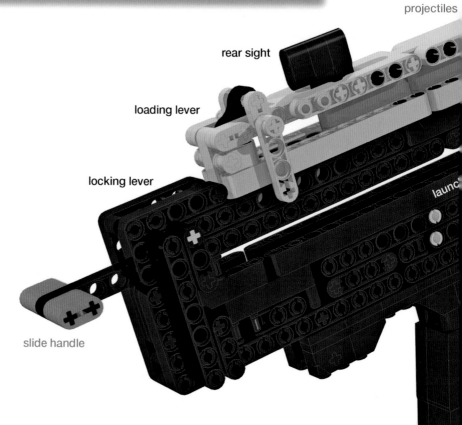

projectiles

rear sight

loading lever

locking lever

launch

slide handle

grip

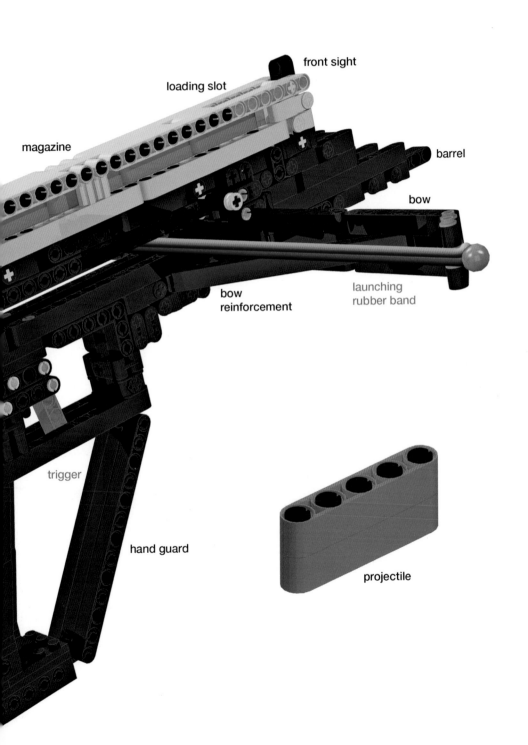

front sight

loading slot

magazine

barrel

bow

launching
rubber band

bow
reinforcement

trigger

hand guard

projectile

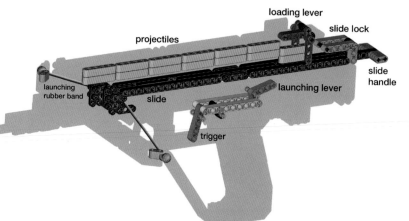

**loading lever**

**slide lock**

**projectiles**

**slide handle**

**launching rubber band**

**slide**

**launching lever**

**trigger**

HAMMERHEAD SENIOR at its ground state: No projectile is inside the launch rail. The launching rubber band is not taut. The slide is held in its foremost position by the slide lock. The magazine is fully loaded with seven projectiles. The rearmost projectile is in loading position.

Now the slide gets pulled, which raises the slide lock and pulls taut the launching rubber band.

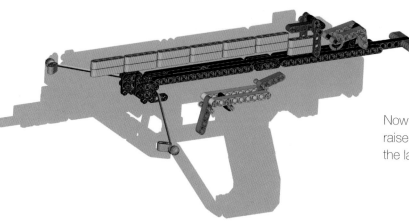

Shortly after the slide has pulled the launching rubber band behind the rearmost projectile, it touches the locking lever and makes it turn. The locking lever will then do two things: 1. push the rearmost projectile from loading position to launching position, and 2. prevent the next projectile from sliding into loading position before the slide is pushed forward again.

The slide gets pushed to its basic position, and the slide lock snaps in again. The taut launching rubber band exerts force to the projectile (which is now in firing position inside the running rail), but it is locked in place by the launching lever. HAMMERHEAD SENIOR is ready to fire.

Pulling the trigger lowers the launching lever—the projectile is released and catapulted forward.

After every shot, the HAMMERHEAD SENIOR's nose has to be raised some inches for the next projectile to slide under the loading lever.

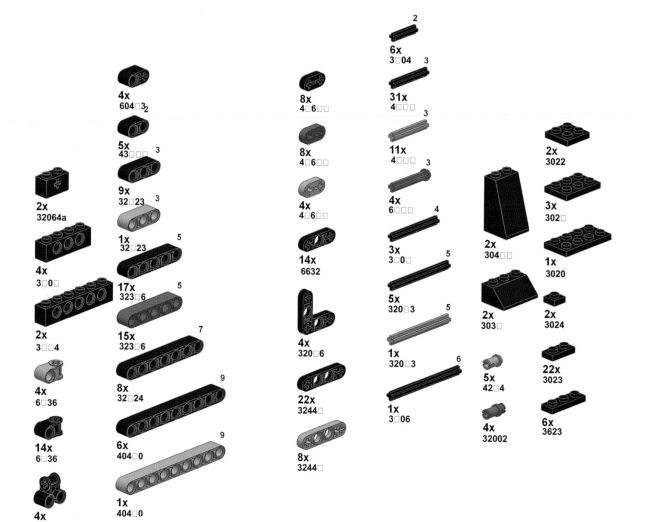

**2**
**6x**
3□04

**4x**
604□3₂

**8x**
4□6□□

**3**
**31x**
4□□□

**5x**
43□□□

**3**
**8x**
4□6□□

**3**
**11x**
4□□□

**2x**
3022

**9x**
32□23

**3**
**4x**
4□6□□

**3**
**4x**
6□□□

**3x**
302□

**2x**
32064a

**1x**
32□23

**5**
**14x**
6632

**4**
**3x**
3□0□

**2x**
304□□

**4x**
3□0□

**17x**
323□6

**5**
**5x**
320□3

**5**
**2x**
3022

**1x**
3020

**2x**
3□4

**15x**
323□6

**7**
**4x**
320□6

**1x**
320□3

**2x**
303□

**2x**
3024

**4x**
6□36

**8x**
32□24

**9**
**22x**
3244□

**6**
**5x**
42□4

**22x**
3023

**14x**
6□36

**6x**
404□0

**9**
**1x**
3□06

**4x**
32002

**6x**
3623

**4x**
322□□

**1x**
404□0

**8x**
3244□

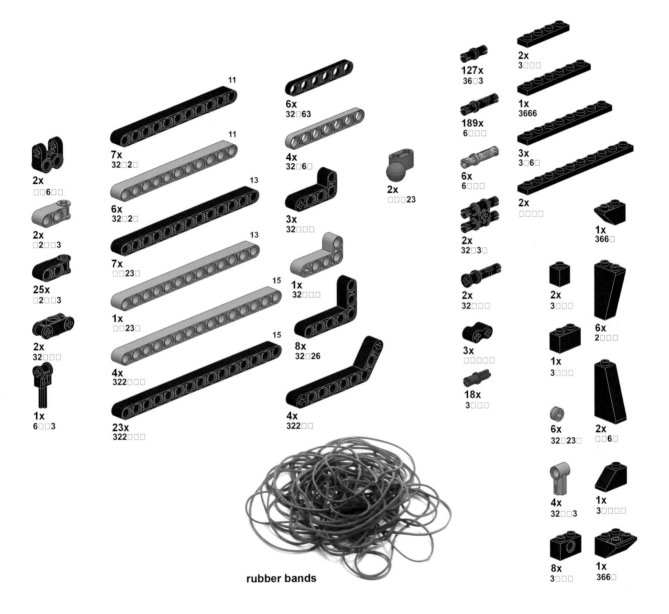

2x
□6□□

2x
□2□□3

25x
□2□□3

2x
32□□□

1x
6□□3

7x
32□2□

6x
32□2□

7x
□23□

1x
□23□

4x
322□□□

23x
322□□□

11

11

13

13

15

15

6x
32□63

4x
32□6□

3x
32□□□

1x
32□□□

8x
32□26

4x
322□□

2x
□□23

127x
36□3

189x
6□□□

6x
6□□□

2x
32□3□

2x
32□□□

3x
□□□□□

18x
3□□□

6x
32□23□

4x
32□□3

8x
3□□□

2x
3□□□

1x
3666

3x
3□6□

2x
□□□□

1x
366□

2x
3□□□

6x
2□□□

1x
3□□□

6x
32□23□

2x
□□6□

1x
3□□□□

1x
366□

rubber bands

# BUILDING INSTRUCTIONS

**1**

1x
1x **9**
1x **11**
3x 2x

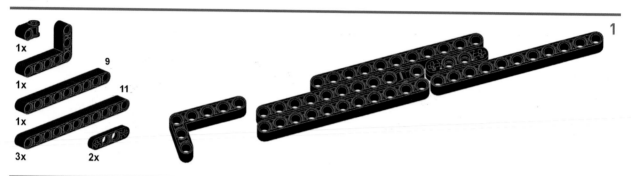

**2**

**3**
2x
**22x**
**4x**

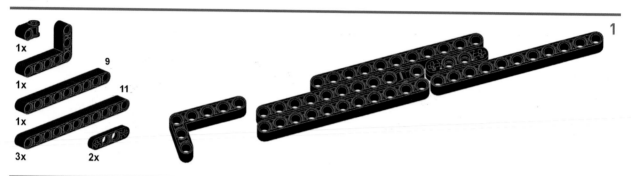

**3**

**2**
1x **7**
1x **1x**
1x **9**
2x 2x 1x **1x**

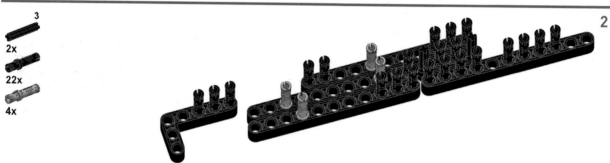

**4**

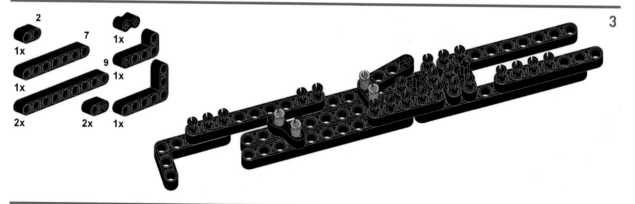

1x
2x

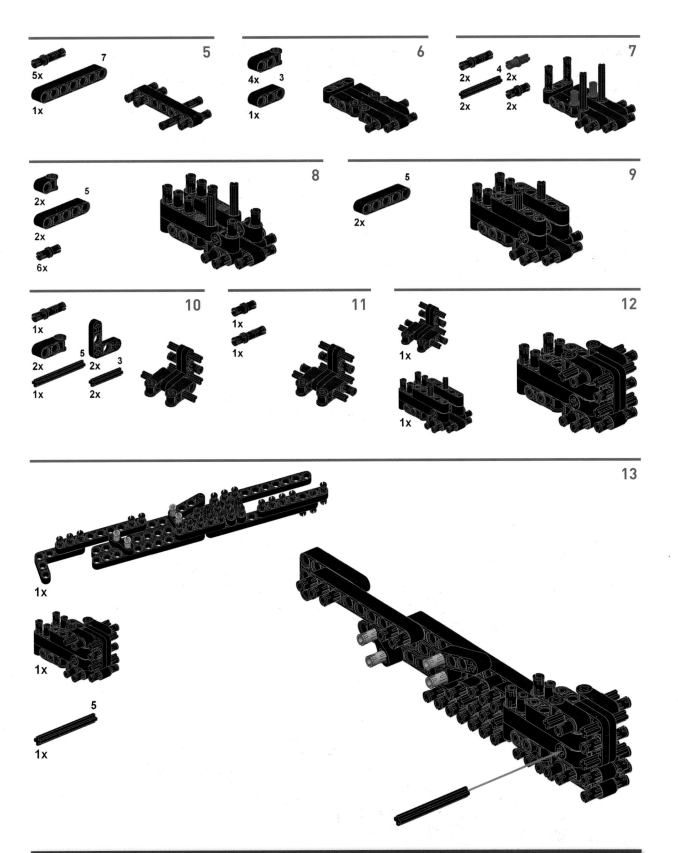

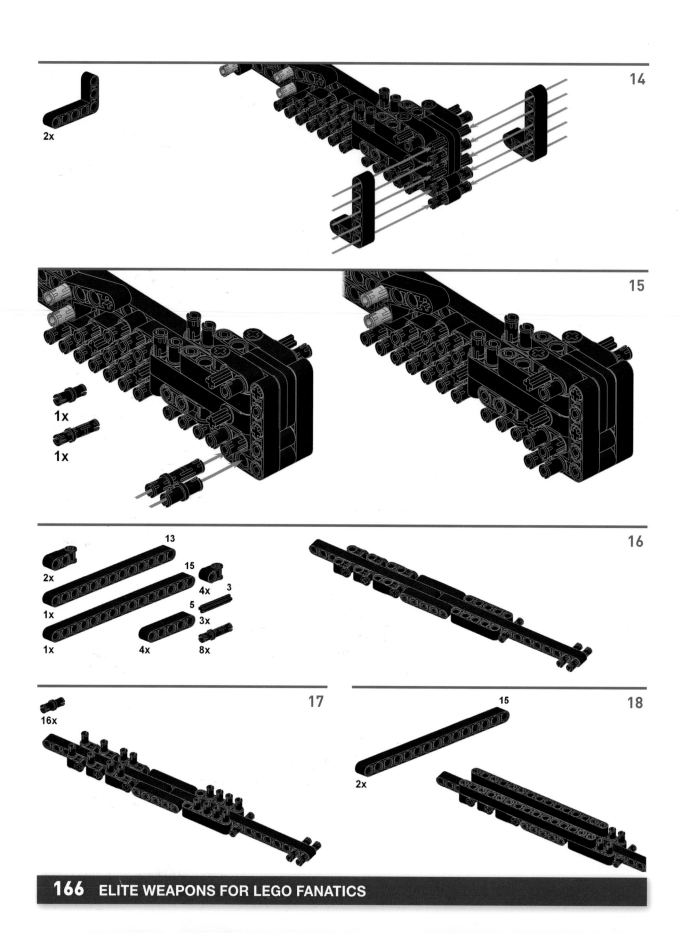

14

15

16

13
2x
15
1x
4x 3
5
1x
4x
3x
8x

17
16x

18
15
2x

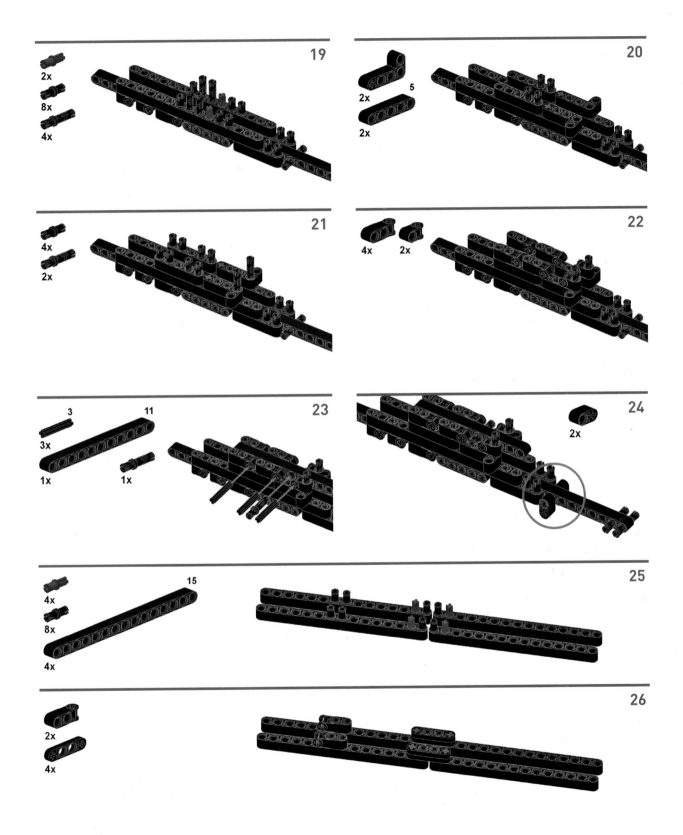

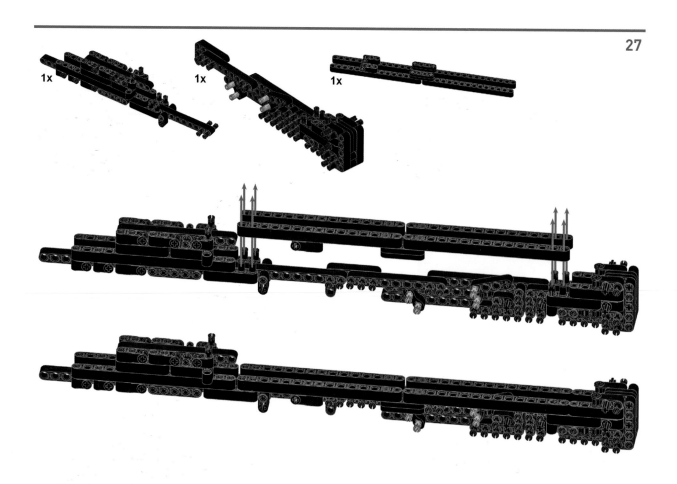

1x  1x  1x

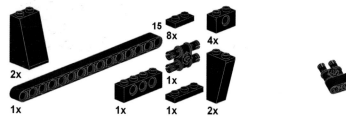

2x  15  8x  4x
1x  1x  1x  2x

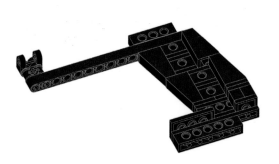

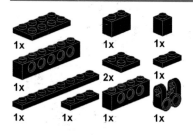

1x  1x  1x
1x  2x  1x
1x  1x  1x  1x

3
1x

13x

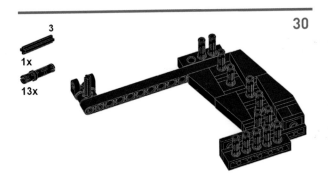

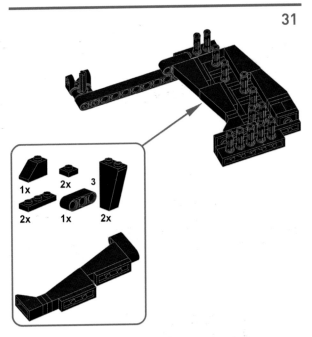

1x    2x    3

2x    1x    2x

9
1x

15
1x

5
1x    1x

7
1x    1x

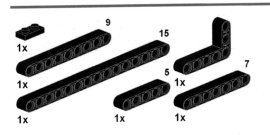

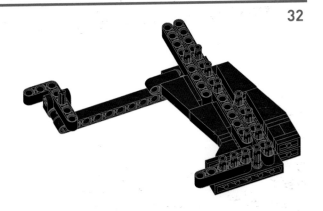

## 33

2x

15

1x    8x    4x

1x    1x

1x    2x    2x    2x    2x    1x    2

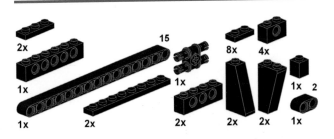

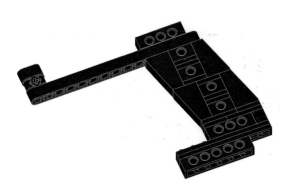

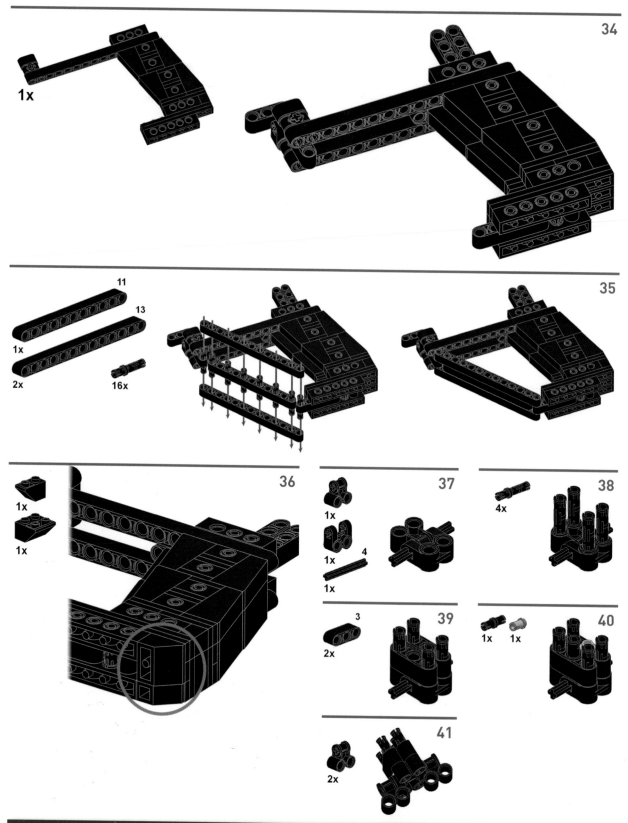

34

1x

35

11
1x

13
2x

16x

36

1x

1x

37

1x

1x

4
1x

38

4x

39

3
2x

40

1x  1x

41

2x

**42**

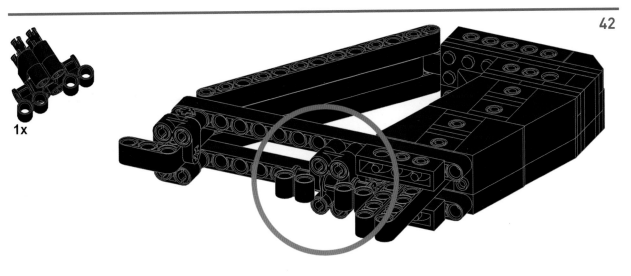

1x

**43**

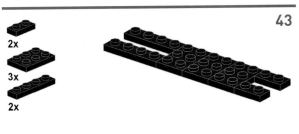

2x
3x
2x

**44**

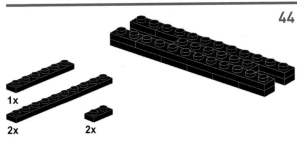

1x
2x
2x

**45**

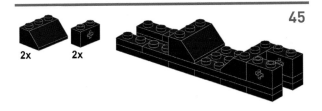

2x
2x

**46**

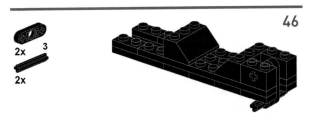

2x 3
2x

**47**

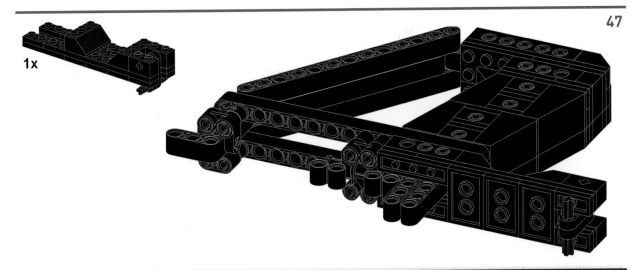

1x

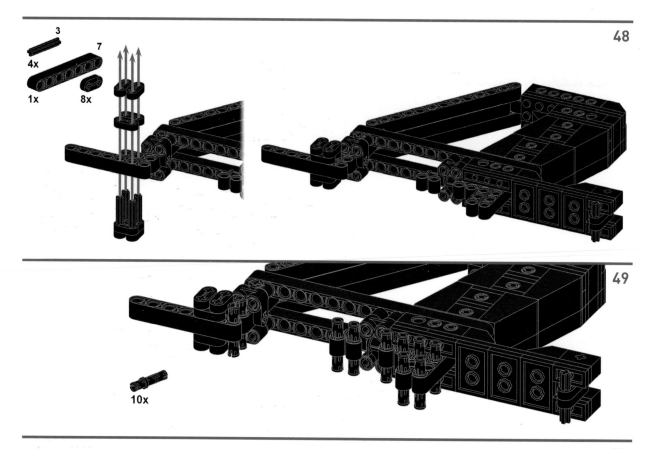

3
4x
7
1x
8x

10x

1x

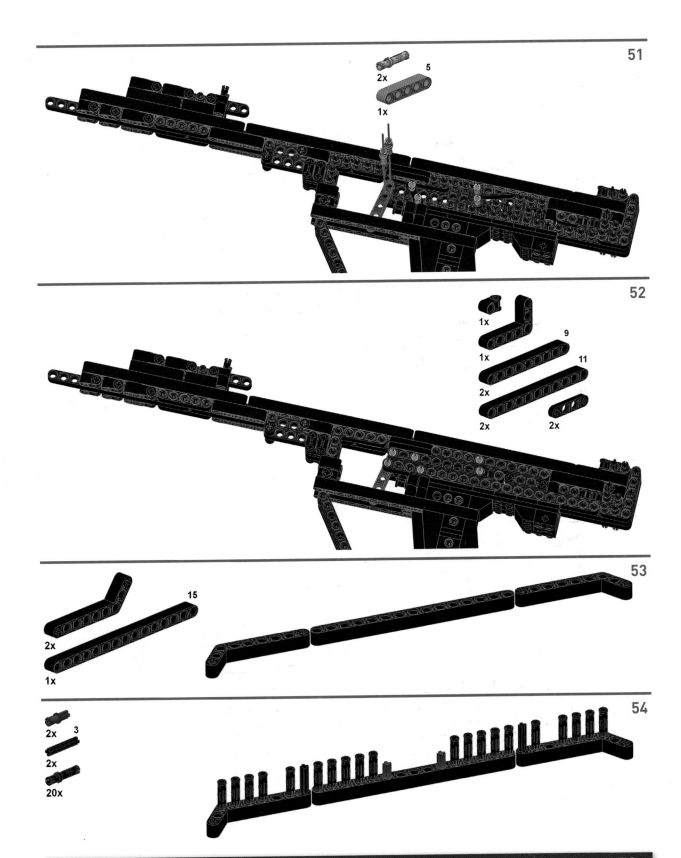

**51**

2x

5

1x

**52**

1x

1x

9

2x

11

2x

2x

**53**

15

2x

1x

**54**

2x  3

2x

20x

7

13

2x

2x

3

2x

2x

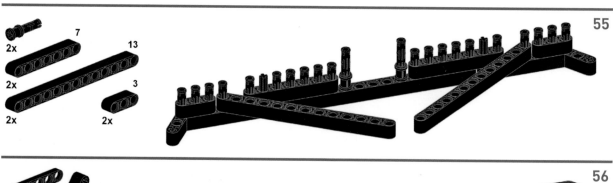

4x

2x 2x

2x 3

4x

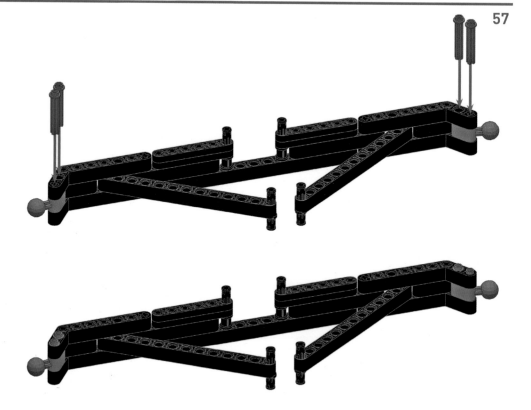

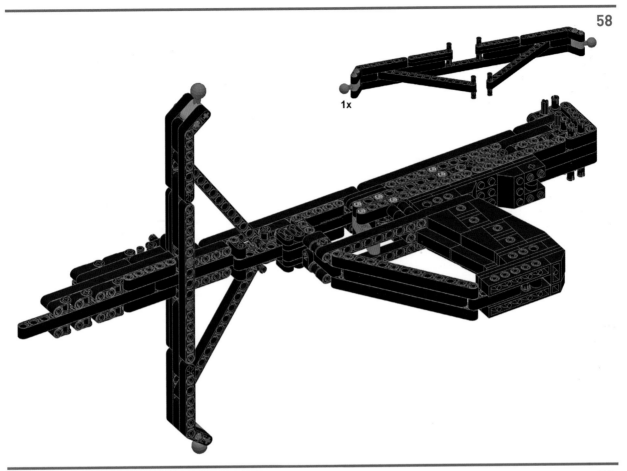

1x

3
4x
2x

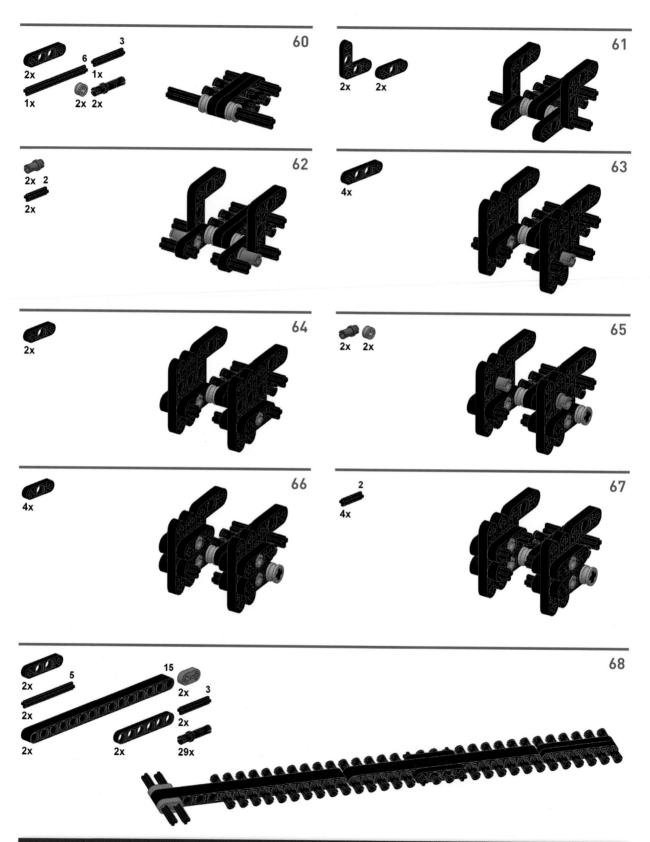

60

2x
3
6
1x
1x
2x 2x

61

2x 2x

62

2x 2
2x

63

4x

64

2x

65

2x 2x

66

4x

67

2
4x

68

2x
5
2x
2x
15
2x
3
2x
2x 29x

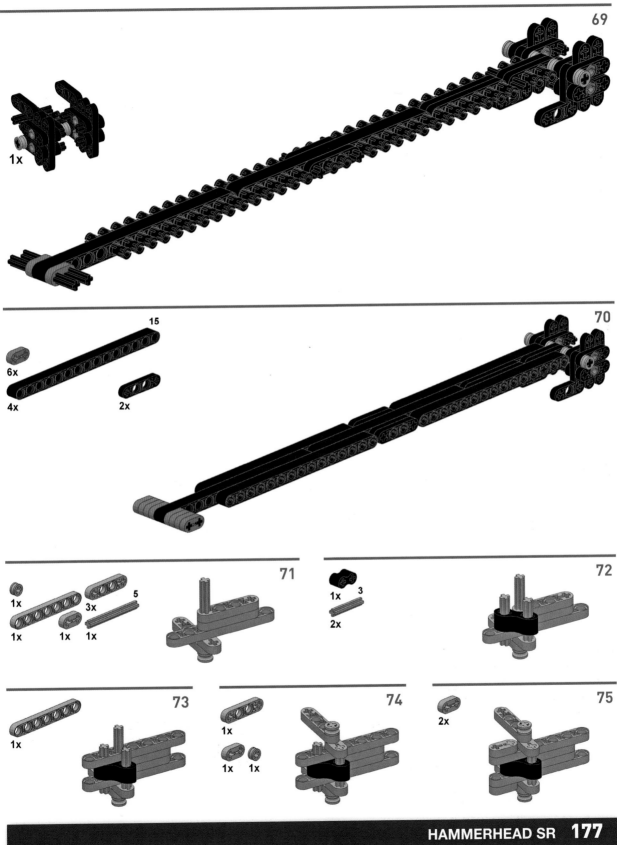

69

1x

70

15

6x

4x

2x

71

1x

1x

1x

1x

3x

5

72

1x

3

2x

73

1x

74

1x

1x

1x

75

2x

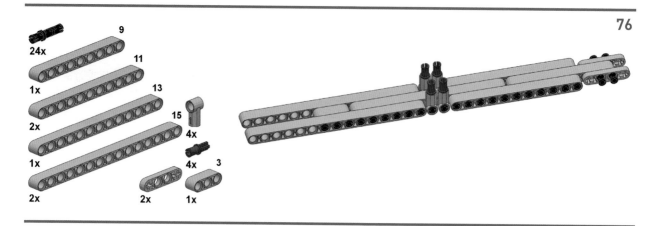

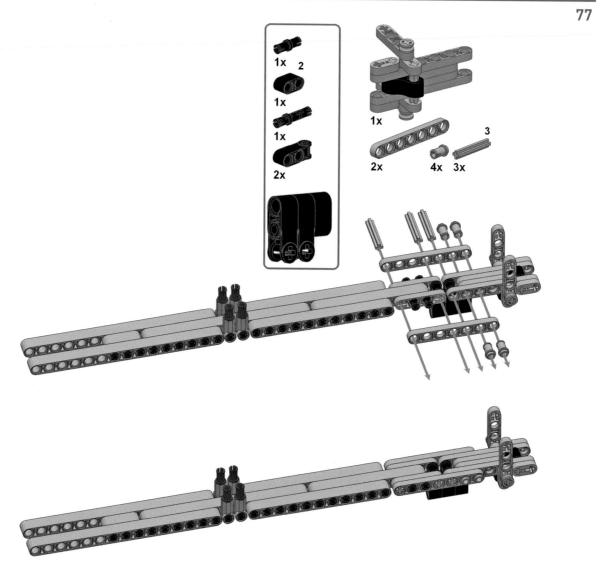

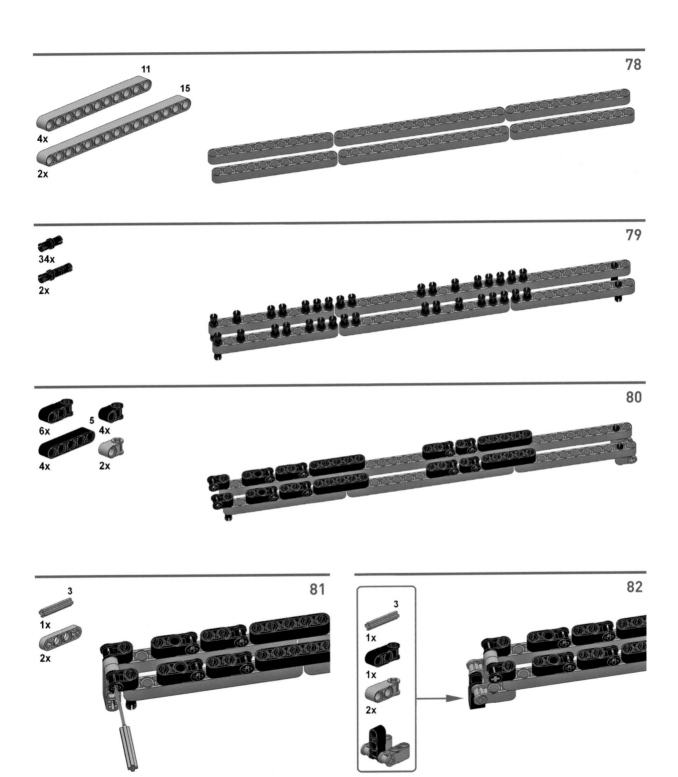

78

11
4x

15
2x

79

34x

2x

80

6x

5

4x

4x

2x

81

3
1x

2x

82

3
1x

1x

2x

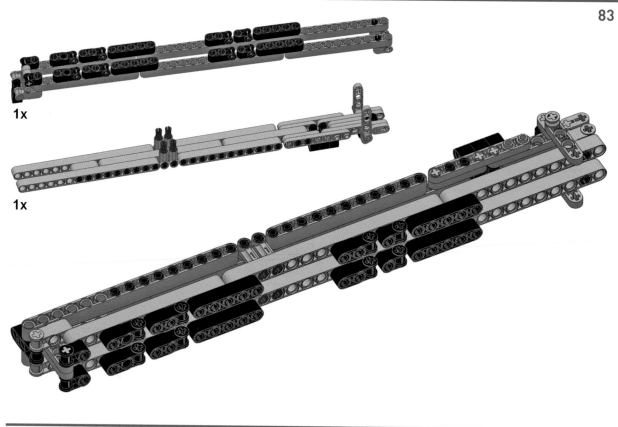

1x

1x

13

1x        7x

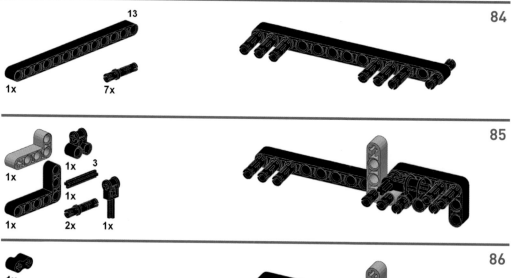

1x

1x    3

1x

1x    2x    1x

1x

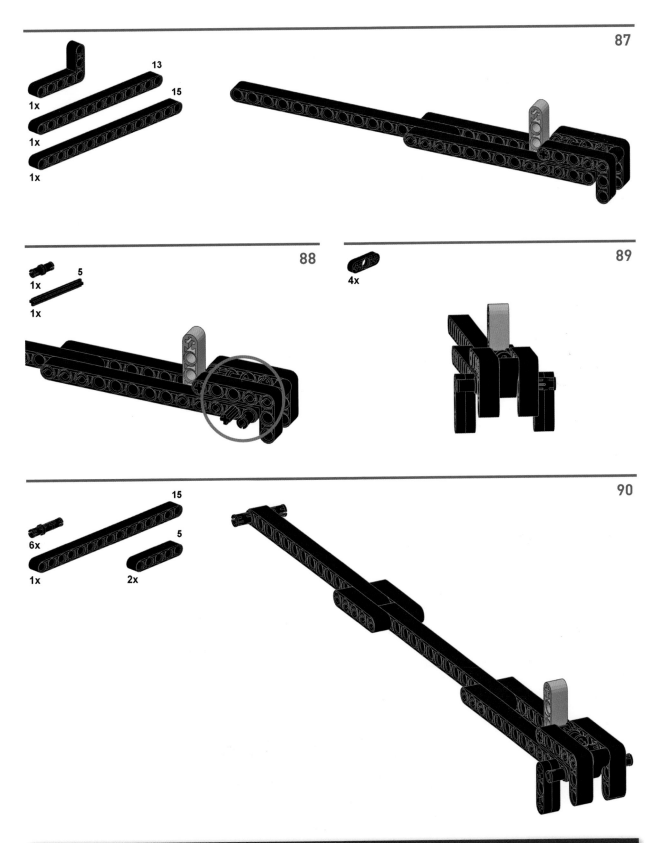

13
1x

15
1x

1x

5
1x

1x

4x

15

6x

5

1x

2x

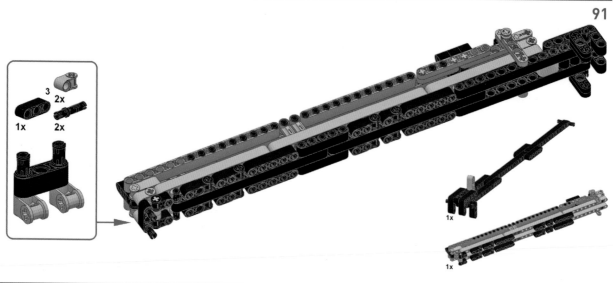

91

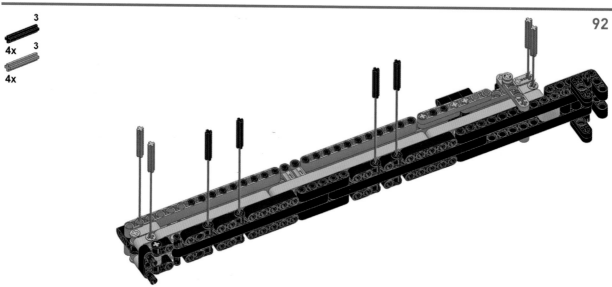

92

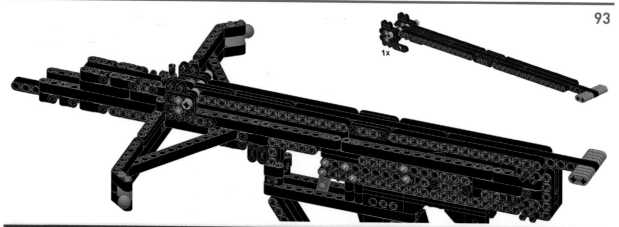

93

1x
2
2x
3
2x
7
2x

5x

5

2x

7x

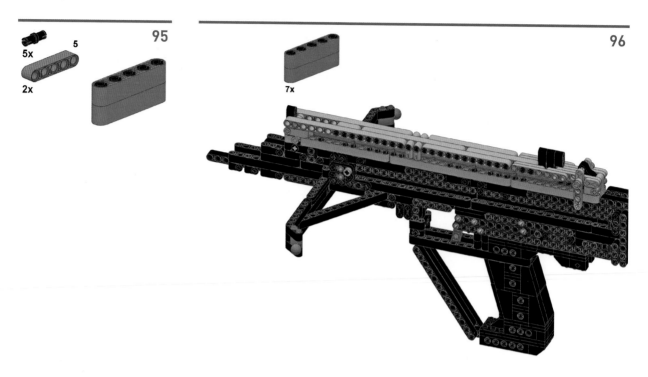

1x

Twisting the rubber band
is important for the firing
mechanism to work well.

# HOW IT'S LOADED

Drop the projectile into the loading slot.

Push the projectile down into the magazine.

To cock the gun, pull the slide all the way back and then push it forward again.

# TIPS

Tuning Tip: Put some metal into your projectiles, like this pin from a cupboard.

Or even add hot soldering tin.

## The effect will be devastating.

# PART 8

... my arsenal shouldn't lack automatic firepower. The next two guns seem to be just the right tools to ruin a SMERT's day!

# DINOSAUR SUPERIOR

## ✛ SPECS

| NAME | DINOSAUR SUPERIOR |
|---|---|
| TYPE | Fully Automatic Assualt RIfle (12 Shots) |
| PARTS | 1610 |
| SIZE | 26.0" x 2.2" x 13.4" |
| SKILL LEVEL | Master |

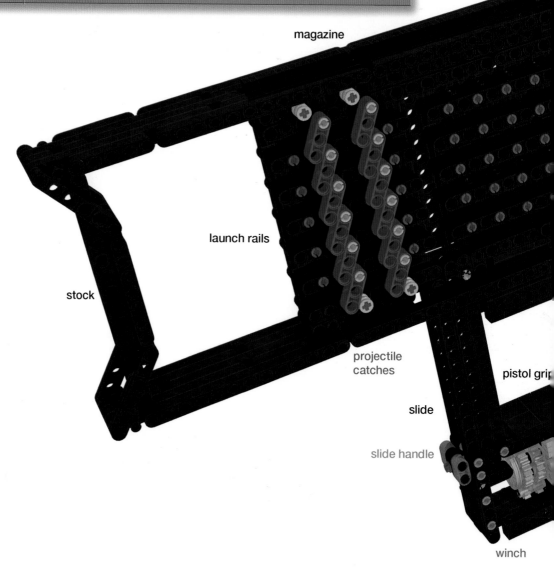

rear sight

magazine

launch rails

stock

projectile catches

pistol grip

slide

slide handle

winch

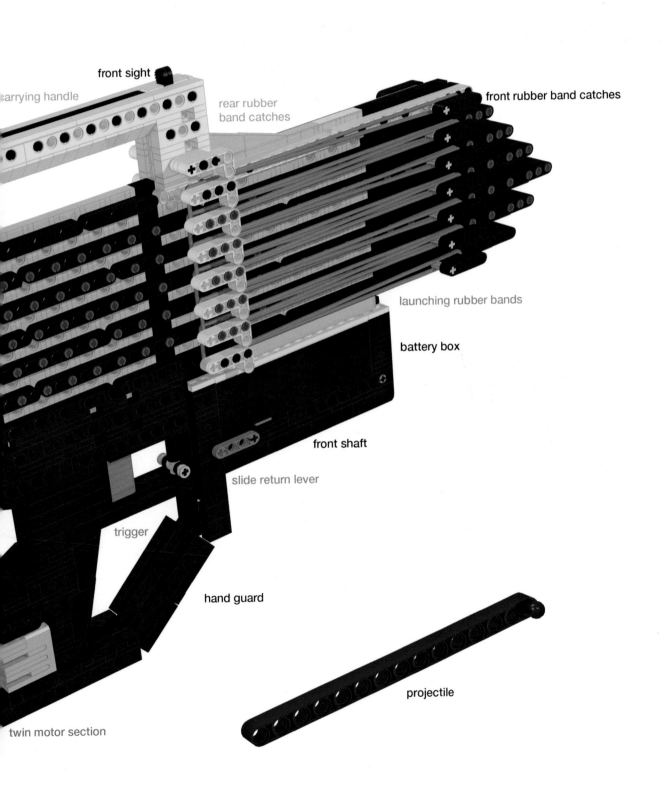

front sight

carrying handle

rear rubber band catches

front rubber band catches

launching rubber bands

battery box

front shaft

slide return lever

trigger

hand guard

projectile

twin motor section

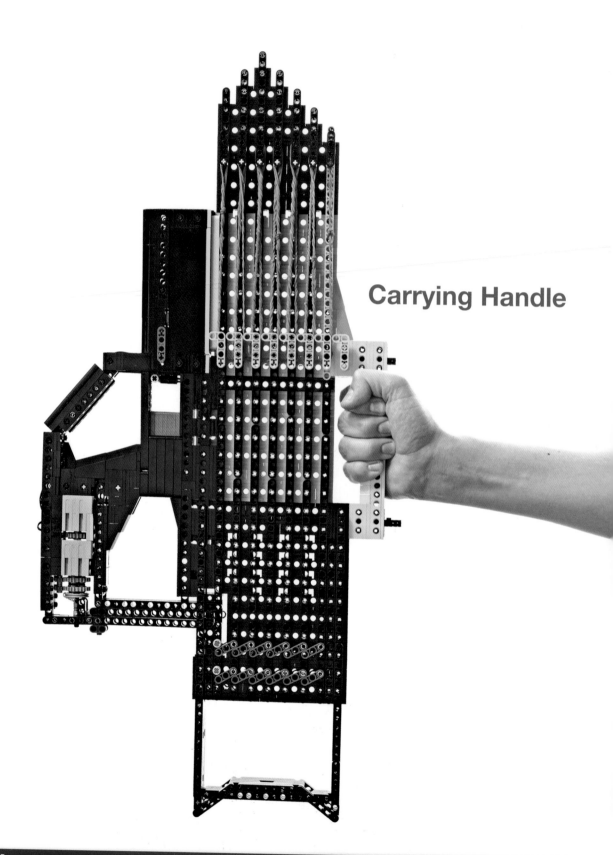

Carrying Handle

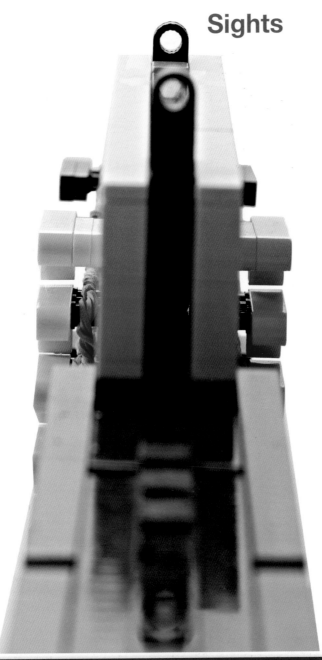

Sights

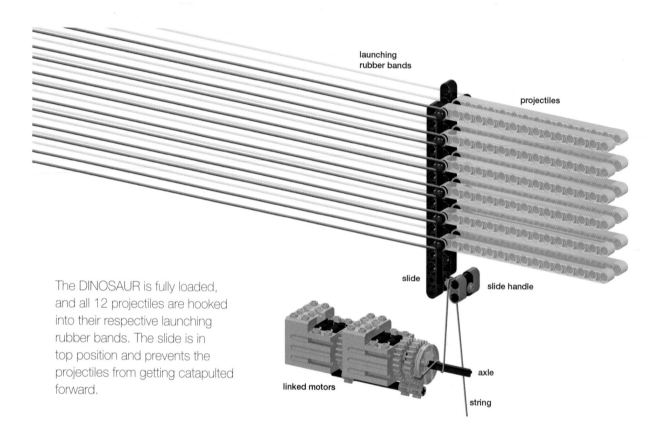

launching
rubber bands

projectiles

The DINOSAUR is fully loaded, and all 12 projectiles are hooked into their respective launching rubber bands. The slide is in top position and prevents the projectiles from getting catapulted forward.

slide

slide handle

linked motors

axle

string

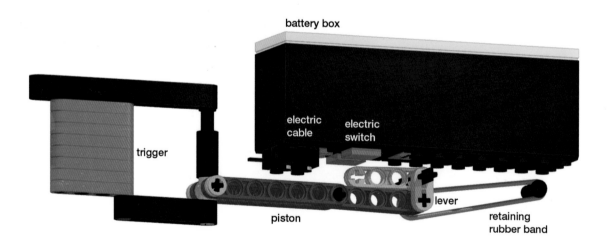

battery box

electric cable

electric switch

trigger

piston

lever

retaining rubber band

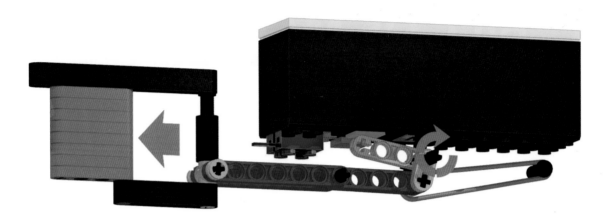

Now, the trigger is pulled, and the movement gets transferred via the piston to the lever, which actuates the electric switch of the battery box. This results in electric current being applied to the motors.

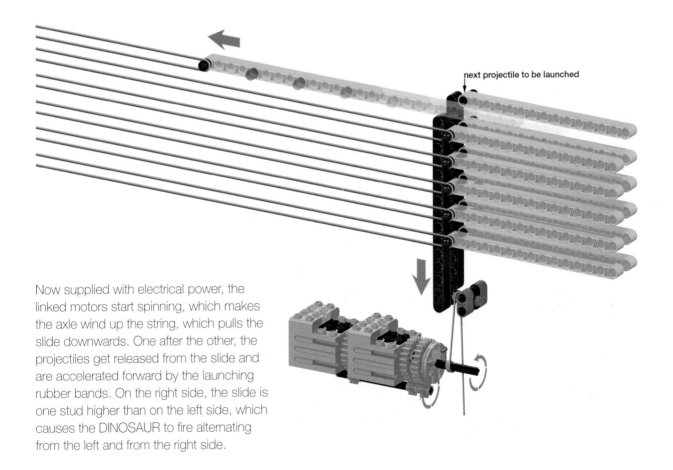

next projectile to be launched

Now supplied with electrical power, the linked motors start spinning, which makes the axle wind up the string, which pulls the slide downwards. One after the other, the projectiles get released from the slide and are accelerated forward by the launching rubber bands. On the right side, the slide is one stud higher than on the left side, which causes the DINOSAUR to fire alternating from the left and from the right side.

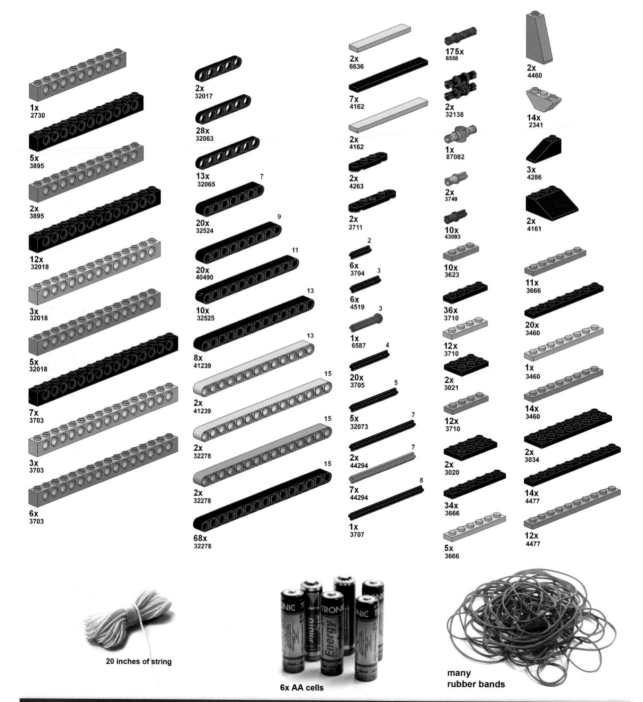

1x
2730

5x
3895

2x
3895

12x
32018

3x
32018

5x
32018

7x
3703

3x
3703

6x
3703

2x
32017

28x
32063

13x
32065          7

20x
32524          9

20x
40490          11

10x
32525          13

8x
41239          13

2x
41239          15

2x
32278          15

2x
32278          15

68x
32278

2x
6636

7x
4162

2x
4162

2x
4263

2x
2711

6x          2
3704

6x          3
4519

1x          3
6587

20x          4
3705

5x          5
32073

2x          7
44294

7x          7
44294          8

1x
3707

175x
6558

2x
32138

1x
87082

2x
3749

10x
43093

10x
3623

36x
3710

12x
3710

2x
3021

12x
3710

2x
3020

34x
3666

5x
3666

2x
4460

14x
2341

3x
4286

2x
4161

11x
3666

20x
3460

1x
3460

14x
3460

2x
3034

14x
4477

12x
4477

20 inches of string

6x AA cells

many
rubber bands

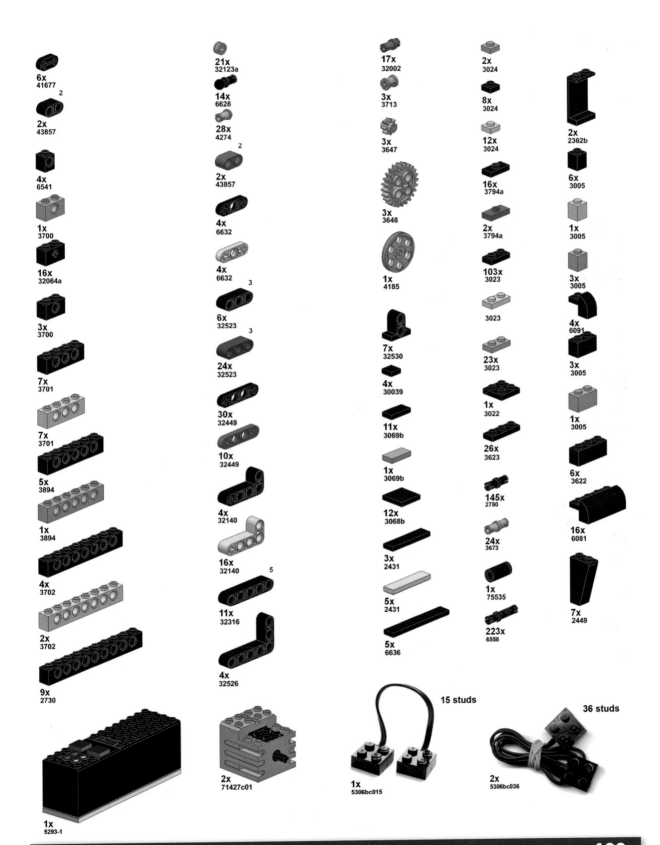

6x
41677

2

2x
43857

4x
6541

1x
3700

16x
32064a

3x
3700

7x
3701

7x
3701

5x
3894

1x
3894

4x
3702

2x
3702

9x
2730

21x
32123a

14x
6628

28x
4274

2

2x
43857

4x
6632

4x
6632

3

6x
32523

3

24x
32523

30x
32449

10x
32449

4x
32140

16x
32140

5

11x
32316

4x
32526

17x
32002

3x
3713

3x
3647

3x
3648

1x
4185

7x
32530

4x
30039

11x
3069b

1x
3069b

12x
3068b

3x
2431

5x
2431

5x
6636

2x
3024

8x
3024

12x
3024

16x
3794a

2x
3794a

103x
3023

3023

23x
3023

1x
3022

26x
3623

145x
2780

24x
3673

1x
75535

223x
6558

2x
2362b

6x
3005

1x
3005

3x
3005

4x
6091

3x
3005

1x
3005

6x
3622

16x
6081

7x
2449

1x
5293-1

2x
71427c01

15 studs

1x
5306bc015

36 studs

2x
5306bc036

**1**

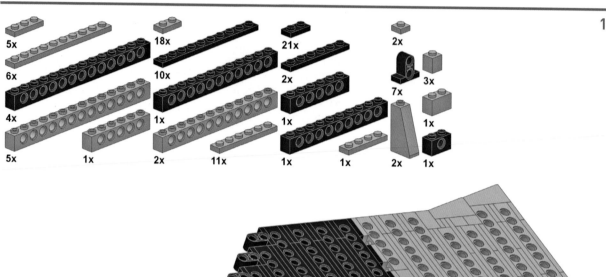

5x
6x
4x
5x
18x
10x
1x
2x
11x
21x
2x
1x
1x
1x
7x
3x
1x
2x
2x
1x

**2**

22x
66x

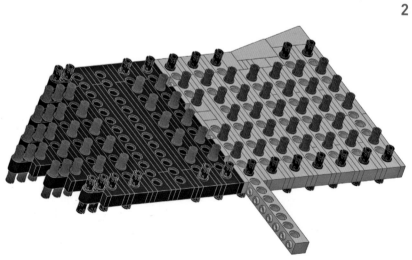

Going forward, when you see this symbol, apply the listed parts mirror-symmetrically on both sides of the model.

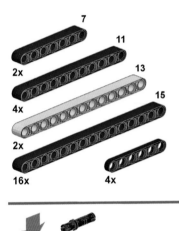

7

11

2x

13

4x

15

2x

16x

4x

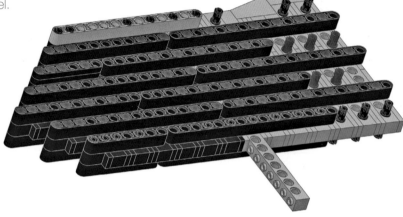

 14x

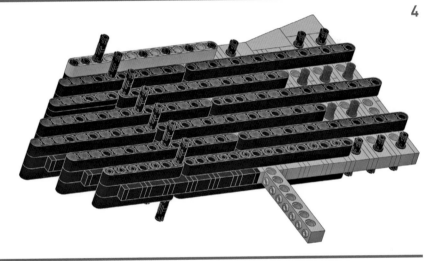

 14x

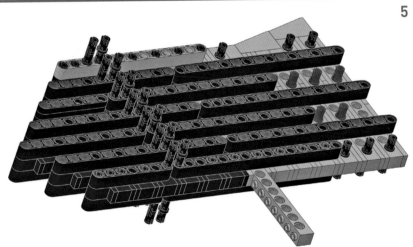

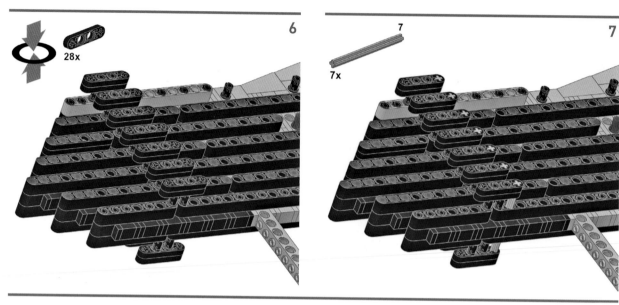

6
7
7
28x
7x

8

14x
4x
3x
6x 6x

5x
8x
1x
2x
1x 2x

2x
1x
1x
2x
1x
1x
2x
2x
6x
2x 1x 11x 3x 1x

1x
2x
1x
2x
1x
1x
2x

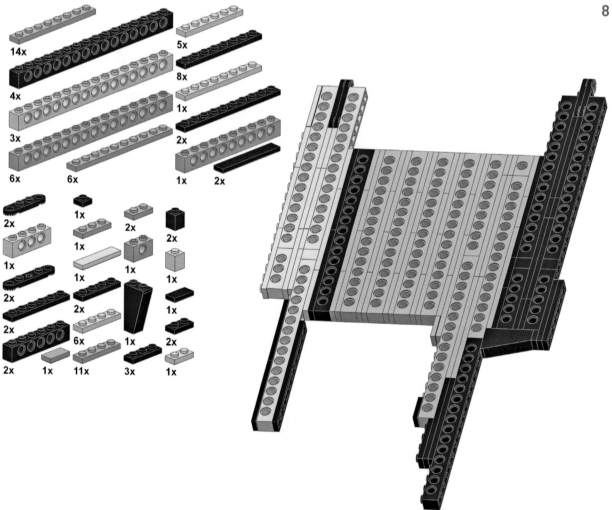

**37x**

**44x**

**15**

**6x**     **4x**

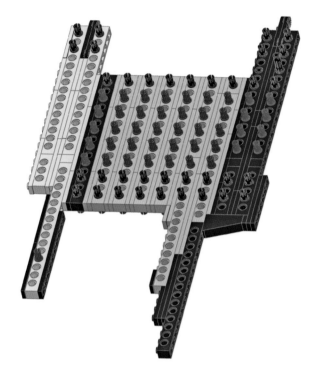

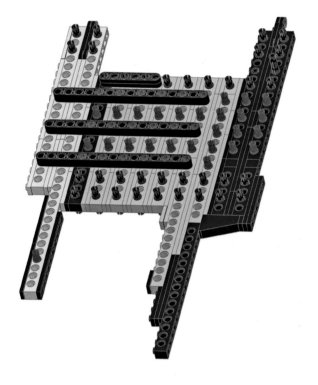

**3x**

**1x**

**1x**     **1x**

**1x**

**3x**

**1x**     **6x**     **3x**

**6x**

**7x**

**2x**

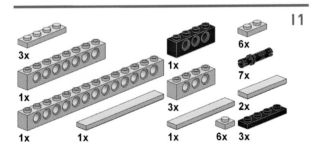

**1x**

**1x**     **1x**

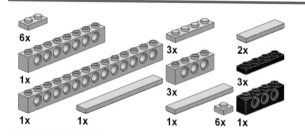

6x
1x
1x
1x

3x
3x

2x
3x
6x 1x

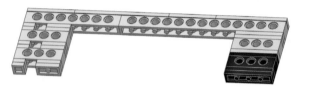

1x

1x

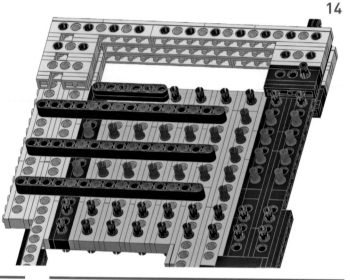

14x

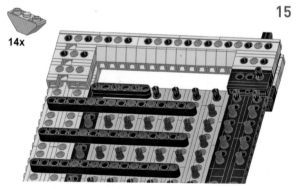

4x

7

2x 2x

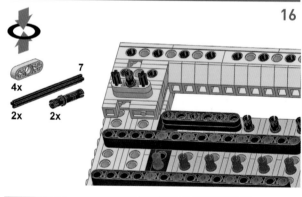

2x

13

1x 1x

1x

3

1x 1x

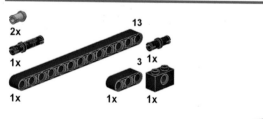

7

1x 3x

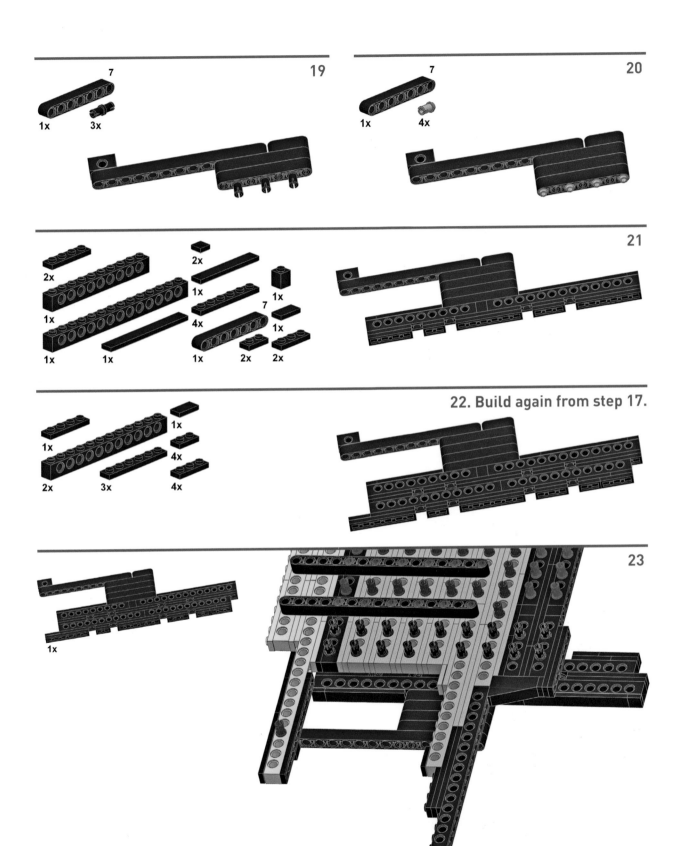

19

7
1x  3x

20

7
1x  4x

21

2x
2x
1x
1x
1x
1x
7
4x
1x
1x  1x  2x  2x

**22. Build again from step 17.**

1x
1x
4x
2x  3x  4x

23

1x

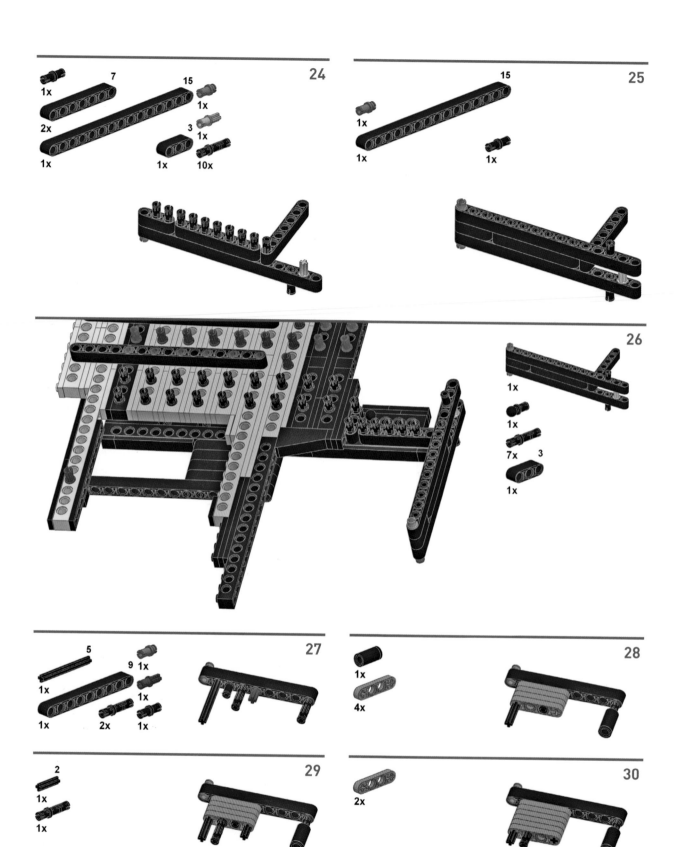

24

1x
7
2x
15
1x
1x
3
1x
1x
10x

25

1x
15
1x
1x

26

1x
1x
7x
3
1x

27

5
9
1x
1x
1x
1x
2x
1x

28

1x
4x

29

2
1x
1x

30

2x

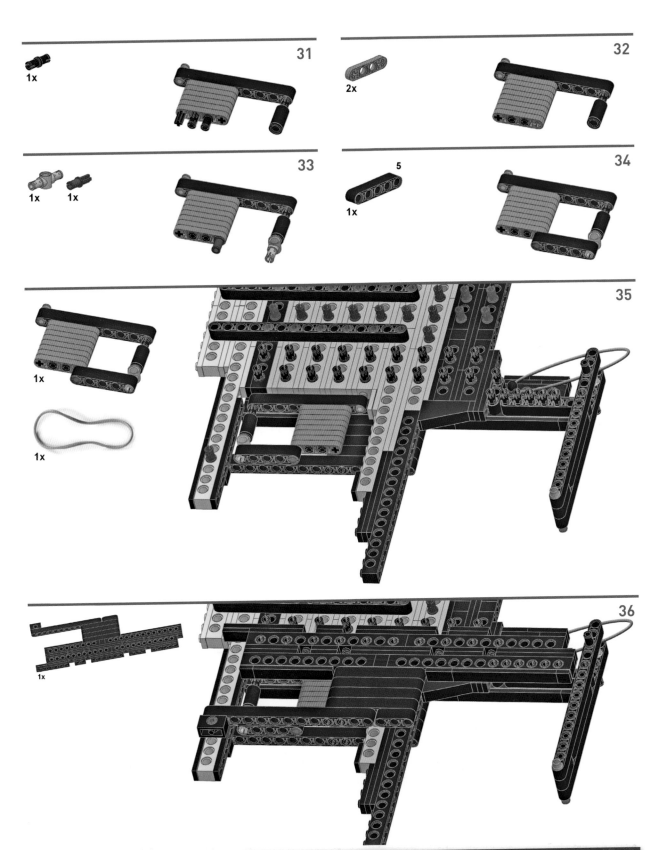

**31** 1x

**32** 2x

**33** 1x 1x

**34** 5 1x

**35** 1x 1x

**36** 1x

16x

37

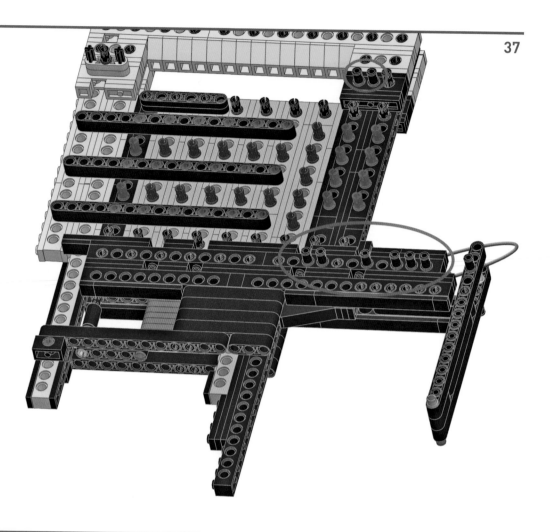

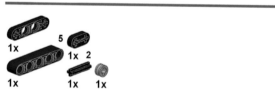

38

1x

1x

1x

1x

2x 4

1x

1x

5

2x

1x 1x 1x 1x

1x

1x

1x

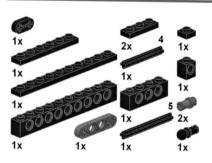

39

1x

1x

5

1x 2

1x 1x

**40**

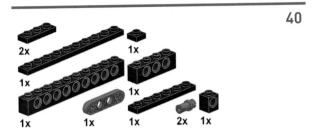

2x  1x  1x  1x  1x  1x  2x  1x

**41**

4x  1x

**42**

20x  8x  4x

**43**

14x

**44**

15

2x

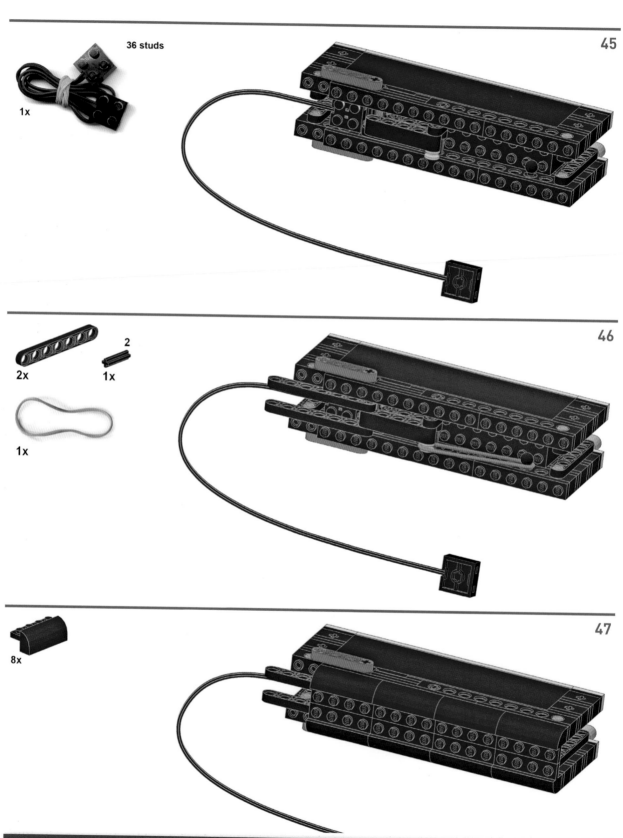

8x

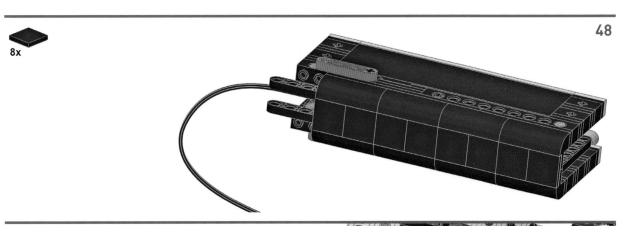

2x
3
1x
4
2x

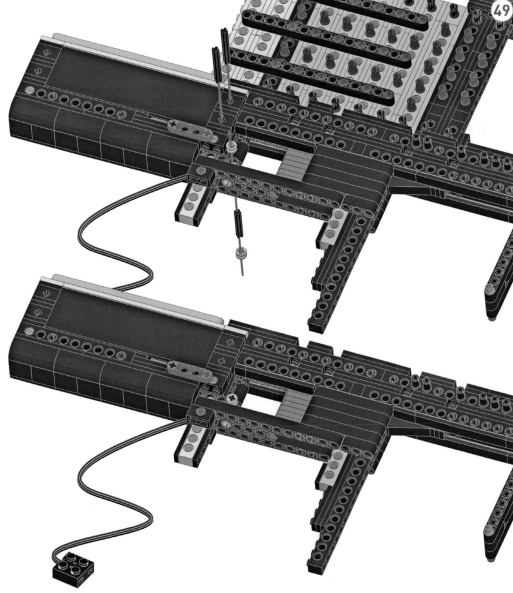

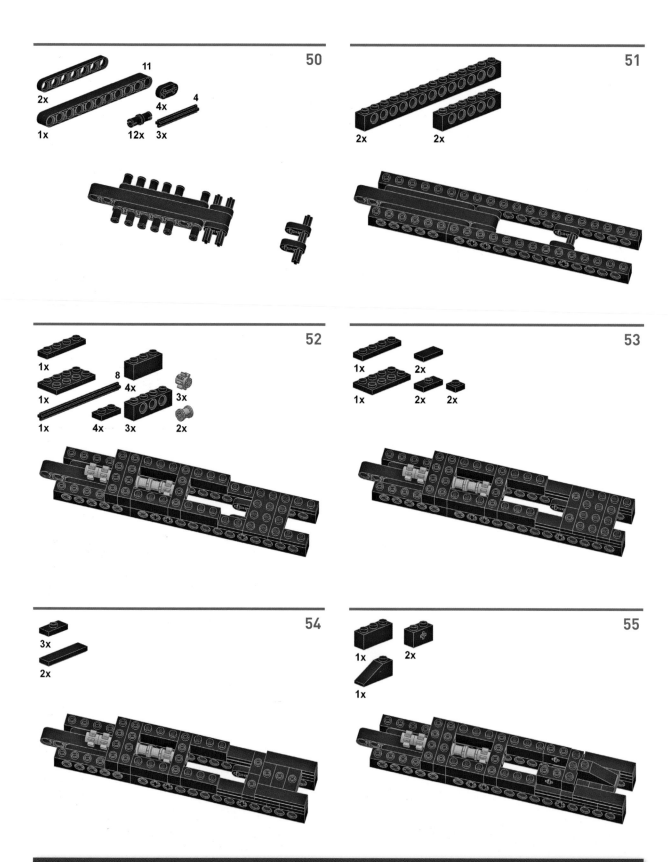

50

2x
11
1x
4x
12x 3x
4

51

2x 2x

52

1x
1x
1x
8
4x
4x 3x
3x
2x

53

1x
1x
2x
2x 2x

54

3x
2x

55

1x
2x
1x

**56**

2x

2x

2x

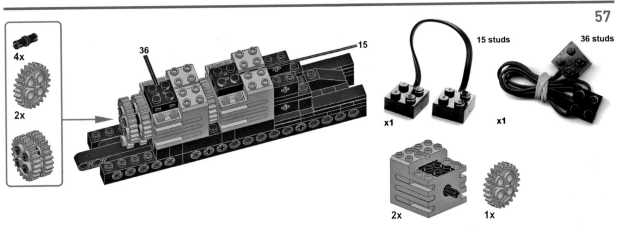

**57**

4x

2x

15 studs

36 studs

x1

x1

36

15

2x

1x

**58**

1x

3x

3x

4x

3x

Lay the cables through the gap in front of the motors.

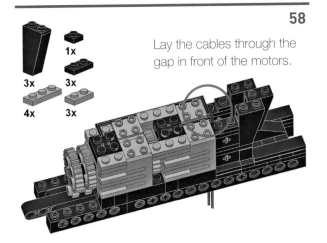

**59**

18x

2x

1x

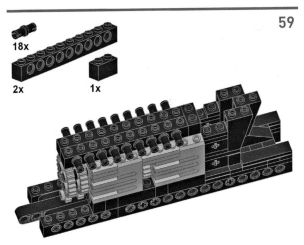

**60**

4x

11x

1x

2x

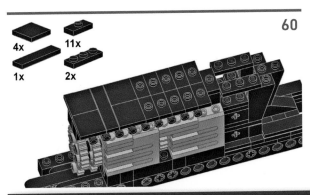

**61**

1x

2x

1x

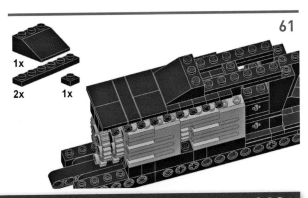

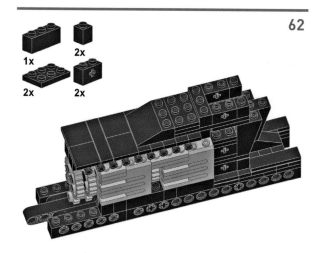

1x
2x
2x
2x

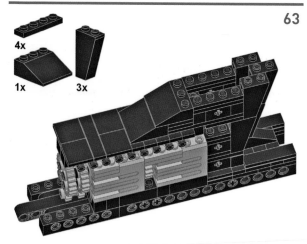

4x
1x
3x

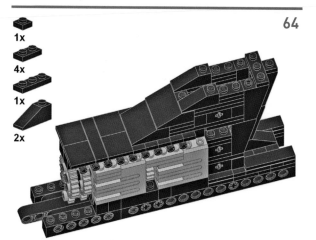

1x
4x
1x
2x

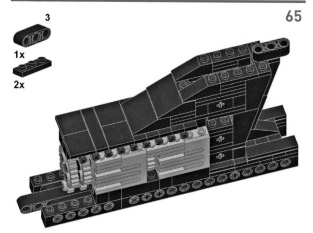

3
1x
2x

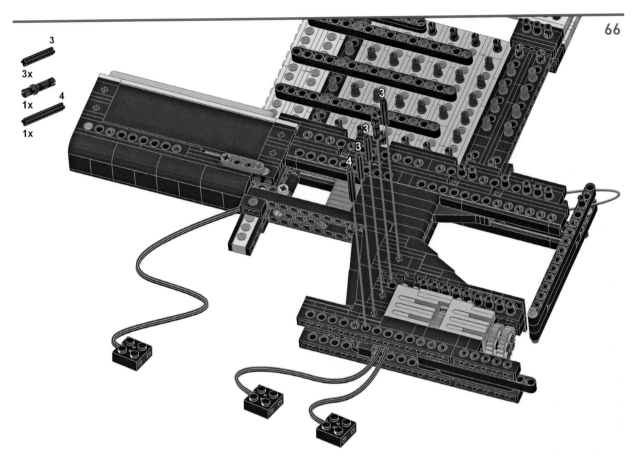

3
3x

4

1x

1x

3

3

4

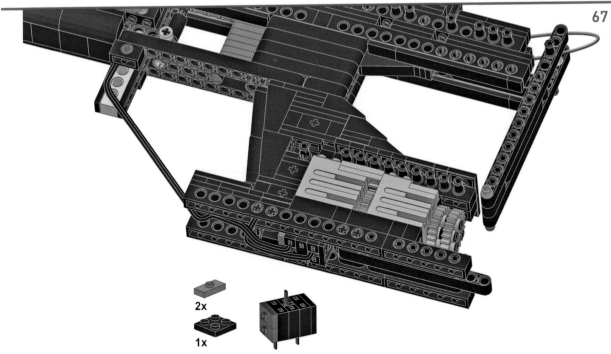

2x

1x

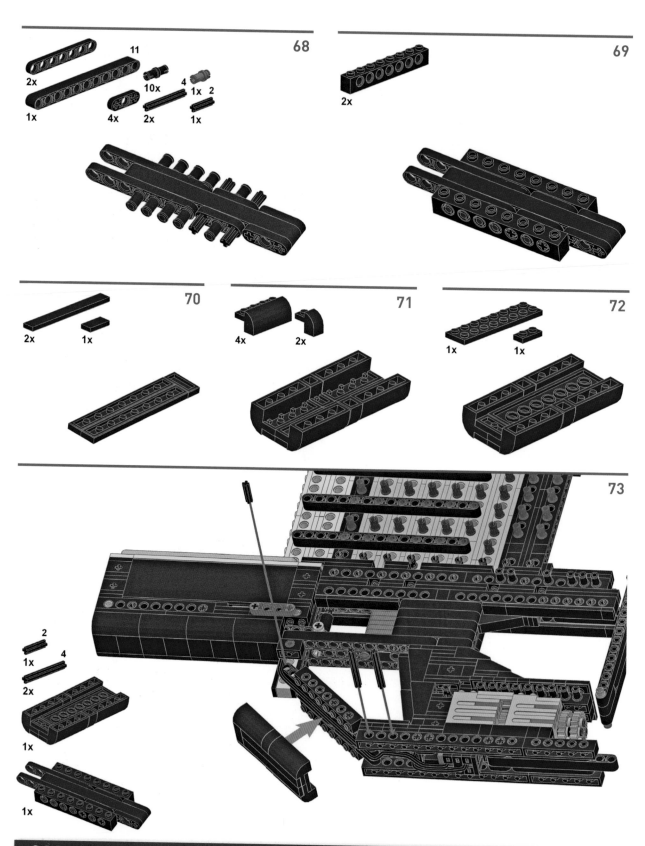

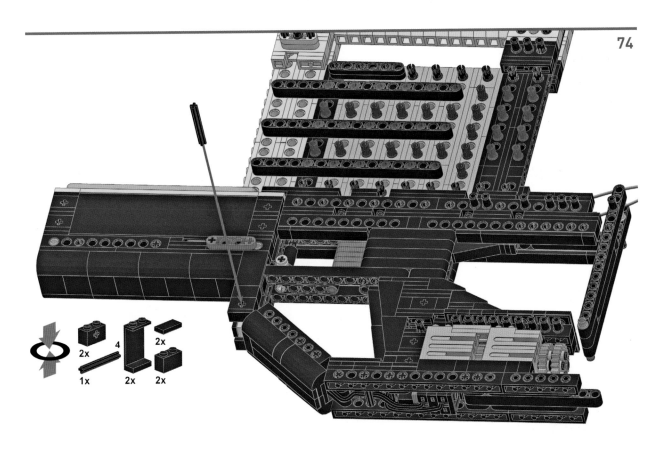

74

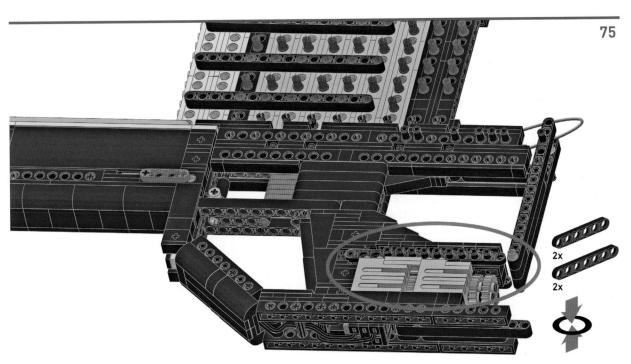

75

**DINOSAUR SUPERIOR** 217

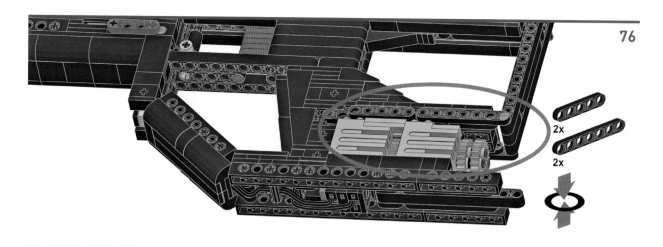

2x

2x

15

2x

2x

3

1x

2

2x

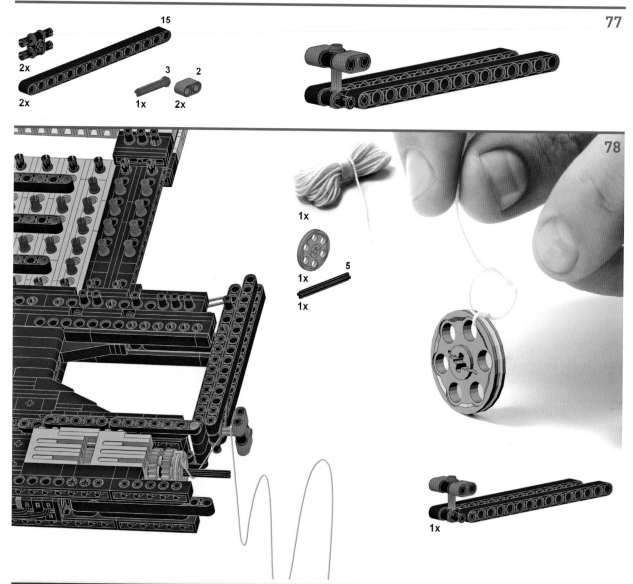

1x

1x

5

1x

1x

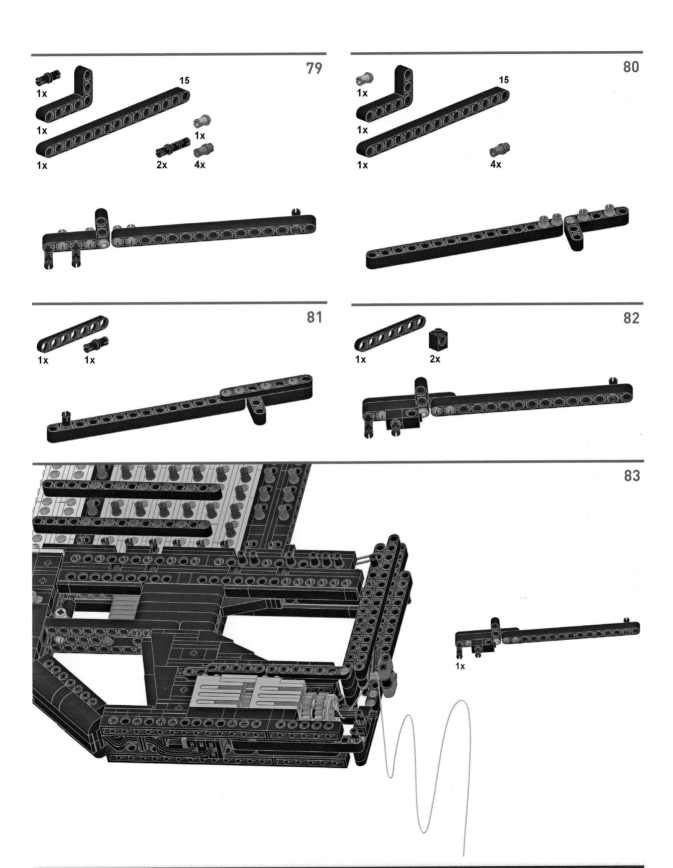

**79**

15

1x
1x
1x
1x
2x
4x

**80**

15

1x
1x
1x
4x

**81**

1x
1x

**82**

1x
2x

**83**

1x

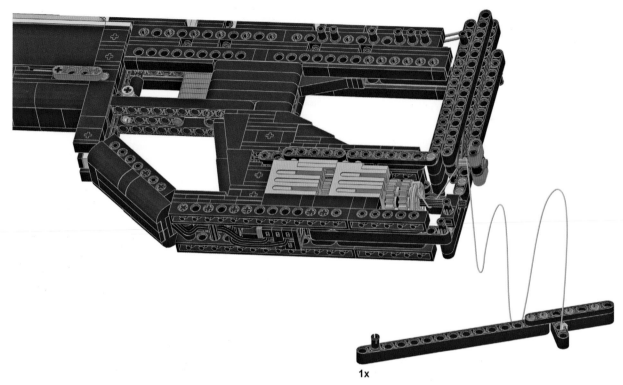

1x

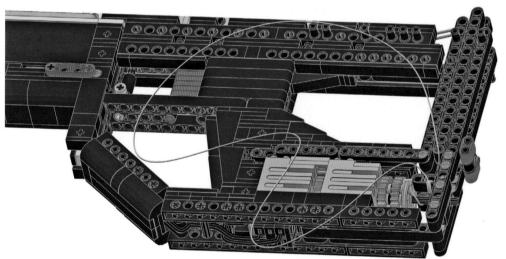

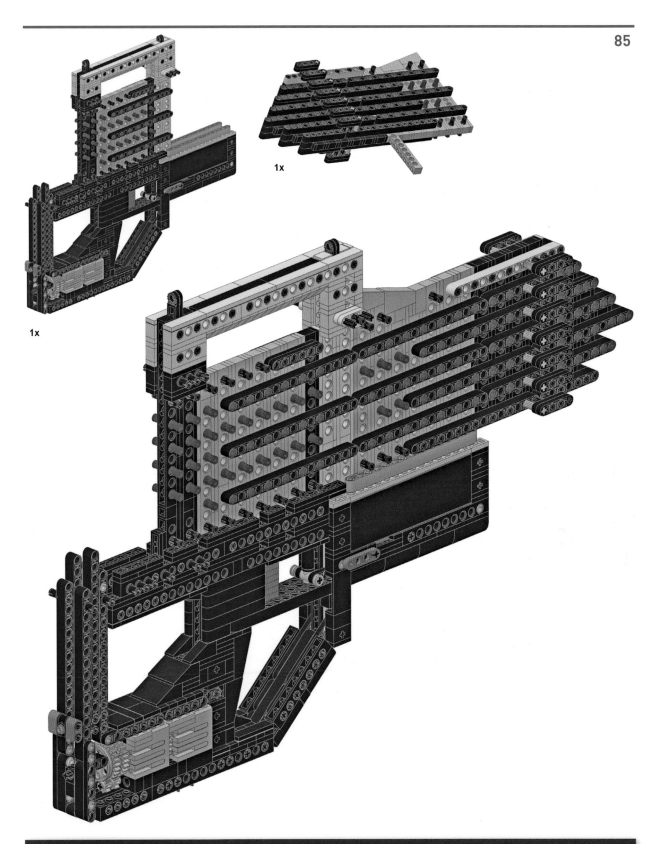

1x

1x

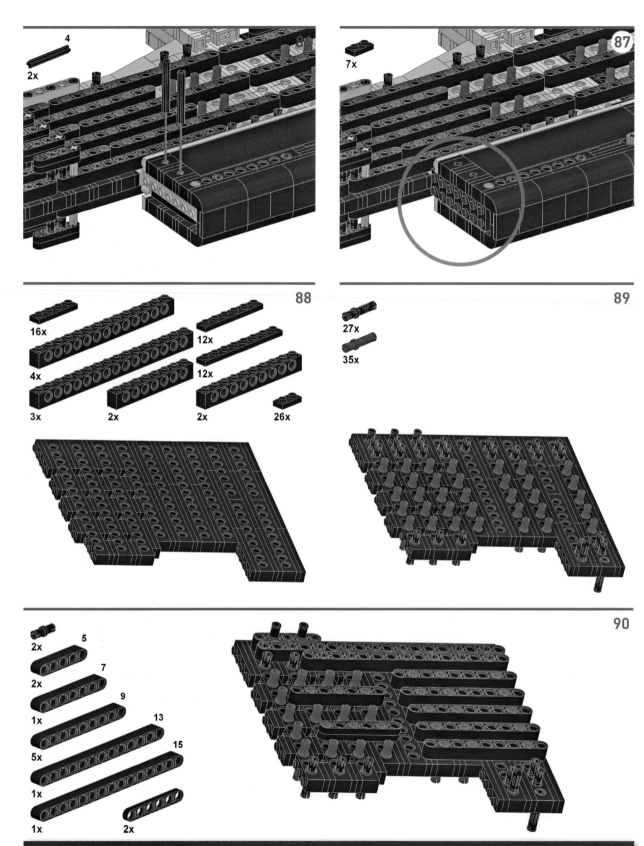

9
2x

13

5

6x

7

3x

1x

2x

1x

7
1x

1x

9
1x

1x

5x   1x   1x

1x

7
1x

3

2x

1x

1x   1x

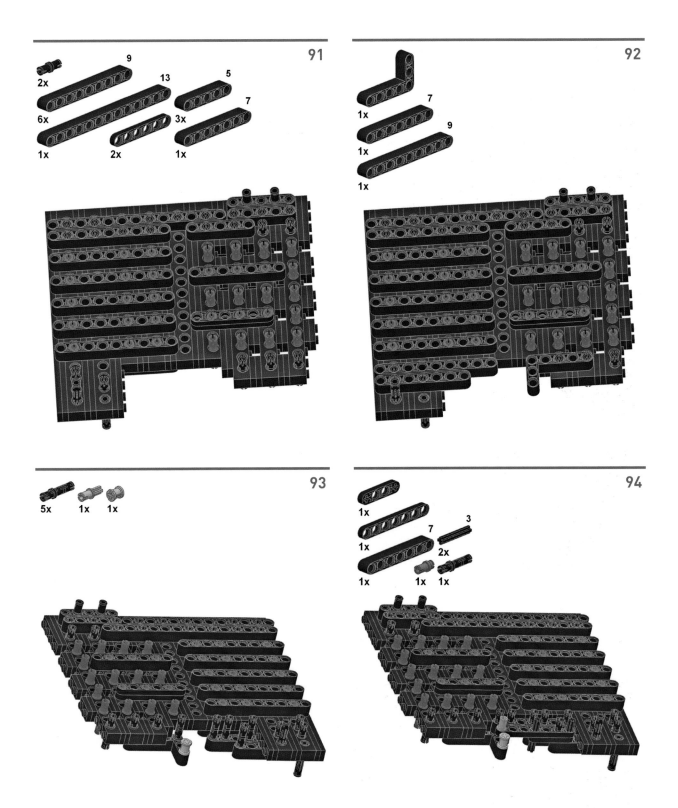

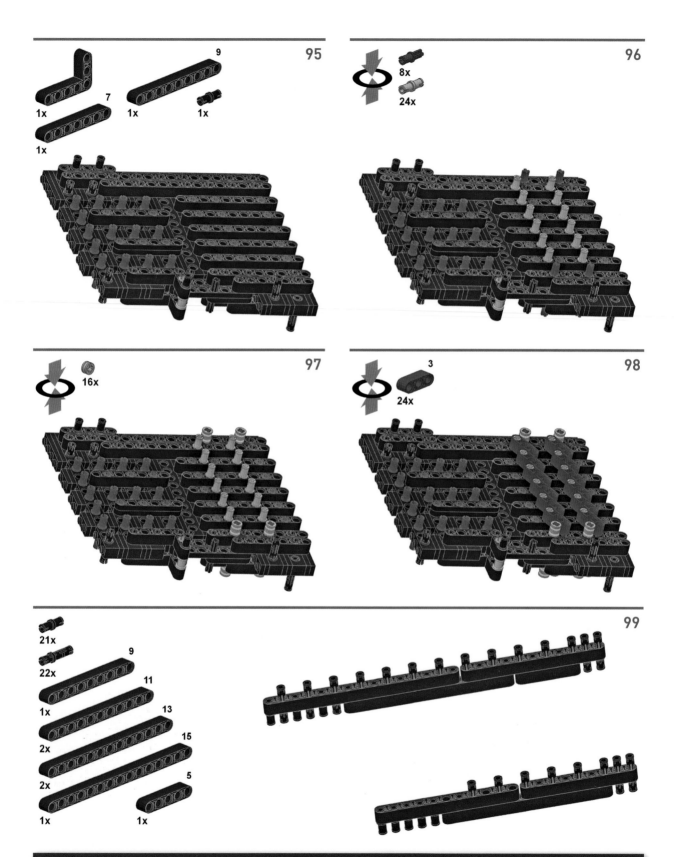

95

9

7

1x

1x

1x

1x

1x

96

8x

24x

97

16x

98

3

24x

21x

22x

9

1x

11

2x

13

2x

15

1x

5

1x

99

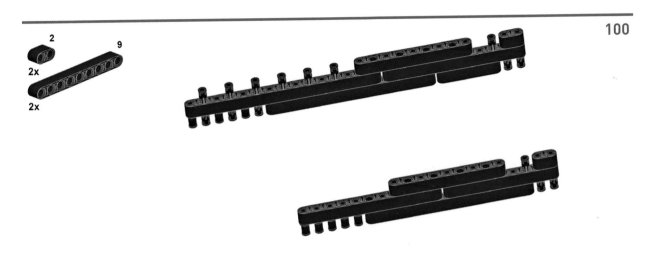

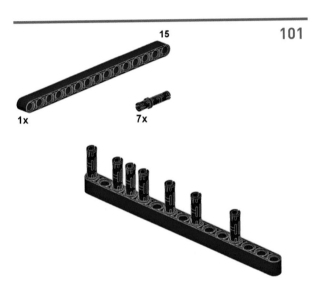

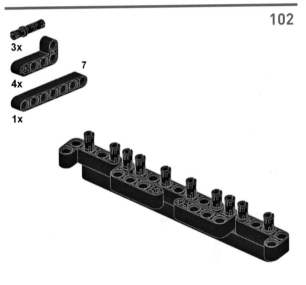

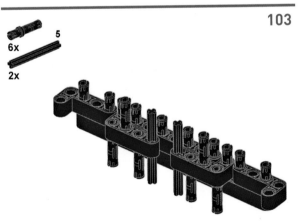

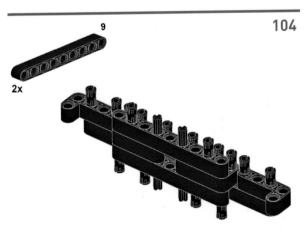

**105**

7x

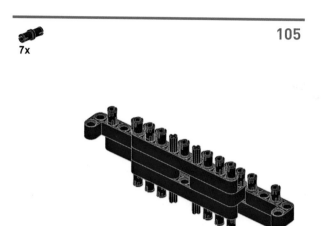

**106**

1x

7

15

2x

1x

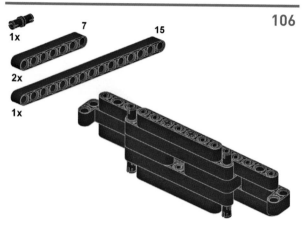

**107. Combine parts from steps 100 and 106.**

**108**

9x

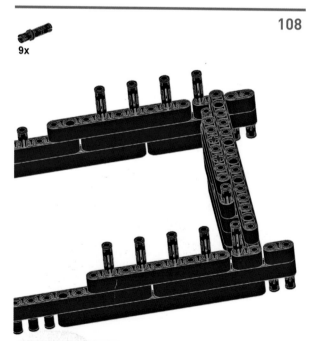

**109**

9

11

1x

1x

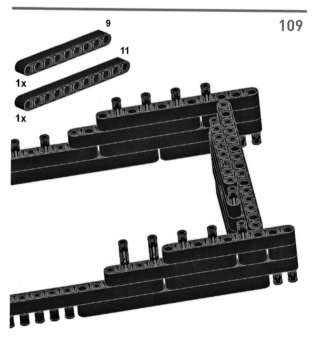

**110**

13x

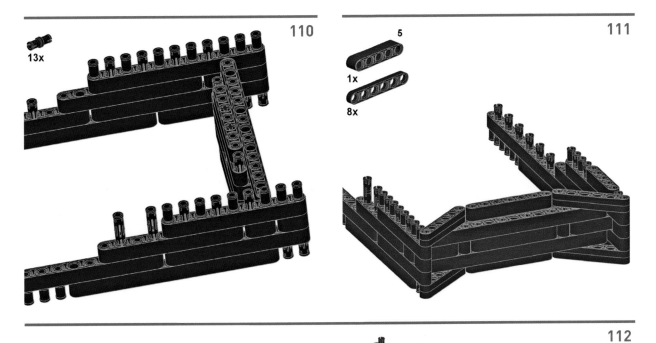

**111**

5

1x

8x

**112**

1x

1x

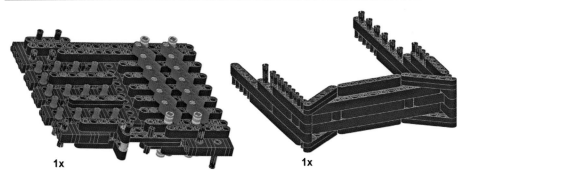

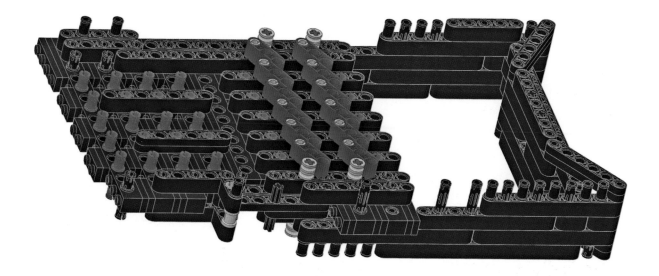

**113**

11

15

1x

1x

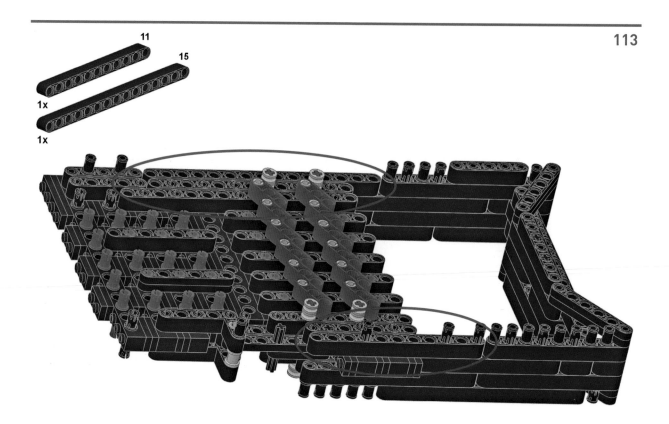

**114**

18x

10x

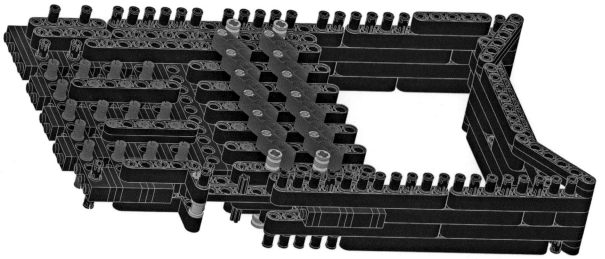

## 115

**13**

**2x**

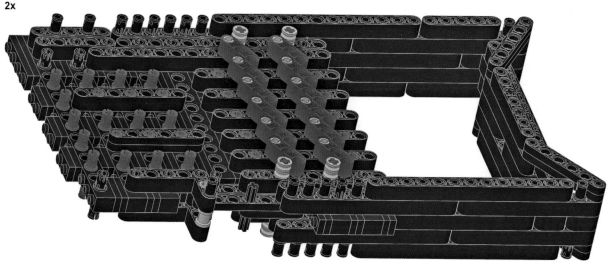

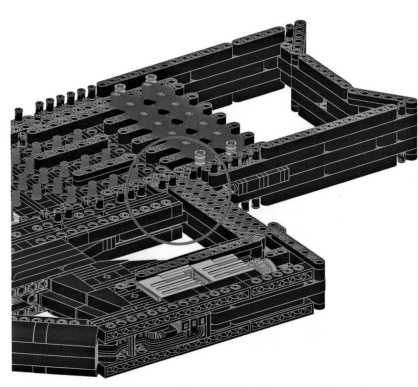

Make sure the slide retaining rubber band is installed like this.

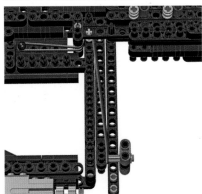

It's a bit difficult to connect the parts here. You've got to stretch them a bit.

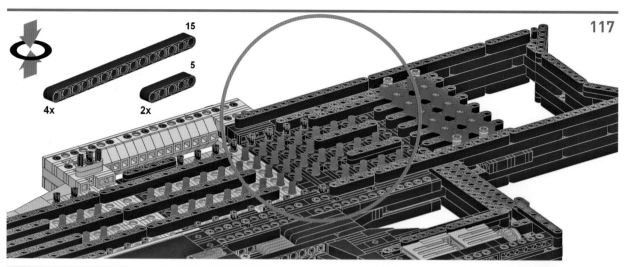

117

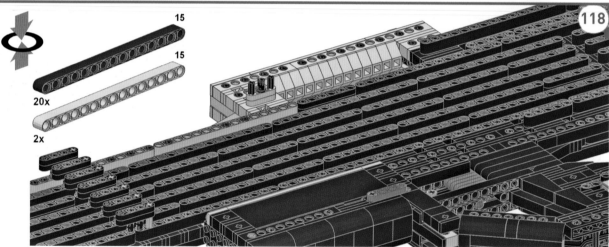

118

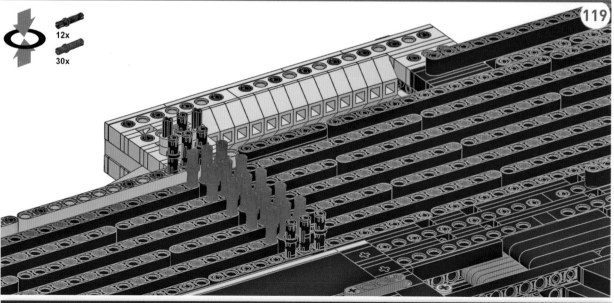

119

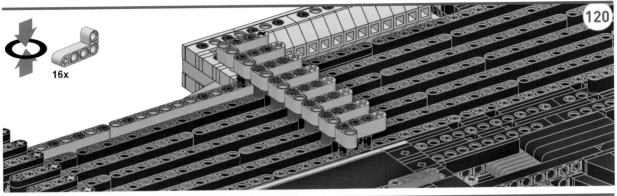

**120**

16x

**121**

6x

**122**

6x

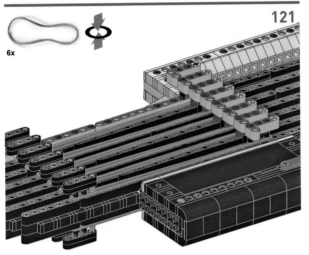

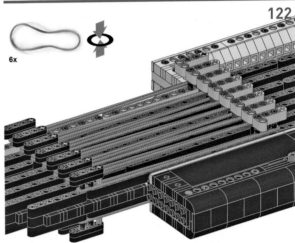

## Tips for adding the rubber bands:

It's important to twist the rubber bands for the gun to work well.

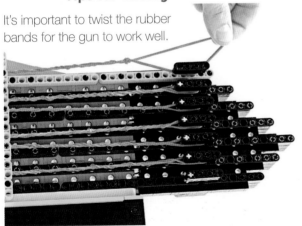

Make sure the rubber bands overlap like this.

## 123. Projectile: build 12x

15

1x

1x

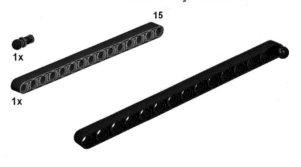

**1**

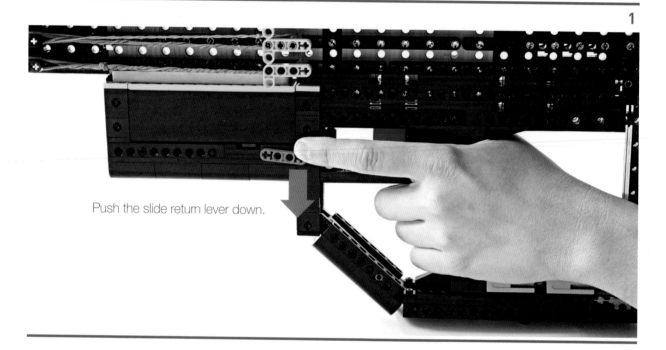

Push the slide return lever down.

**2**

So you can push the slide up.

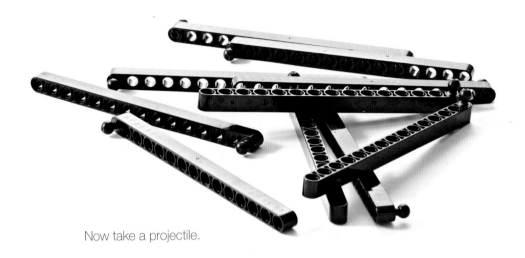

Now take a projectile.

And hook it into a rubber band.

Pull the projectile back.

Let it snap into the projectile catch.

# TIPS

Use hot soldiering tin to add weight to the projectiles.

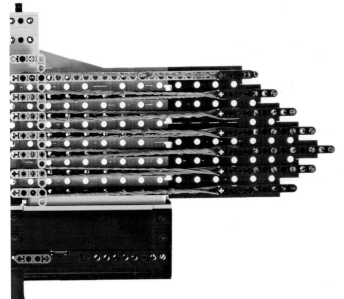

**This will turn the DINOSAUR SUPERIOR into a real beast!**

# MELODY

| SPECS | |
|---|---|
| **NAME** | **MELODY** |
| **TYPE** | **Rubber Band Machine Pistol (40 shots)** |
| **PARTS** | **404** |
| **SIZE** | **13.72" x 1.97" x 7.38"** |
| **SKILL LEVEL** | **Expert** |

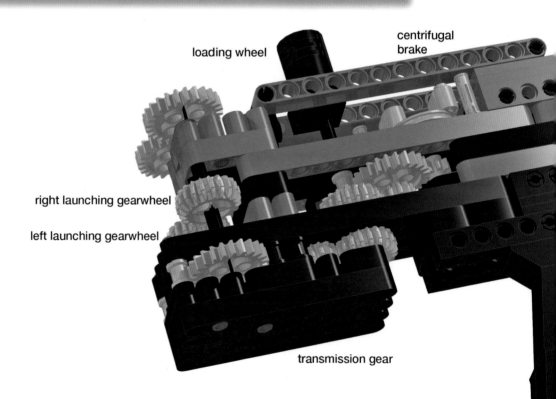

loading wheel

centrifugal brake

right launching gearwheel

left launching gearwheel

transmission gear

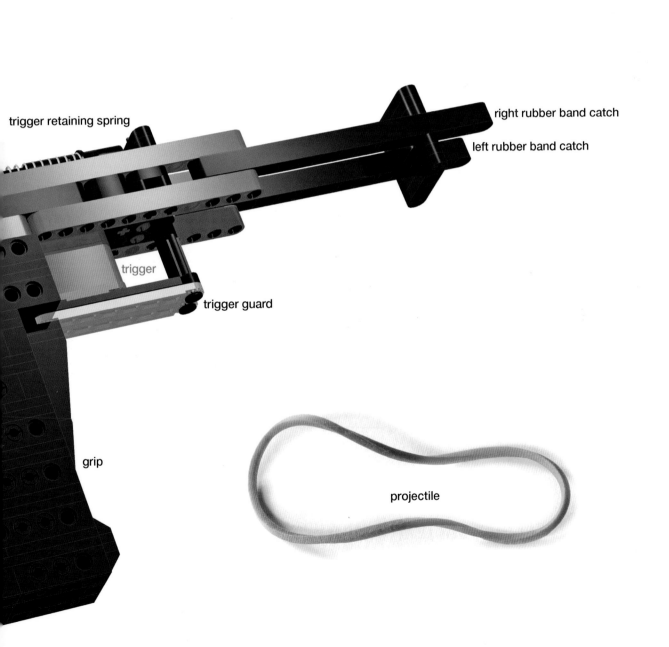

trigger retaining spring

right rubber band catch

left rubber band catch

trigger

trigger guard

grip

projectile

# HOW IT WORKS

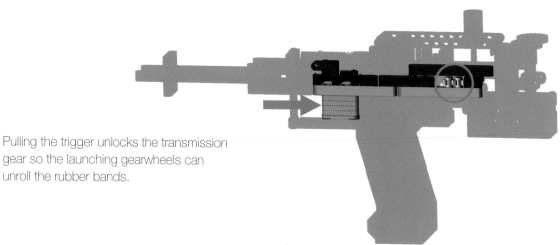

Pulling the trigger unlocks the transmission gear so the launching gearwheels can unroll the rubber bands.

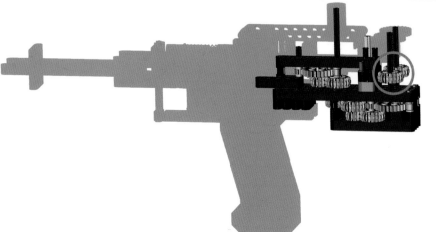

The unrolling rubber bands turn the launching gearwheels. This rotary movement gets accelerated by the transmission gear.

The transmission gear lets the centrifugal brake spin at high speed. The centrifugal brake is the unique feature of the MELODY: It's a mechanism that forces an accelerated axis to spin at a constant speed. It helps the MELODY to keep its rate of fire constant—no matter how many rubber bands are loaded. You find the same mechanisms inside of rotary phones.

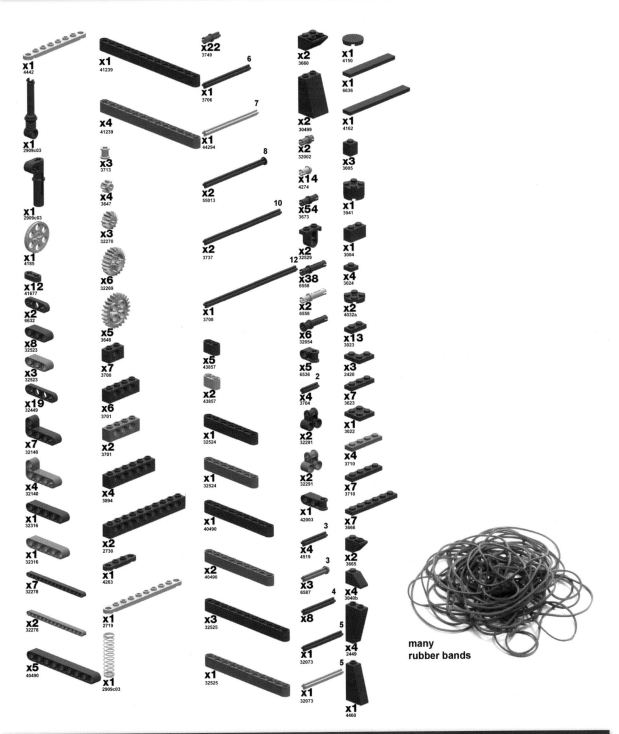

**x1** 4442

**x1** 41239

**x22** 3749

6

**x2** 3660

**x1** 4150

**x1** 2909c03

**x4** 41239

**x1** 3706

**x2** 30499

**x1** 6636

7

**x2** 32002

**x1** 4162

**x1** 2909c03

**x3** 3713

**x1** 44294

**x14** 4274

**x3** 3005

8

**x1** 4185

**x4** 3647

**x2** 55013

**x54** 3673

**x1** 3941

**x12** 41677

**x3** 32270

10

**x2** 32529

**x1** 3004

**x2** 6632

**x6** 32269

**x2** 3737

12

**x38** 6558

**x4** 3024

**x8** 32523

**x5** 3648

**x1** 3708

**x2** 6558

**x2** 4032a

**x3** 32523

**x7** 3700

**x5** 43857

**x6** 32054

**x13** 3023

**x19** 32449

**x6** 3701

**x2** 43857

**x5** 6536

2

**x3** 2420

**x7** 32140

**x2** 3701

**x4** 3704

**x7** 3623

**x4** 32140

**x4** 3894

**x1** 32524

**x2** 32291

**x1** 3022

**x1** 32316

**x2** 2730

**x1** 32524

**x2** 32291

**x4** 3710

**x1** 32316

**x1** 4263

**x1** 40490

**x1** 42003

3

**x7** 3710

**x7** 32278

**x1** 2719

**x2** 40490

**x4** 4519

3

**x7** 3666

**x2** 32278

**x1** 2909c03

**x3** 32525

**x3** 6587

4

**x2** 3665

**x5** 40490

**x1** 32525

**x8**

**x4** 3040b

5

**x1** 32073

**x4** 2449

**x1** 32073

5

**x1** 4460

many rubber bands

# BUILDING INSTRUCTIONS

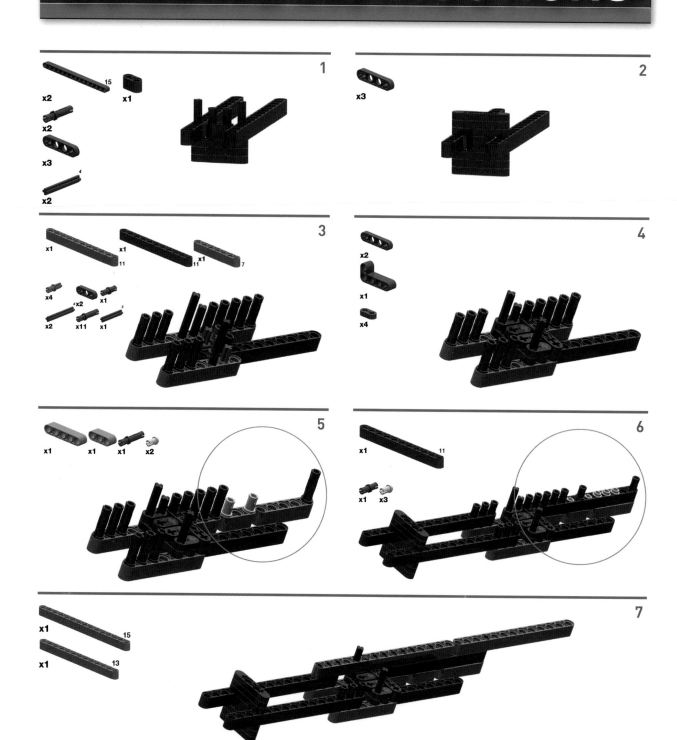

**1**

x2  15
x1
x2
x3
x2  4

**2**

x3

**3**

x1  x1  x1
11  11  7
x4  x2  x1
x2  x11  x1

**4**

x2
x1
x4

**5**

x1  x1  x1  x2

**6**

x1  11
x1  x3

**7**

x1  15
x1  13

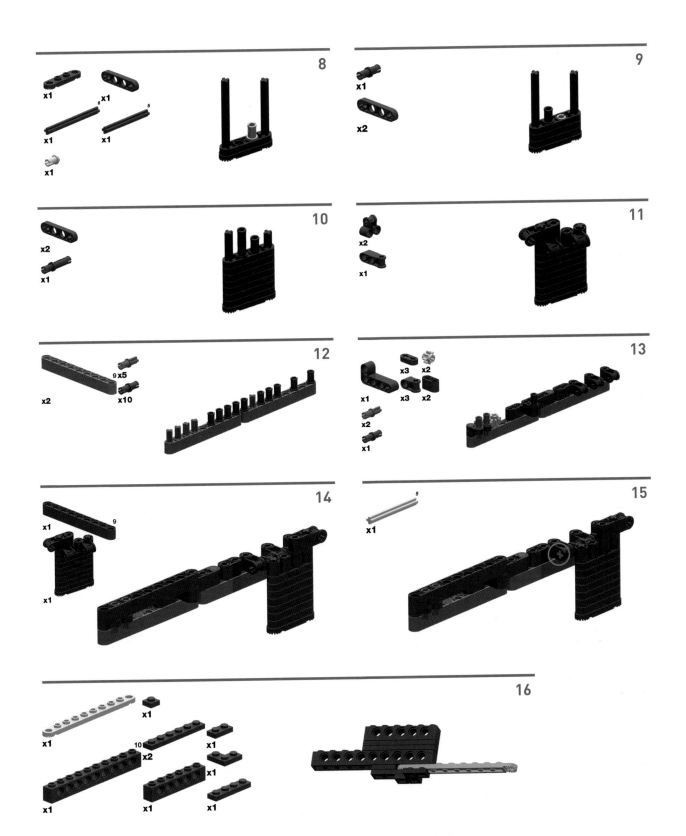

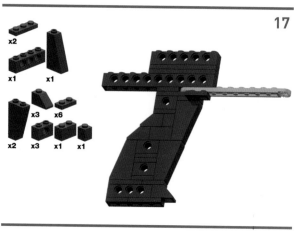

17

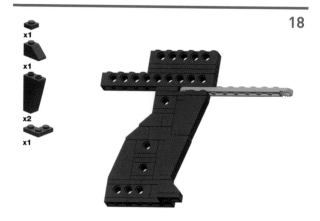

18

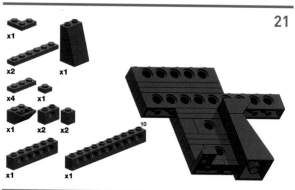

19

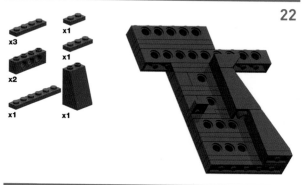

20

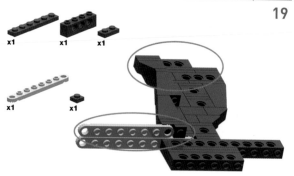

21

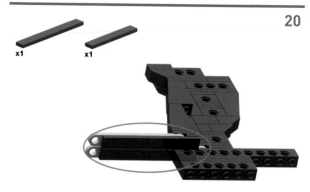

22

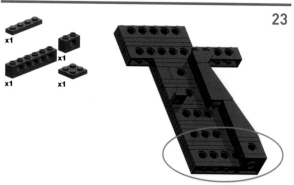

23

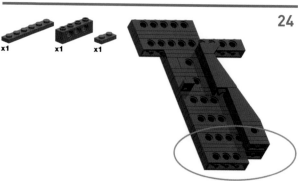

24

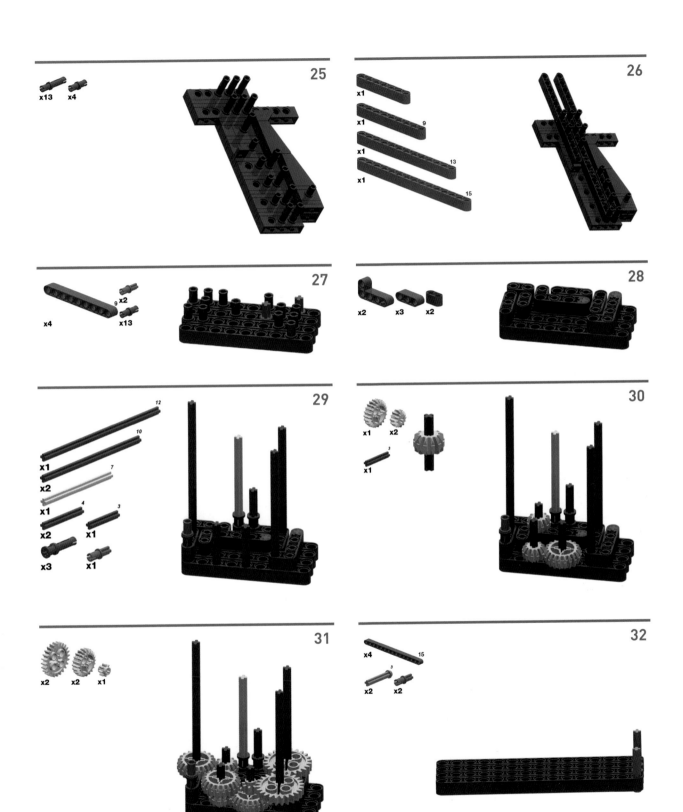

**33**

x2 x2

x2

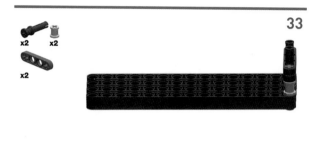

**34**

x1 x4

x1 x2

x4

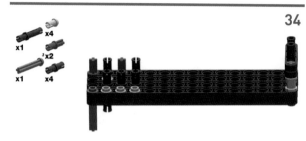

**35**

x2

x2

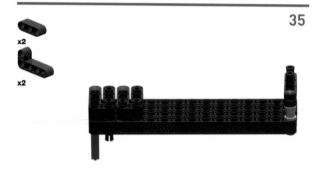

**36**

x1

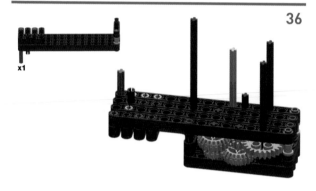

**37**

x3

x2 x6

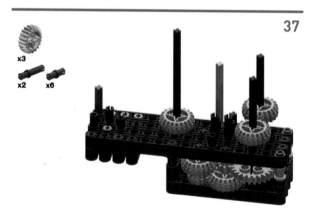

**38**

x1 x1

x1

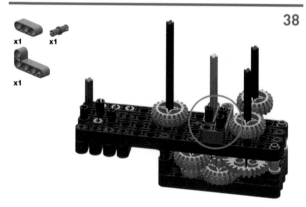

**39**

x1 x1 x2

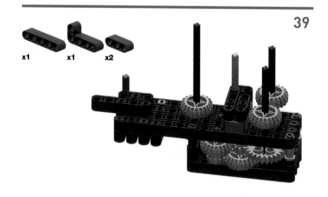

**40**

x1 x1 x2 x1 x1

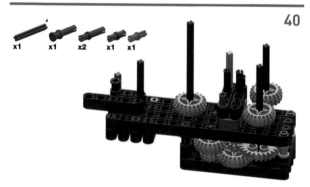

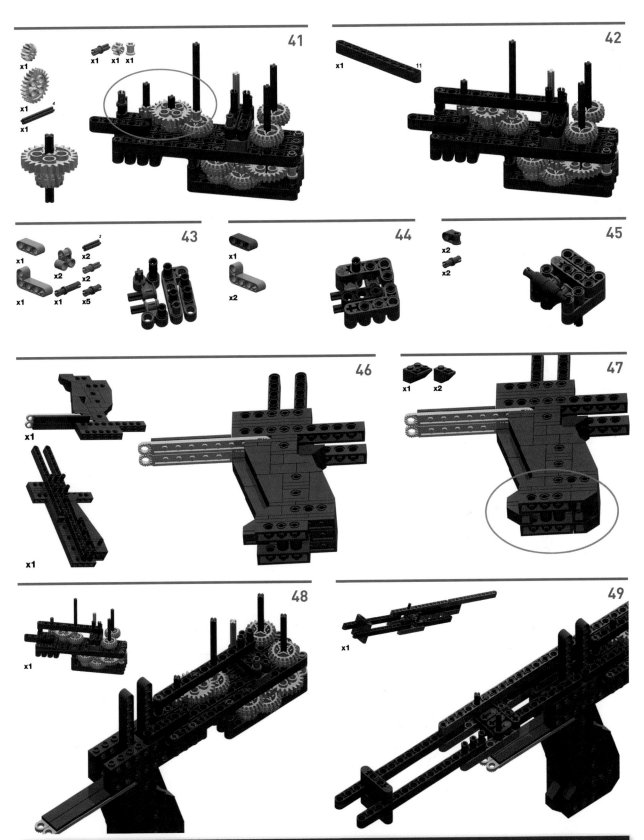

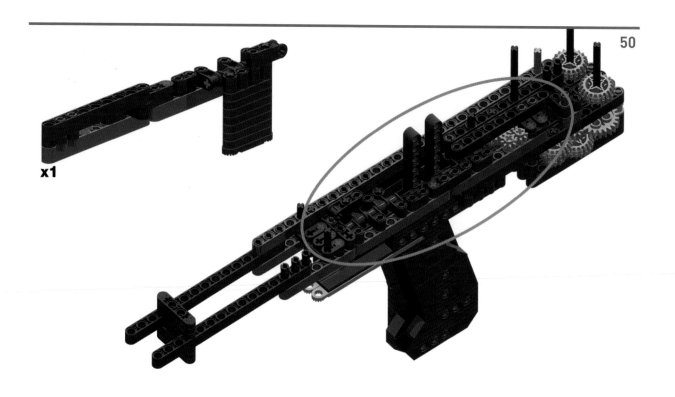

50

x1

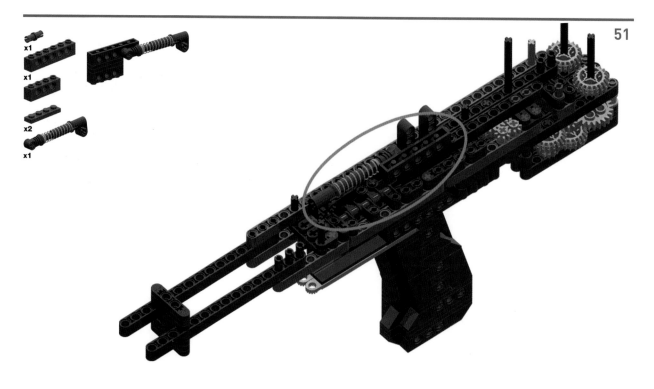

51

x1
x1
x2
x1

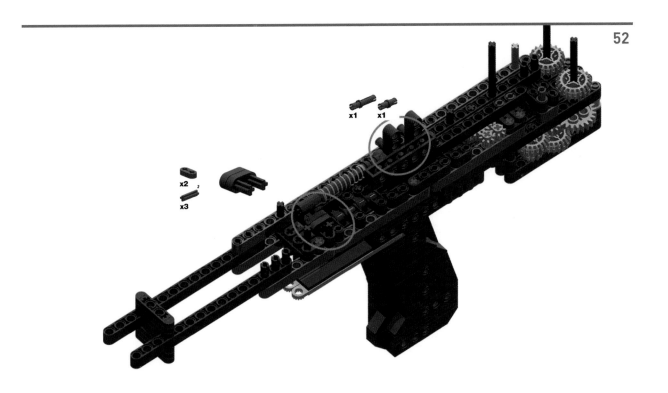

x1 x1

x2 2

x3

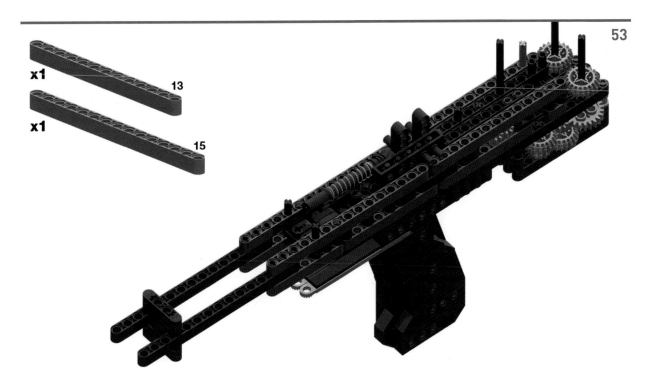

x1 13

x1 15

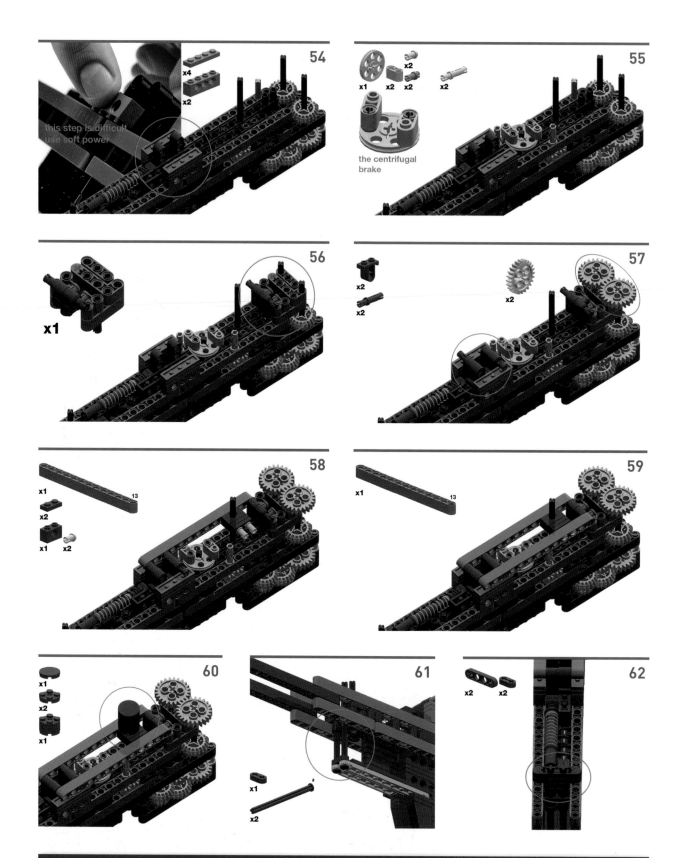

54

this step is difficult
use soft power

x4
x2

55

x1 x2 x2 x2

the centrifugal
brake

56

x1

57

x2

x2
x2

58

x1
13
x2
x1 x2

59

x1
13

60

x1
x2
x1

61

x1

x2

62

x2 x2

# HOW IT'S LOADED

**1**

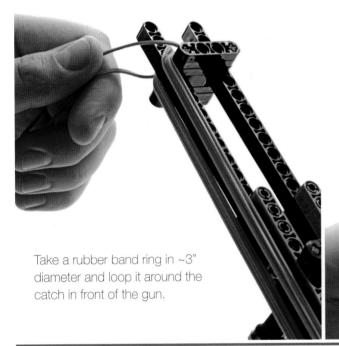

Take a rubber band ring in ~3" diameter and loop it around the catch in front of the gun.

**2**

Pull it back and hook it around a tooth of the gearwheel.

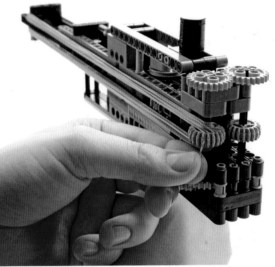

**3**

Now turn the loading wheel on top of the gun counterclockwise, while pulling the trigger at the same time. This readies the gun for the next rubber band to be loaded.

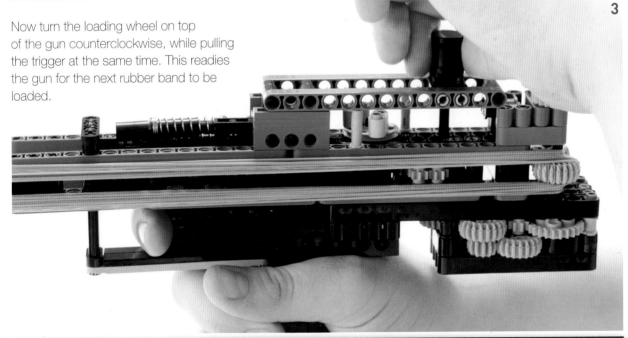

## 4

Repeat step 1-3 until the first gear wheel is full. Then switch sides and do the same thing again.

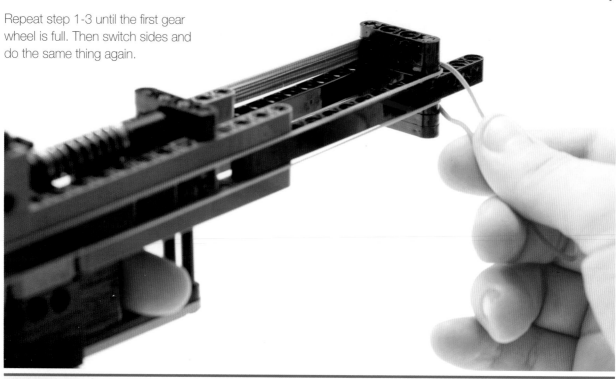

When you're done, 40 rounds are loaded!

# TIPS

Depending on the condition of your LEGO parts, it might be useful to lubricate the moved parts. Only use odorless synthetic oils!

# PART 9

We want to reconcile and sincerely apologize for any misunderstandings.
??

And so once again the search by our galactic scouts for peace and friend-ship was rewarded. hostilities were overcome, borders were opened, and alliances were formed. Long live the cosmic peace!

# BONUS MODEL: HKG3

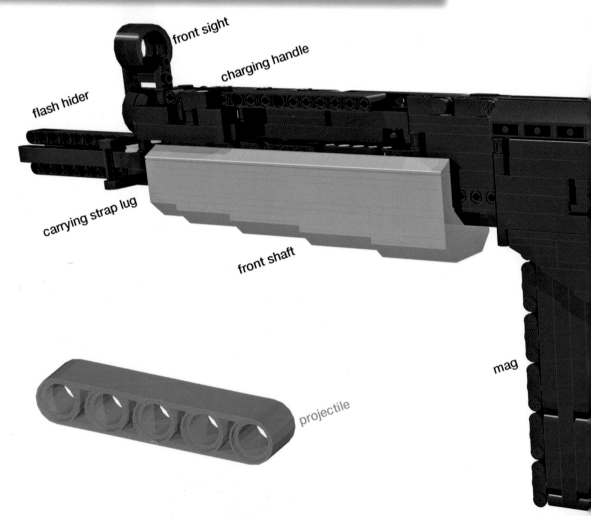

front sight

charging handle

flash hider

carrying strap lug

front shaft

mag

projectile

working red dot sight

electric switch

diopter

retractable stock

select fire switch

carrying strap lug

stock locking lever

mag release lever

trigger

trigger guard

pistol grip

# HOW IT WORKS

The cocking mechanism is in resting position. The select fire switch is on safety. The gun can't be cocked and the trigger can't be moved.

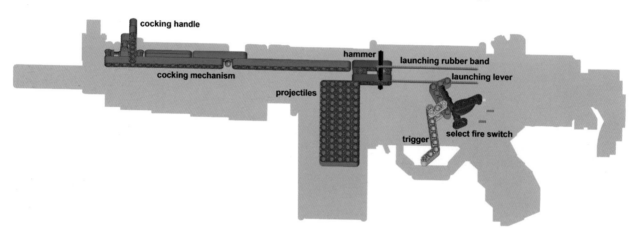

cocking handle

hammer

launching rubber band

cocking mechanism

launching lever

projectiles

trigger     select fire switch

Turning the select fire switch to single shot unlocks the gun. The G3 can now be cocked.

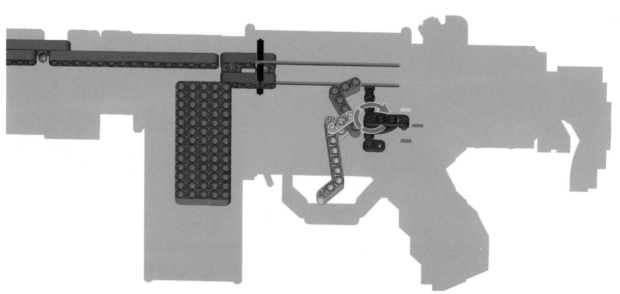

Pulling back the cocking mechanism pushes the hammer behind the launching lever. A new projectile gets pushed into the launch rail.

Releasing the cocking mechanism lets it snap back forward. The launching rubber band is taut. The hammer is blocked by the launching lever. The G3 is ready to fire.

Pulling the trigger lowers the launching lever, which releases the hammer, which then gets catapulted forward, hits the top projectile, and tosses it out of the barrel.

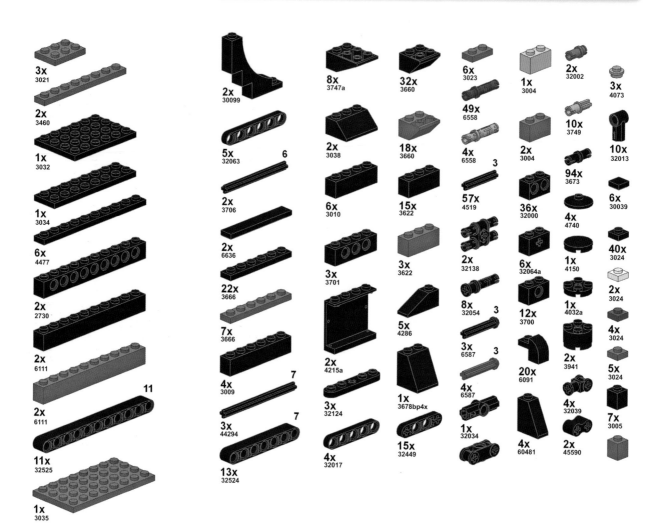

3x
3021

2x
3460

1x
3032

1x
3034

6x
4477

2x
2730

2x
6111

2x
6111

11

11x
32525

1x
3035

2x
30099

5x
32063    6

2x
3706

2x
6636

22x
3666

7x
3666

4x
3009    7

3x
44294

3x
32124    7

13x
32524

8x
3747a

2x
3038

6x
3010

3x
3701

2x
4215a

3x
32124

4x
32017

32x
3660

18x
3660

15x
3622

3x
3622

5x
4286

1x
3678bp4x

15x
32449

6x
3023

49x
6558

4x
6558

57x
4519    3

2x
32138

8x
32054    3

3x
6587    3

4x
6587

1x
32034

4x
60481

1x
3004

2x
3004

36x
32000

6x
32064a

12x
3700

20x
6091

4x
60481

2x
45590

2x
32002

10x
3749

94x
3673

4x
4740

1x
4150

1x
4032a

2x
3941

4x
32039

3x
4073

10x
32013

6x
30039

40x
3024

2x
3024

4x
3024

5x
3024

7x
3005

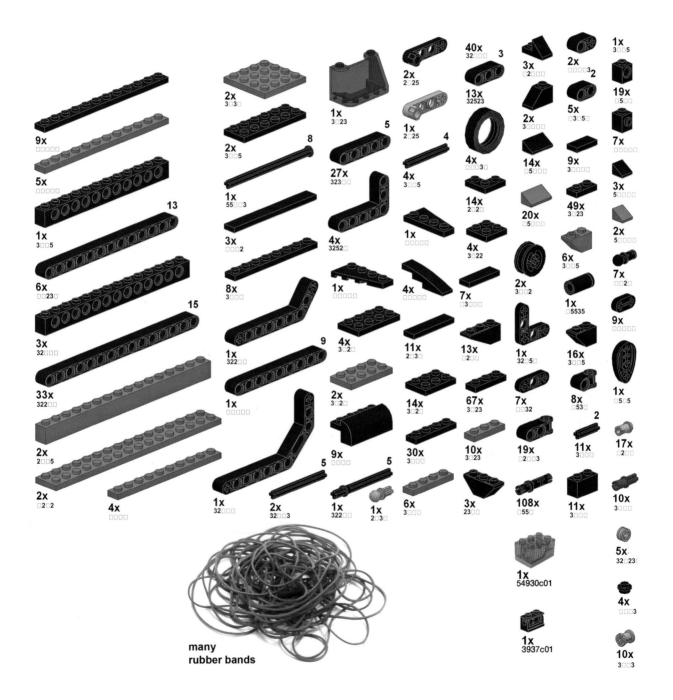

9x

5x

1x 3□5 **13**

6x □□23□

3x 32□□□ **15**

33x 322□□

2x 2□□5

2x □2□2

4x □□□□

2x 3□3□

2x 3□□5 **8**

1x 55□□3

3x □□□2

8x 3□□□

1x 322□□

1x □□□□□

1x 32□□□

2x 32□□□

2x 3□3□ **5**

27x 323□□

4x 3252□

1x □□□□□

4x 3□2□ **9**

2x 3□2□

9x □□□□ **5**

2x 322□□

5

1x 2□25 **5**

4x 3□□5

1x □□□□□

4x □□□□□

11x 2□3□

14x 3□2□

30x 3□□□

1x 322□□ **4**

4x 3□□5

7x □3□□□

13x □2□□

67x 3□23

10x 3□23

1x 2□3□

6x 3□□□

40x 32□□□ **3**

13x 32523

4x □□□3□

14x 2□2□

4x 3□22

2x 3□□2

13x □2□5□

7x □□32

19x □2□□3

3x 23□□

3x □2□□□

2x 3□□□□

14x □5□□□

20x □5□□□

2x 3□□2

1x □5535

1x 32□5□

7x □□□□□

1x 54930c01

2x □□□□3□ **2**

5x □3□5□

9x 3□□□□

49x 3□23

6x 3□□5

1x □5□□

16x 3□□5

8x □53□

11x 3□□□ **2**

108x □55□

11x 3□□□

1x 3937c01

1x 3□□5

19x □5□□

7x □□□□□

3x 5□□□□

3x 5□□□□

2x 5□□□□

7x □□2□

9x □□□□□

1x □5□5

17x □2□□

10x 3□□□

5x 32□23□

4x □□□3

10x 3□□3

**many rubber bands**

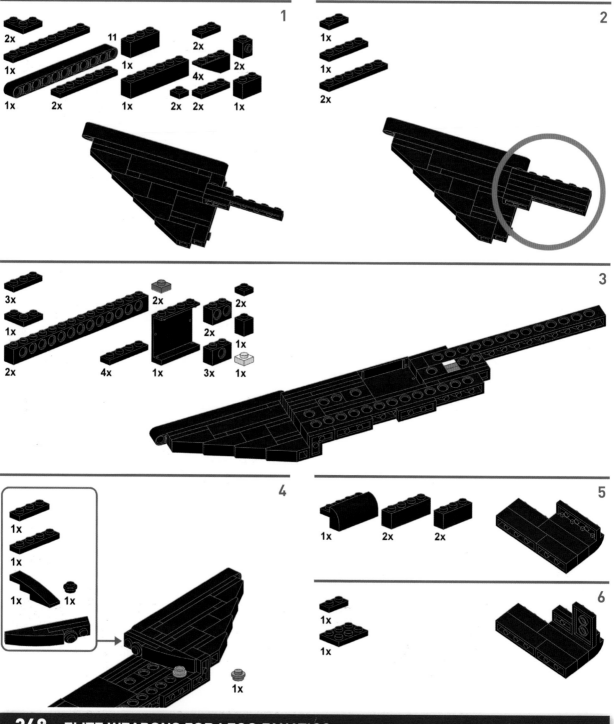

**1**

2x  11  2x
1x  1x  4x  2x
1x  2x  1x  2x  2x  1x

**2**

1x
1x
2x

**3**

3x  2x  2x
1x  2x  2x
2x  4x  1x  3x  1x

**4**

1x
1x
1x  1x

**5**

1x  2x  2x

**6**

1x
1x

1x

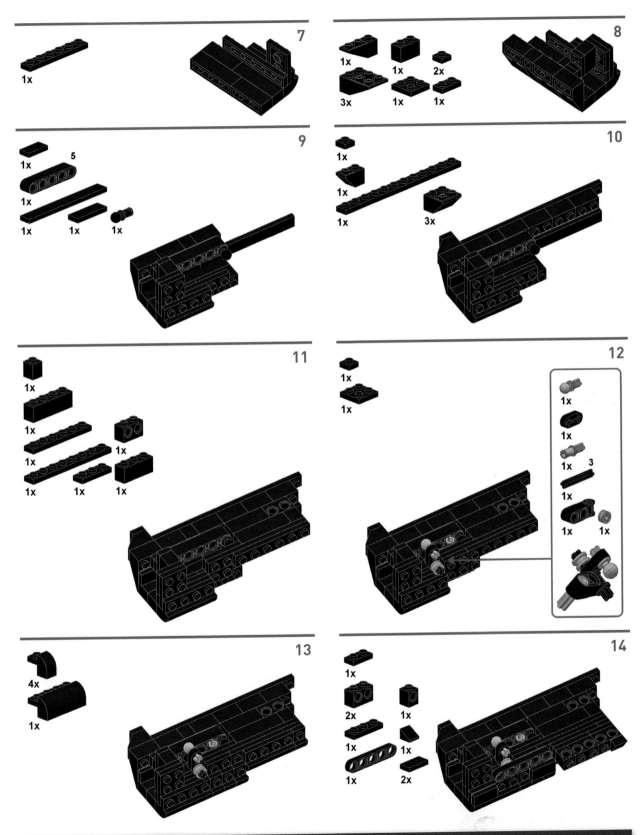

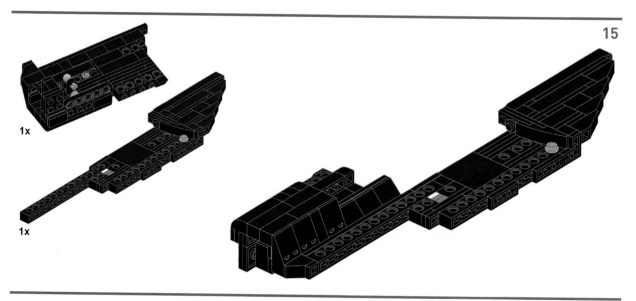

1x

1x

6x

1x

13

1x

1x

1x

1x

1x

1x

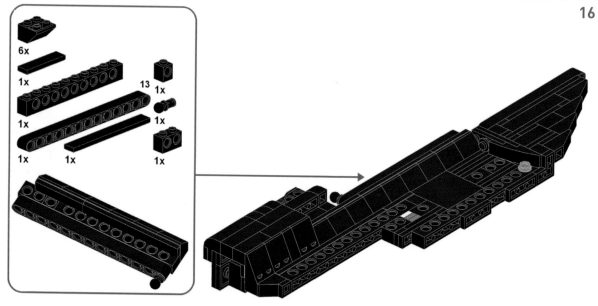

23x

3x

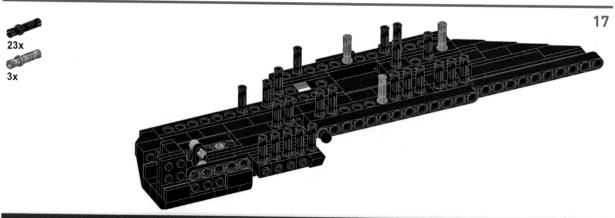

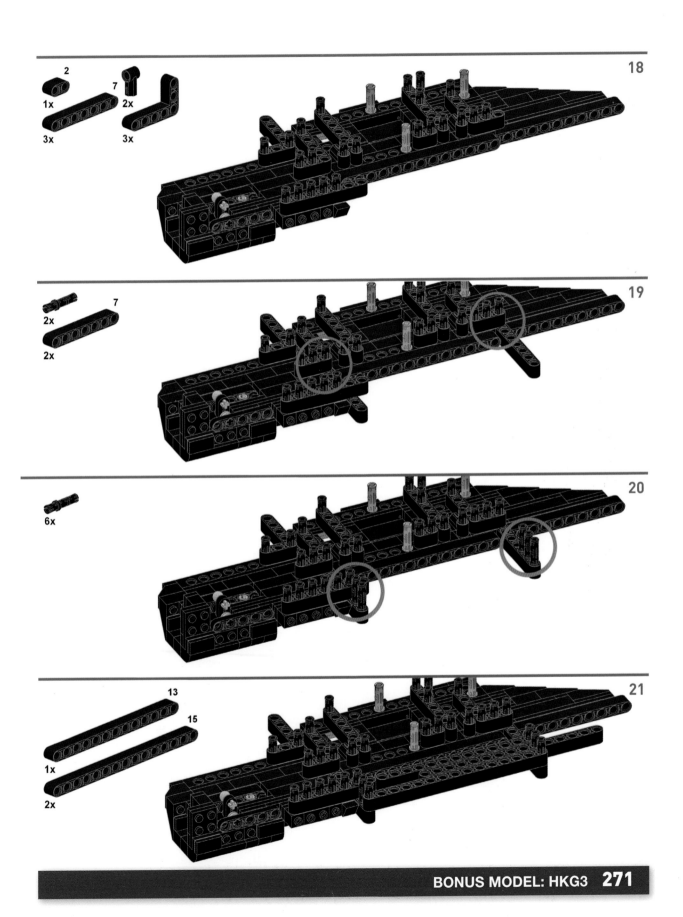

18

2
1x
3x

7
2x
3x

19

2x
2x

7

20

6x

21

13
15
1x
2x

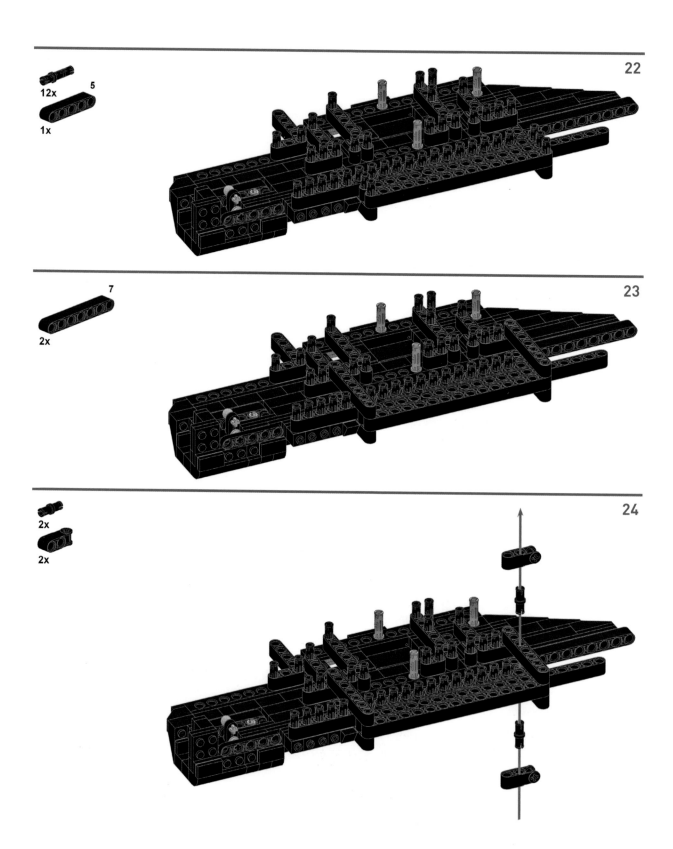

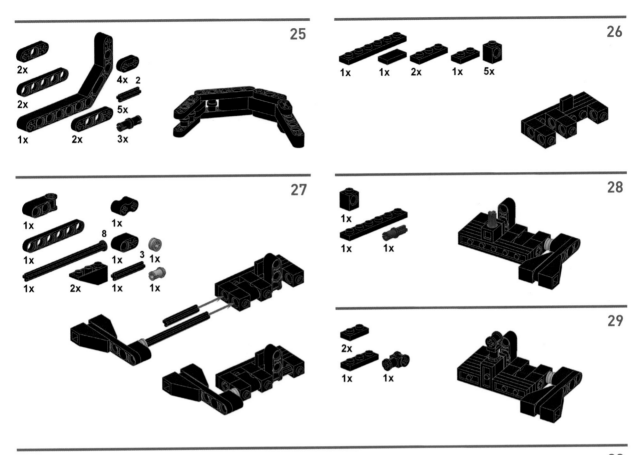

**25**

2x
2x
1x
4x  2
5x
2x  3x

**26**

1x  1x  2x  1x  5x

**27**

1x
1x
1x
2x
1x
8
1x  3
1x  1x
1x

**28**

1x
1x  1x

**29**

2x
1x  1x

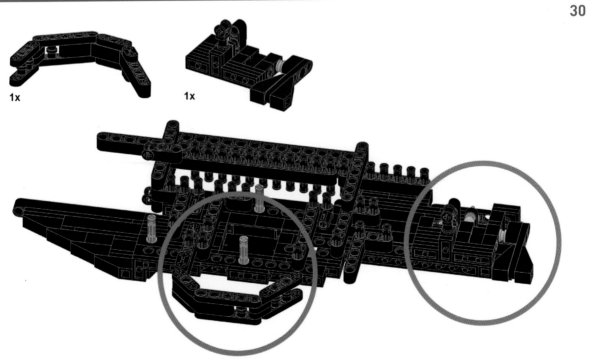

**30**

1x
1x

**31**

1x    1x

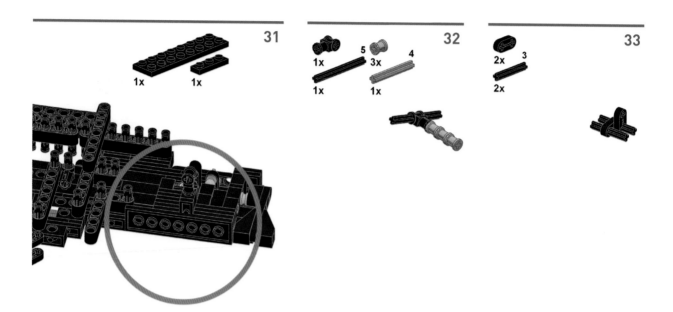

**32**

1x    5    3x    4

1x    1x

**33**

2x    3

2x

**34**

1x    1x

1x

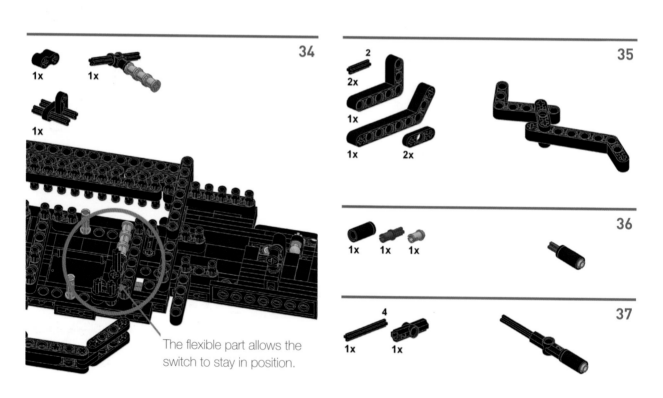

The flexible part allows the switch to stay in position.

**35**

2    2x

1x

1x    2x

**36**

1x    1x    1x

**37**

4

1x    1x

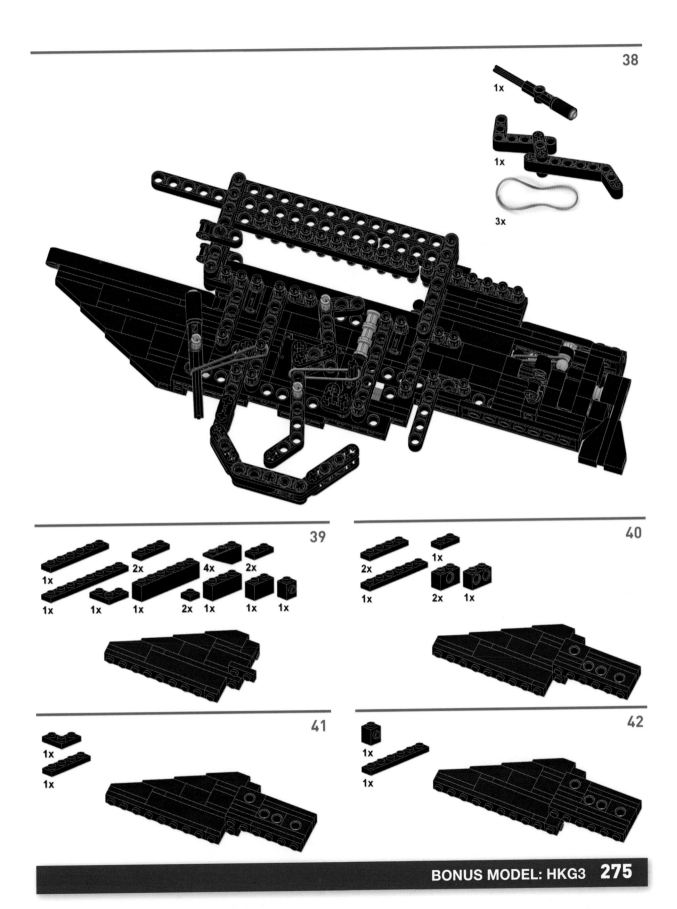

38

1x

1x

3x

39

1x
1x 1x 1x
2x
4x
2x 1x
2x
1x

40

2x
1x
1x
2x 1x

41

1x
1x

42

1x
1x

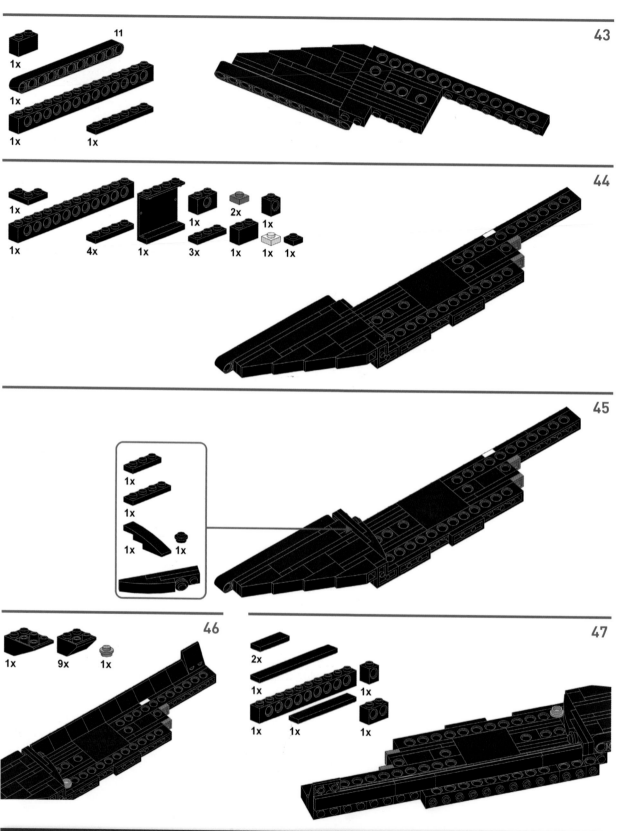

43

11
1x
1x
1x
1x

44

1x
1x
4x
1x
3x
2x
1x
1x
1x
1x

45

1x
1x
1x
1x

46

1x
9x
1x

47

2x
1x
1x
1x
1x

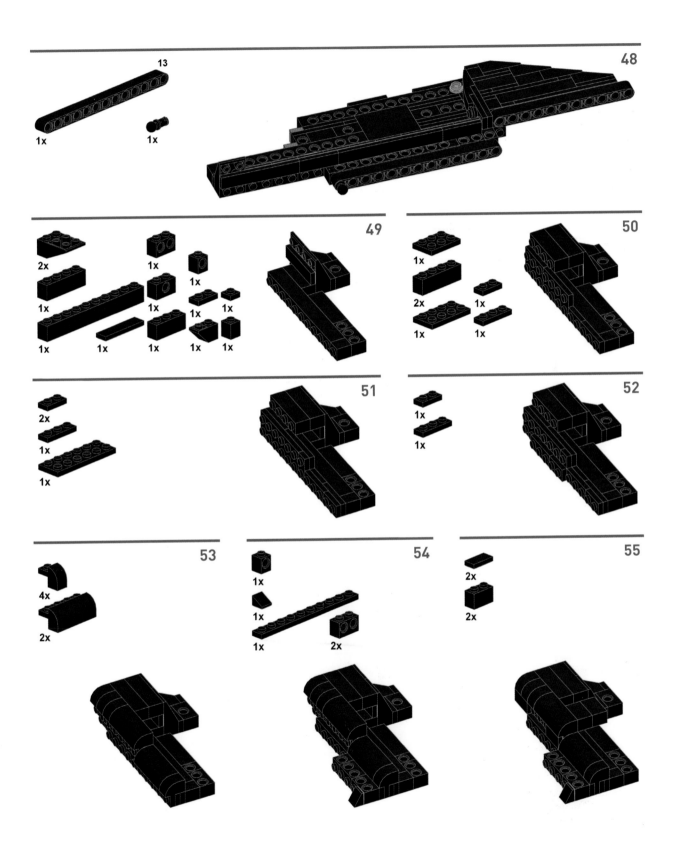

48

13

1x    1x

49

2x    1x    1x

1x    1x    1x    1x

1x    1x    1x    1x    1x

50

1x    1x

2x

1x    1x

51

2x

1x

1x

52

1x

1x

53

4x

2x

54

1x

1x

1x    2x

55

2x

2x

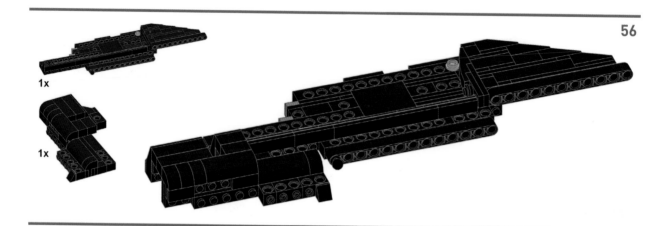

1x

1x

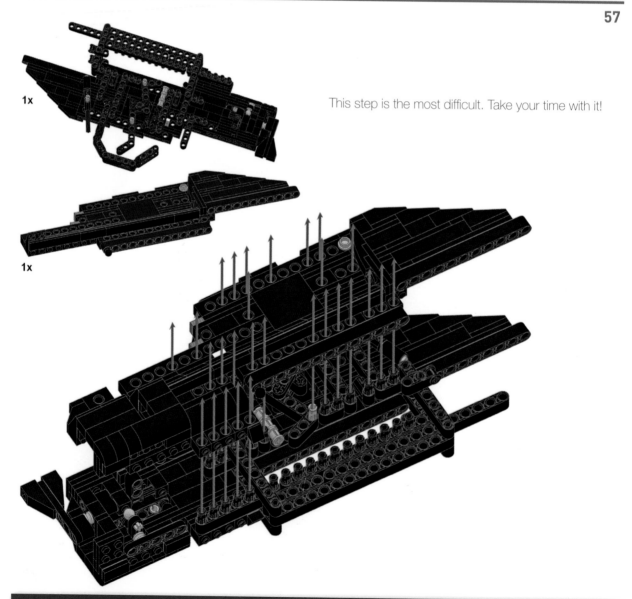

1x

1x

This step is the most difficult. Take your time with it!

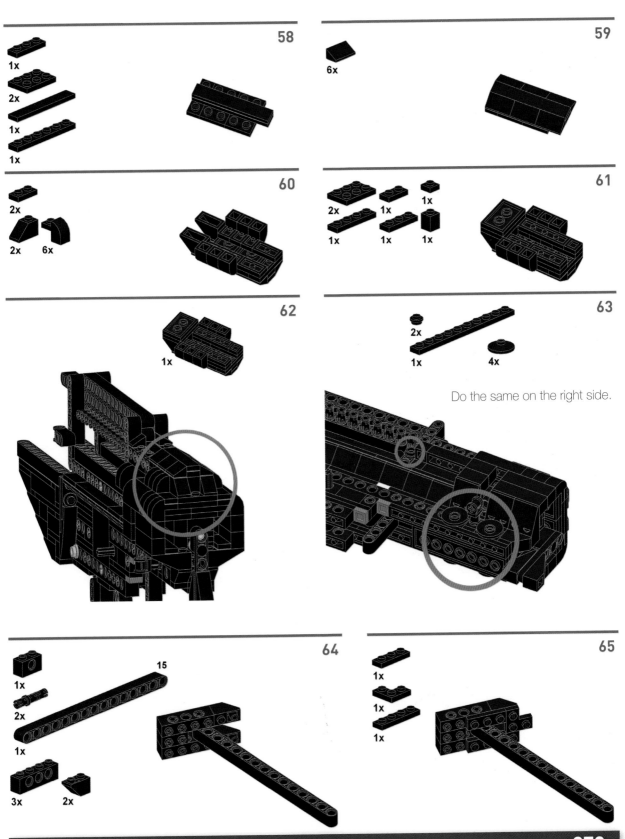

**58**

1x

2x

1x

1x

**59**

6x

**60**

2x

2x 6x

**61**

2x 1x 1x

1x 1x 1x

**62**

1x

**63**

2x

1x 4x

Do the same on the right side.

**64**

1x

2x

1x

15

3x 2x

**65**

1x

1x

1x

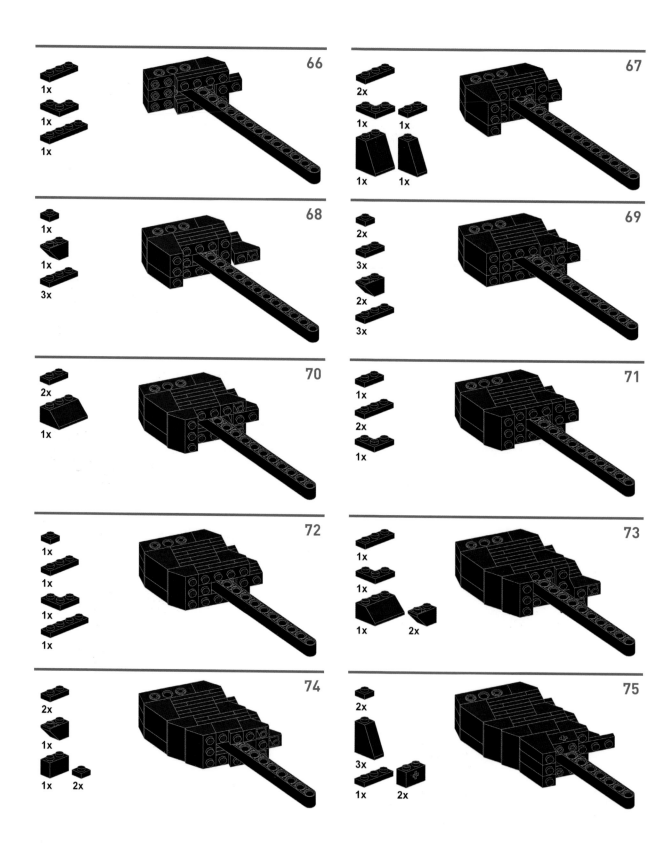

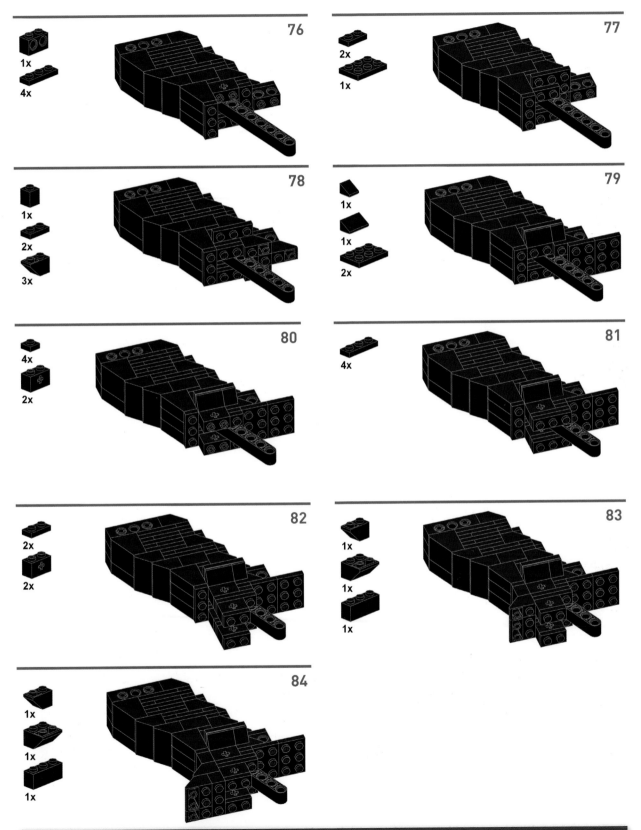

76

1x
4x

77

2x
1x

78

1x
2x
3x

79

1x
1x
2x

80

4x
2x

81

4x

82

2x
2x

83

1x
1x
1x

84

1x
1x
1x

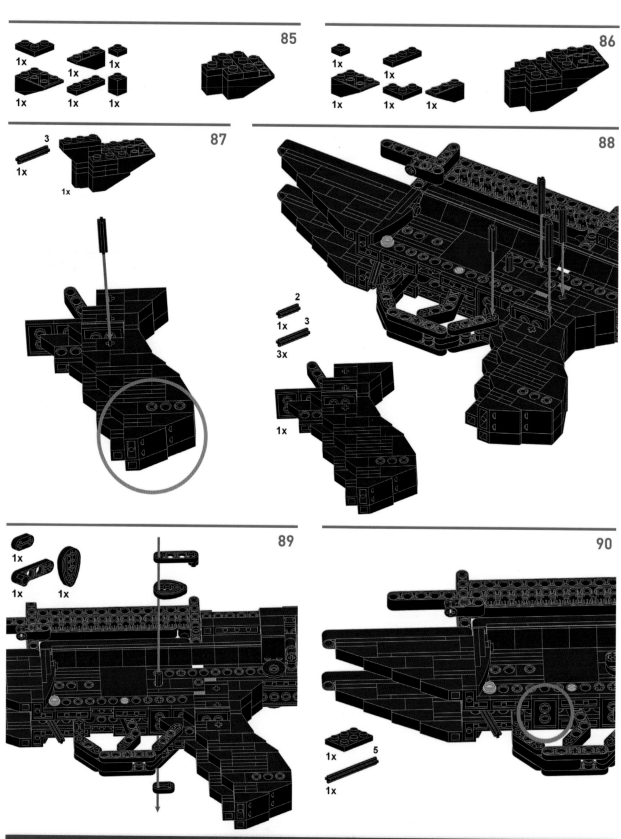

85

1x 1x 1x
1x 1x 1x

86

1x 1x
1x
1x 1x 1x

87

3
1x
1x

88

2
1x 3
3x
1x

89

1x
1x 1x

90

1x 5
1x

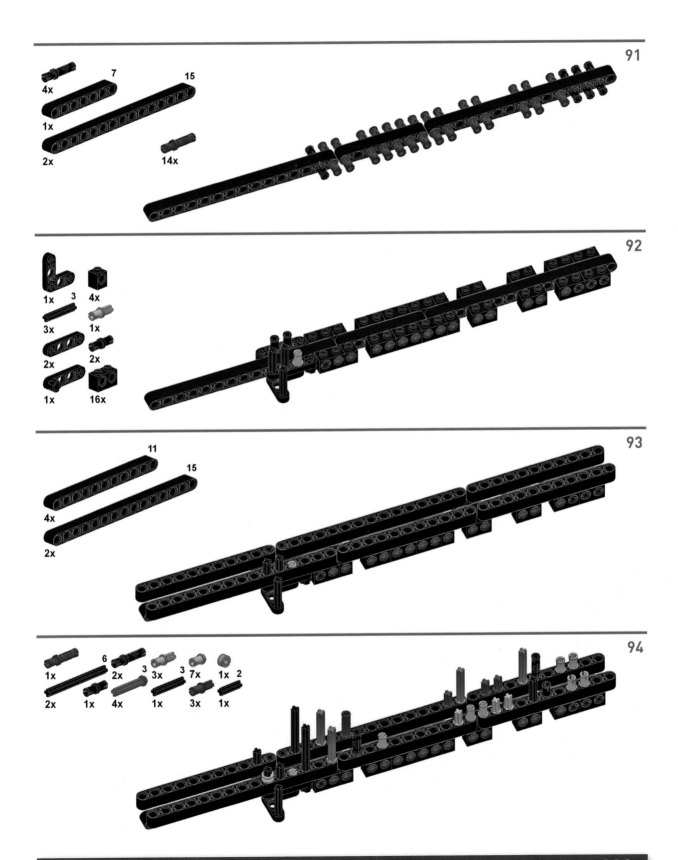

91

7
4x
15
1x
2x
14x

92

1x   3
4x
3x
1x
2x
2x
1x
16x

93

11
15
4x
2x

94

1x
6
2x   3
3x   3
7x
1x   2
2x
1x
4x
1x
3x
1x

**1x**

**4x**

**5**

**2x**

**1x** **3**

**6x**

**15**

**2x**

**4x** **1x**

**7**

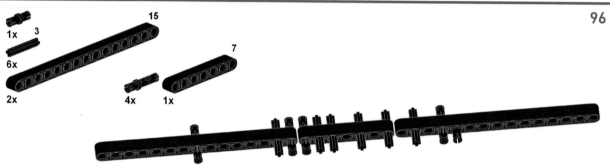

**4x** **5x** **6x**

**1x**

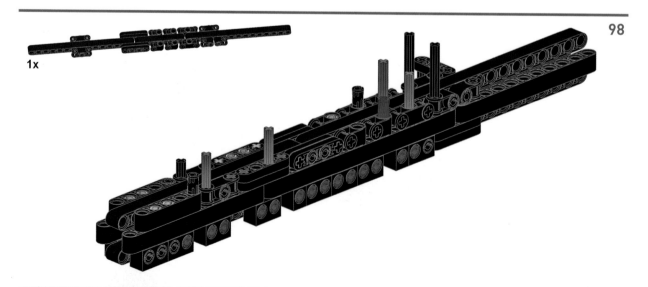

99

1x
5x

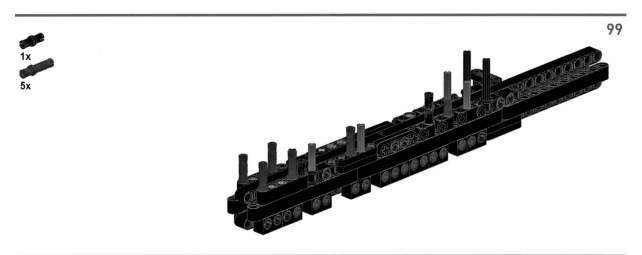

100

13
1x
15
1x
2x
5
2x

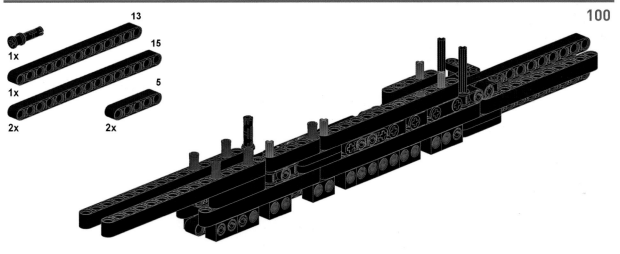

101

1x  1x
5x  7x

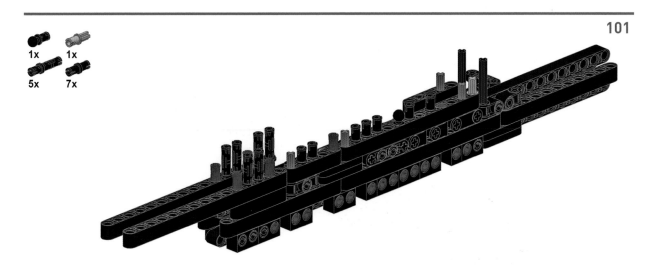

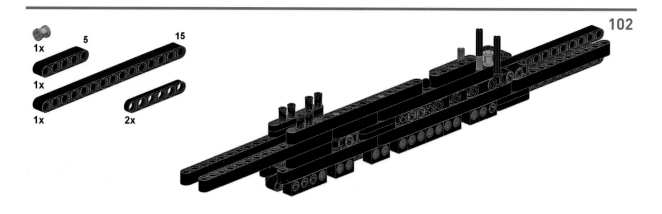

102

103

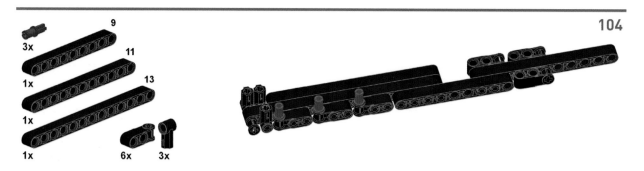

104

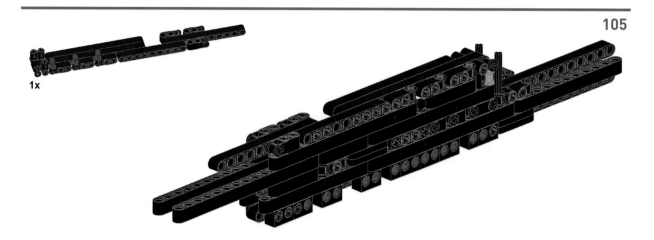

105

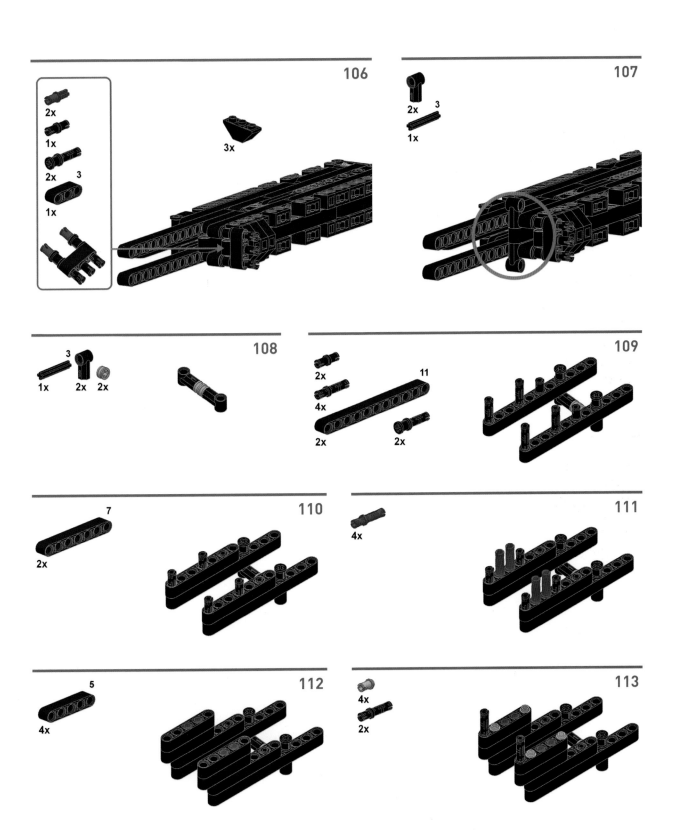

106

2x
1x
2x 3
1x

3x

107

2x
1x 3

108

3
1x 2x 2x

109

2x
4x 11
2x
2x

110

7
2x

111

4x

112

5
4x

113

4x
2x

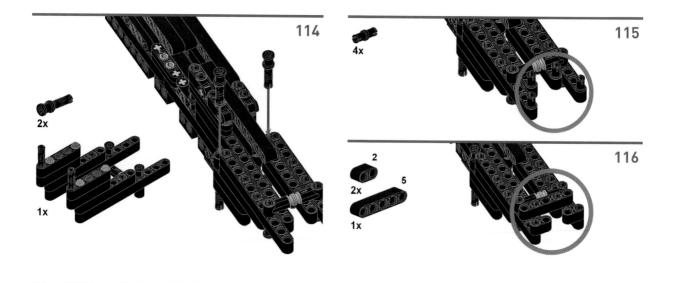

114

2x

1x

115

4x

116

2

2x

5

1x

117

1x

1x

3

2x

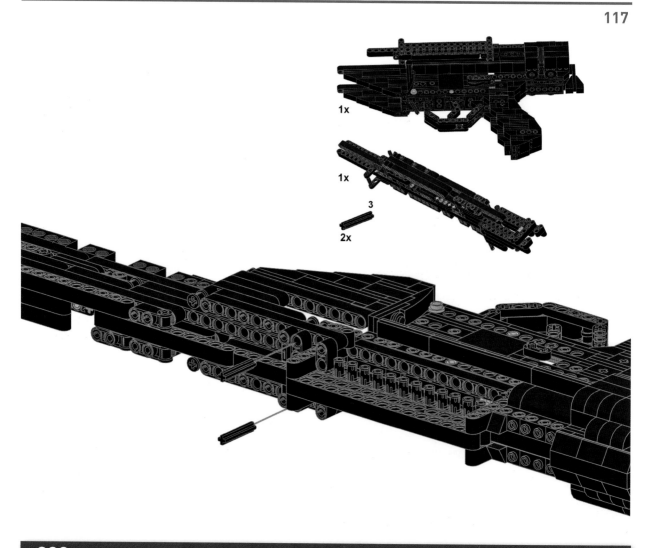

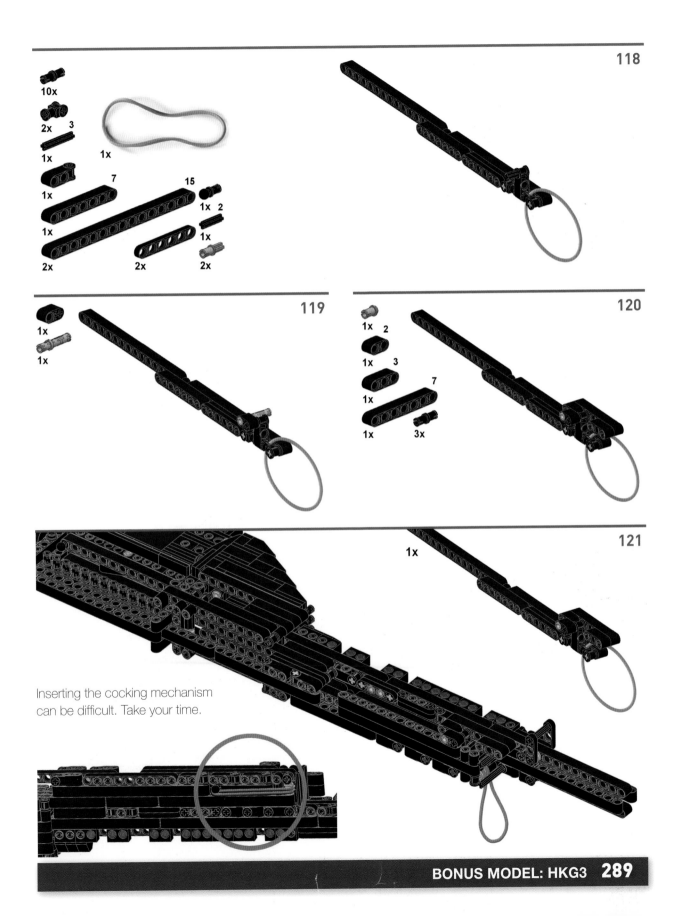

10x

2x 3

1x

1x

1x 2

1x

7

1x

2x

15

2x

1x 2

1x

2x

1x

1x

1x 2

1x 3

1x

7

1x 3x

1x

Inserting the cocking mechanism can be difficult. Take your time.

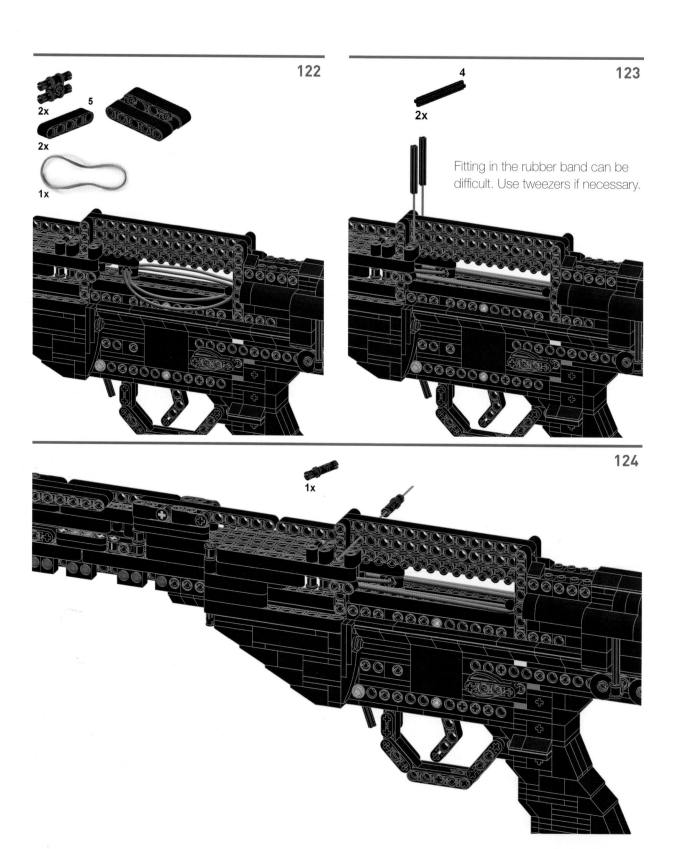

122

2x

5

2x

1x

123

4

2x

Fitting in the rubber band can be difficult. Use tweezers if necessary.

124

1x

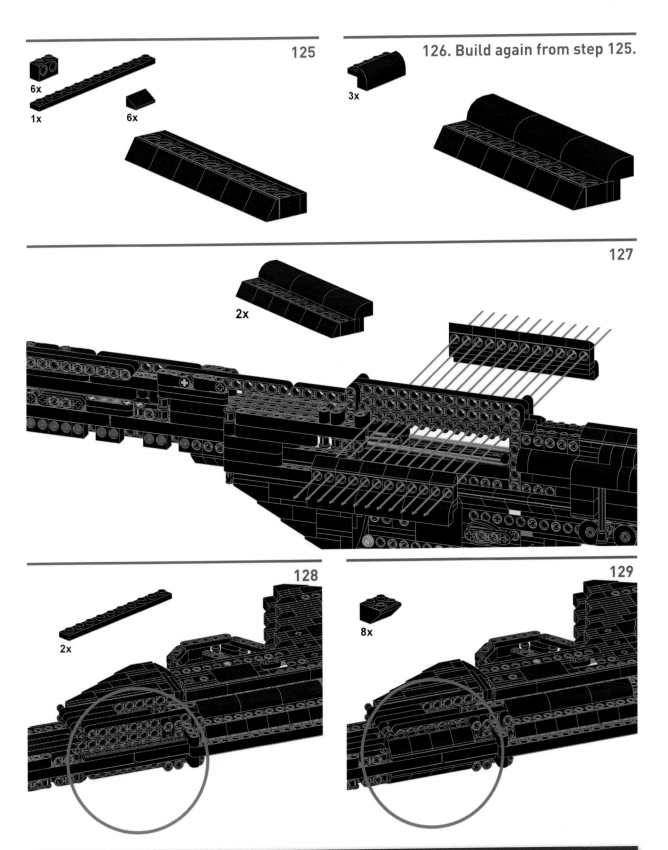

**125**

6x

1x

6x

**126. Build again from step 125.**

3x

**127**

2x

**128**

2x

**129**

8x

130

5

1x

131

3x

2x

2x

132

1x

1x

2x

1x

1x

2x

1x

1x

133

2x

1x

1x

3x

3x

134

6x

2x

1x

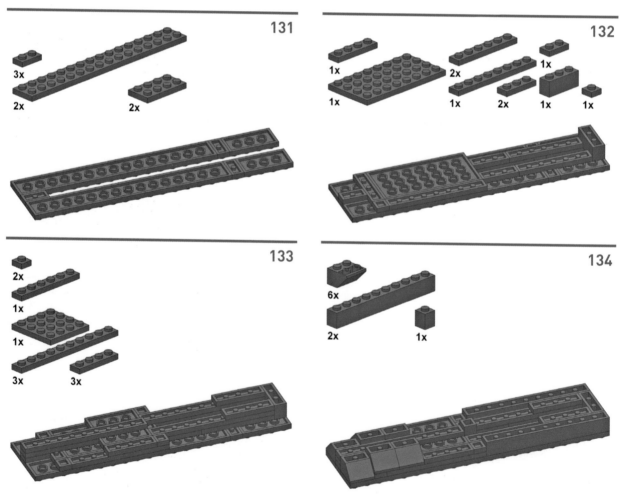

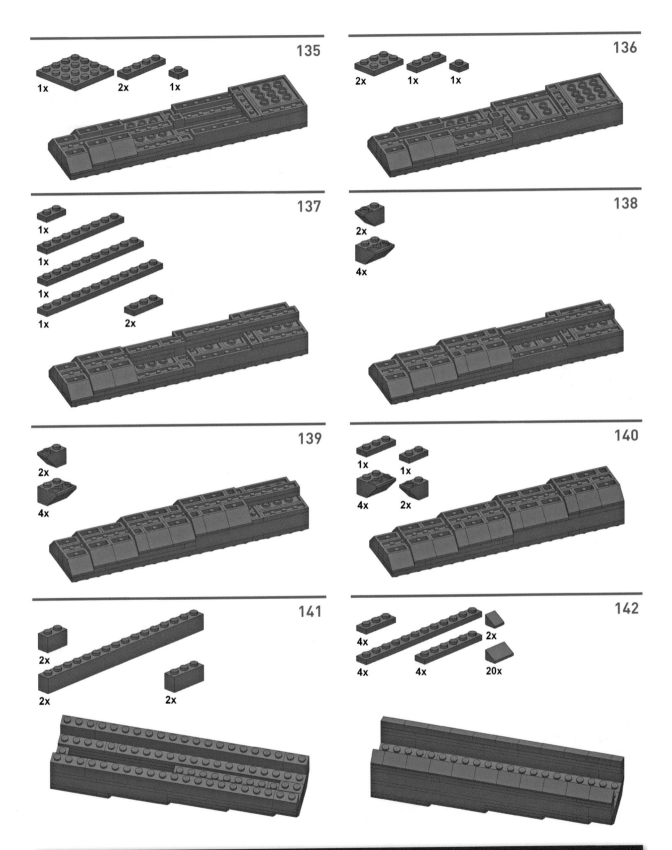

**135**

1x  2x  1x

**136**

2x  1x  1x

**137**

1x
1x
1x
1x  2x

**138**

2x
4x

**139**

2x
4x

**140**

1x  1x
4x  2x

**141**

2x
2x  2x

**142**

4x
4x  4x  2x  20x

**143**
1x  3x  2x

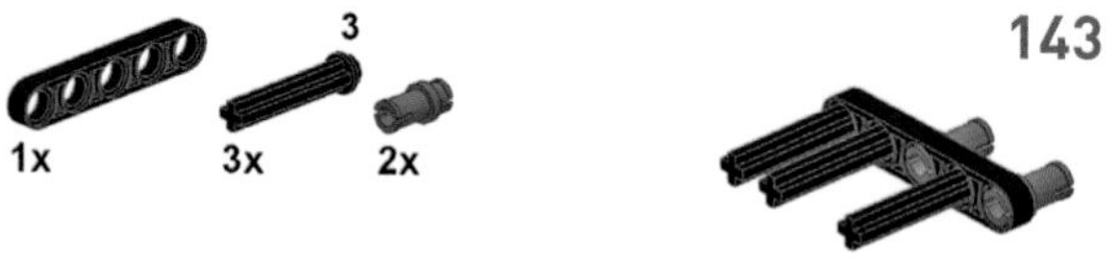

**144**
4x  2x

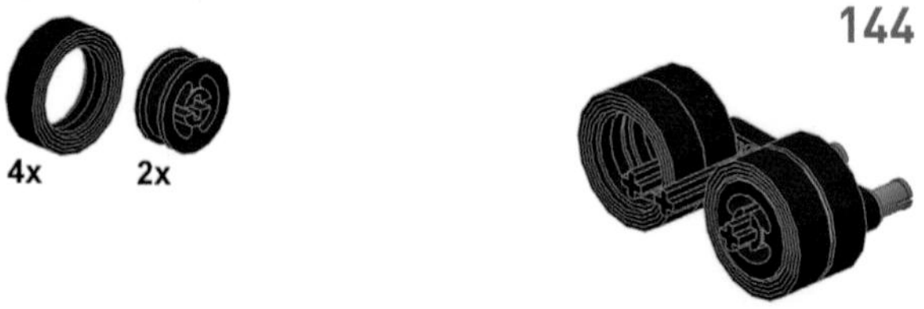

**145**
1x

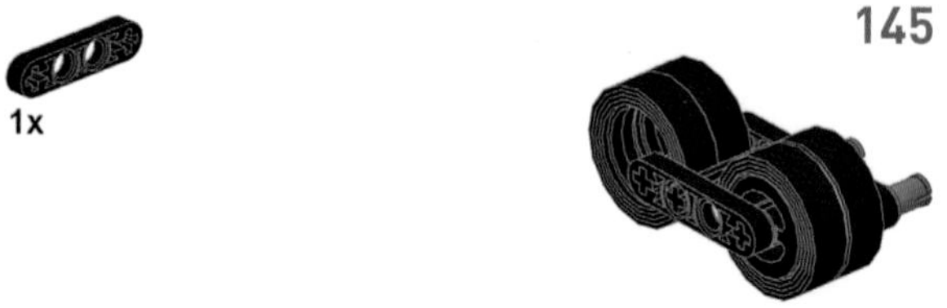

**146**
3x

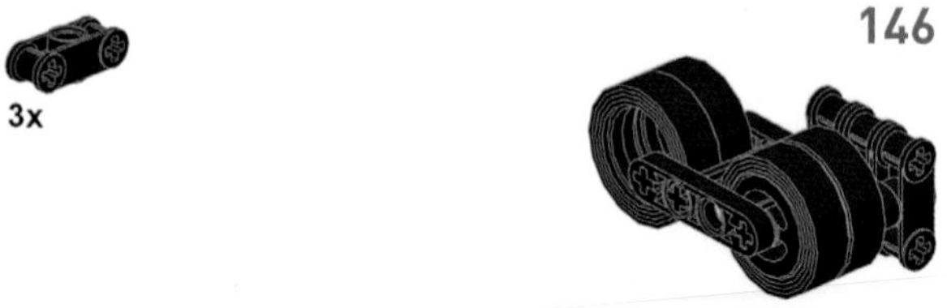

**147**
1x

1x

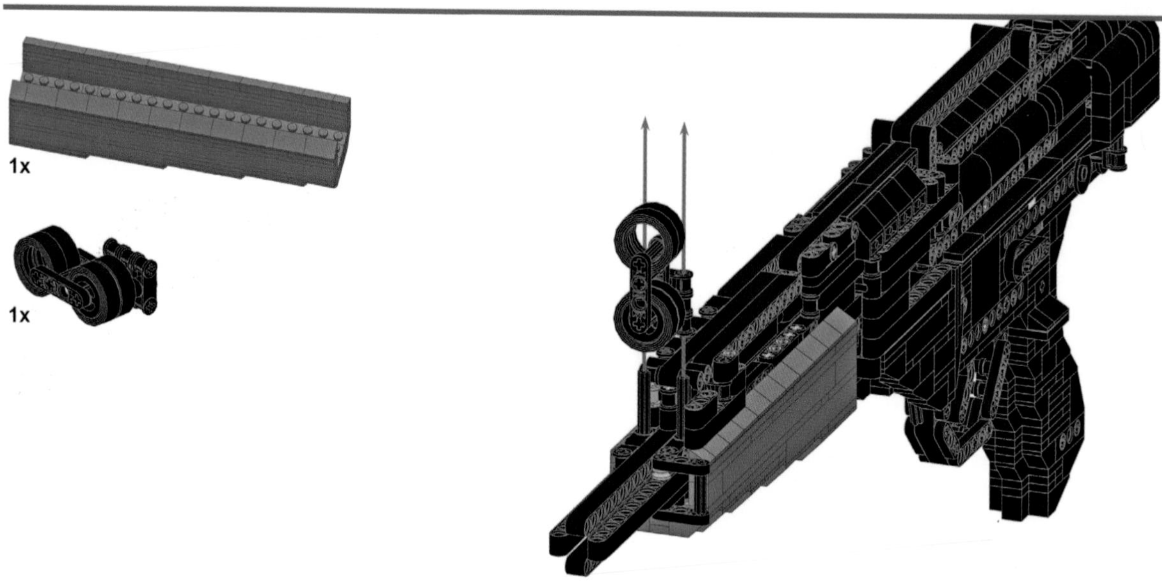

**148**
2x  1x  2x  1x

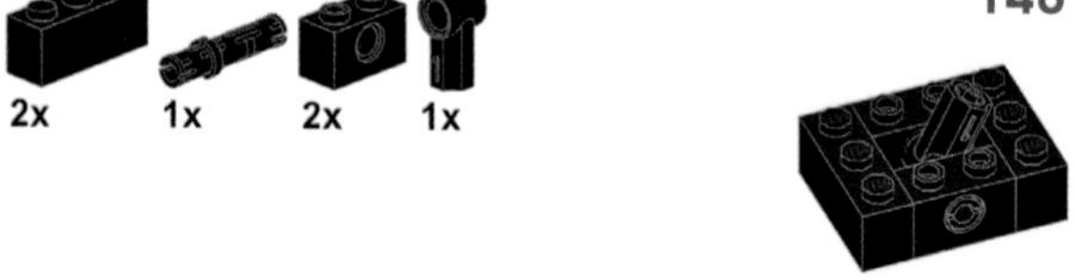

**149**
1x
2x  2x

**150**
2x  1x

**151**
2x
1x

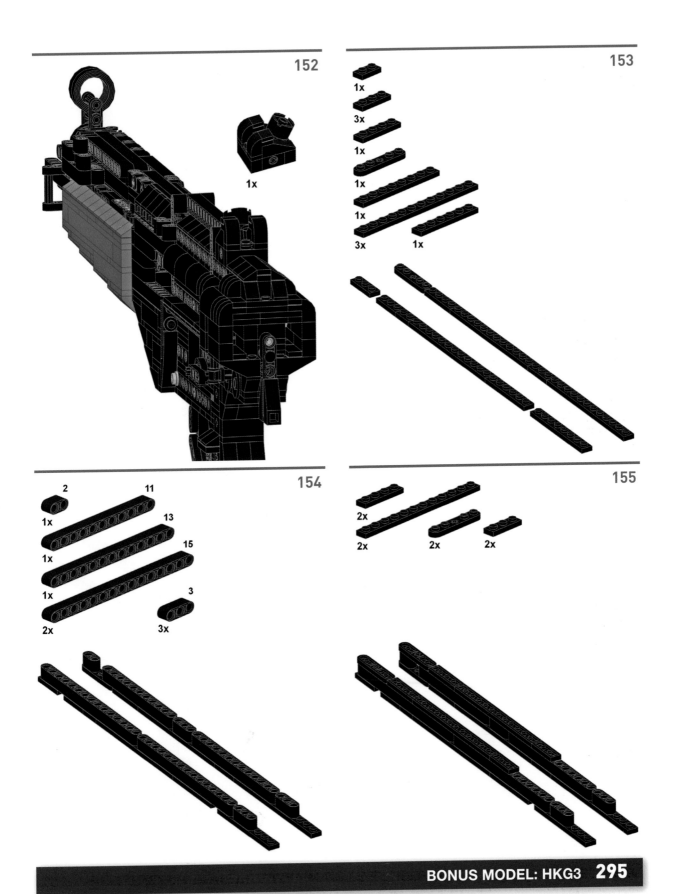

**152**

1x

**153**

1x
3x
1x
1x
1x
3x     1x

**154**

2
1x
11
1x
13
1x
15
2x
3
3x

**155**

2x
2x
2x     2x     2x

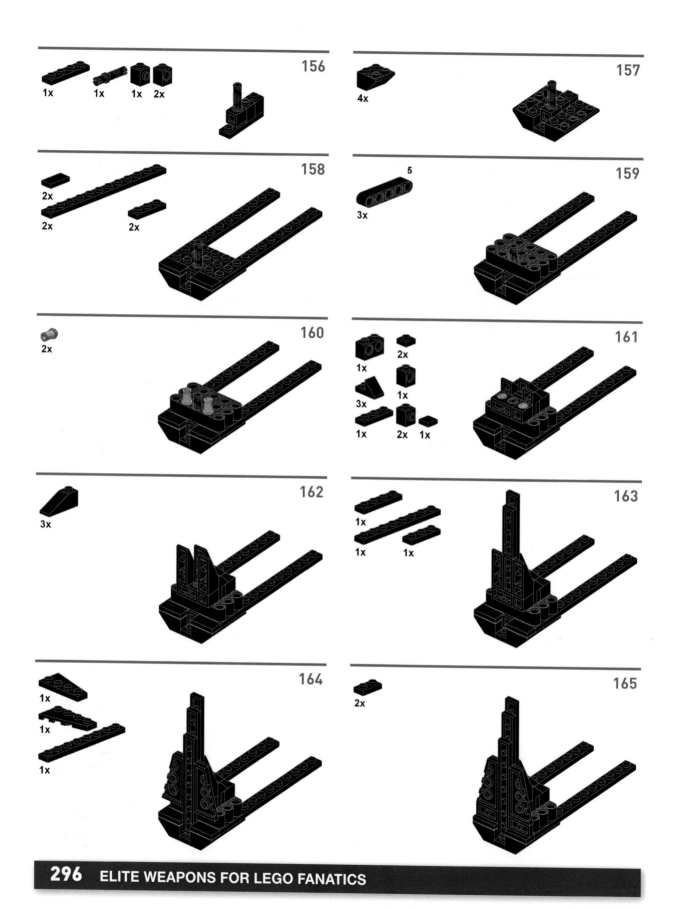

**156**

1x 1x 1x 2x

**157**

4x

**158**

2x
2x 2x

**159**

5
3x

**160**

2x

**161**

1x 2x
3x 1x
1x 2x 1x

**162**

3x

**163**

1x
1x 1x

**164**

1x
1x
1x

**165**

2x

166

1x
1x
1x
1x 1x

167

1x
1x

168

3x
1x

169

1x
2x
2x
3x

170

5x

171. Combine models from steps 155 and 170.

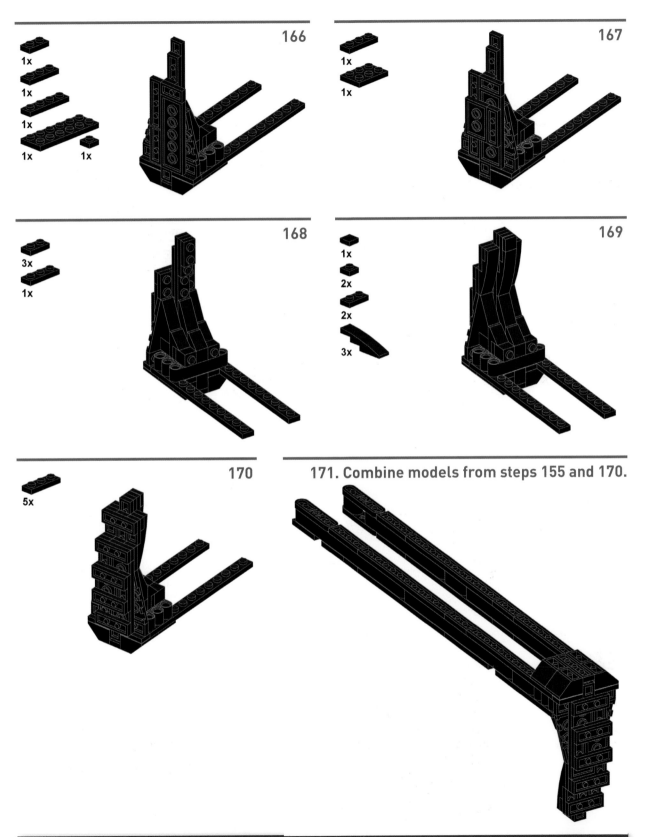

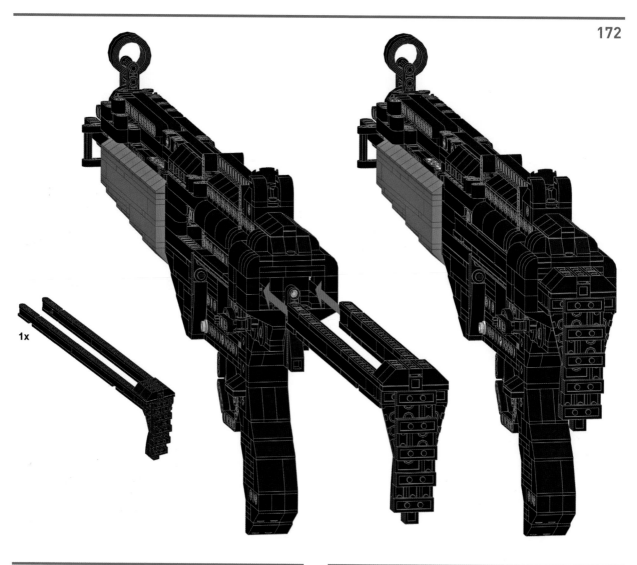

1x

3x  3
15

13x

1x  15x  2x

14x

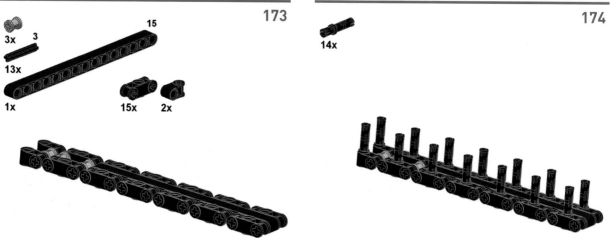

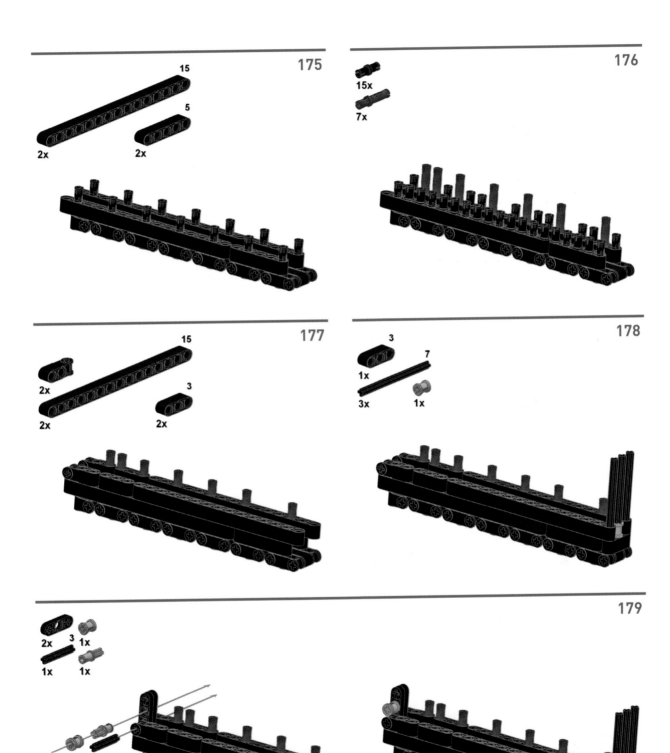

175

15
5
2x
2x

176

15x
7x

177

15
3
2x
2x
2x

178

3
7
1x
1x
3x

179

2x 3 1x
1x 1x

## 180

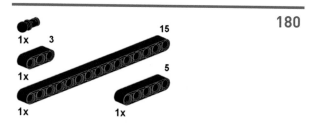

1x    3

1x

1x

15

5

1x

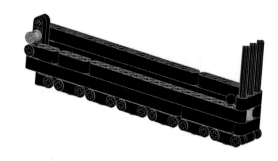

## 181

4x

8x

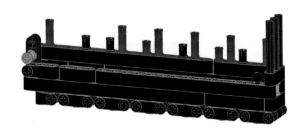

## 182

3

1x

2x

2x

15

3

1x

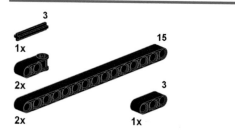

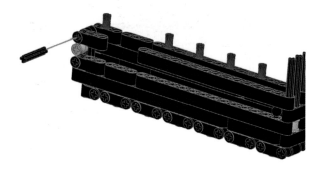

## 183

6x    1x

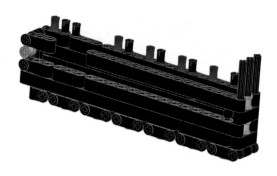

## 184

11x

5x

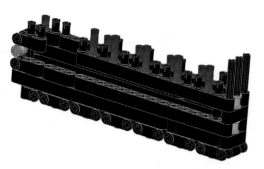

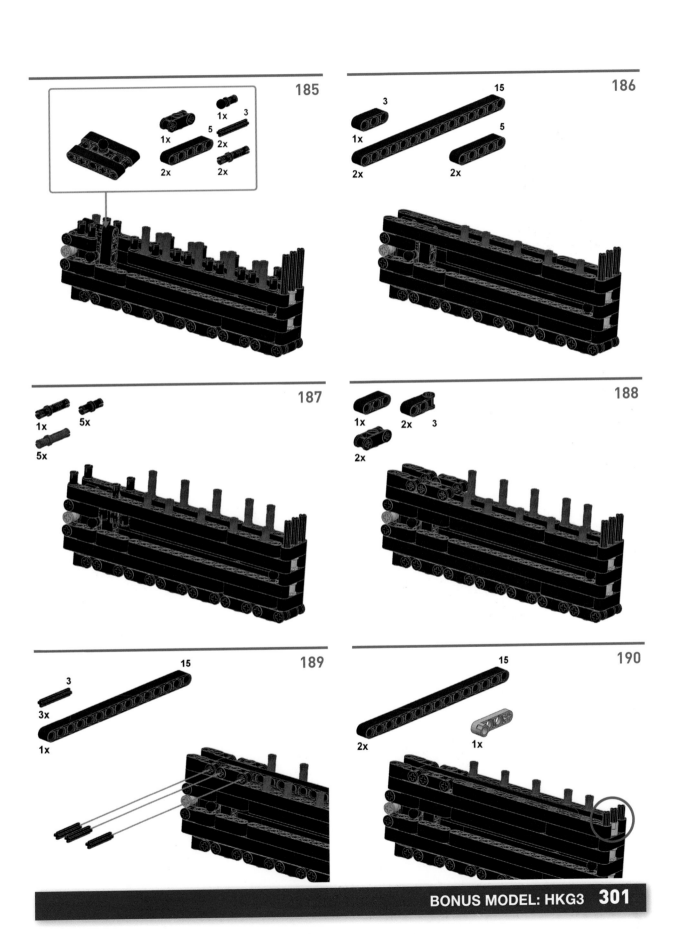

185

186

187

188

189

190

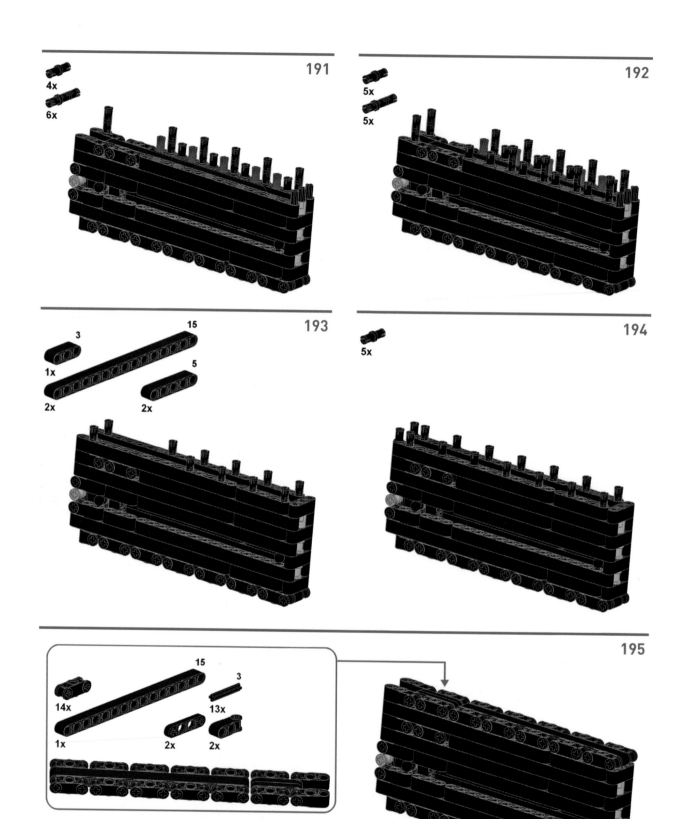

191

4x
6x

192

5x
5x

193

3
1x
15
2x
5
2x

194

5x

195

15
3
14x
13x
1x
2x
2x

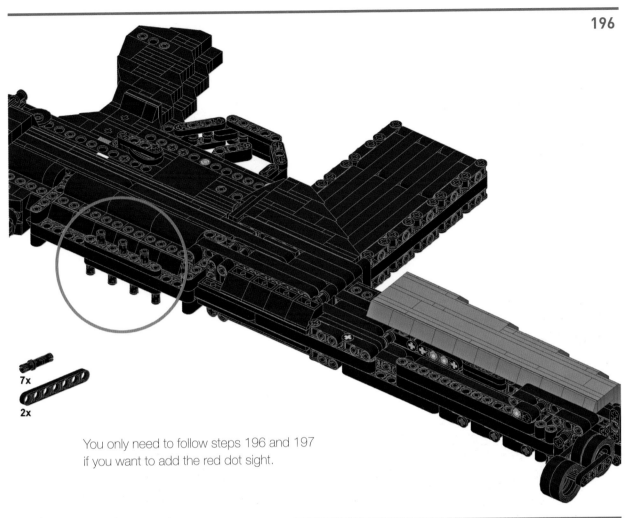

You only need to follow steps 196 and 197
if you want to add the red dot sight.

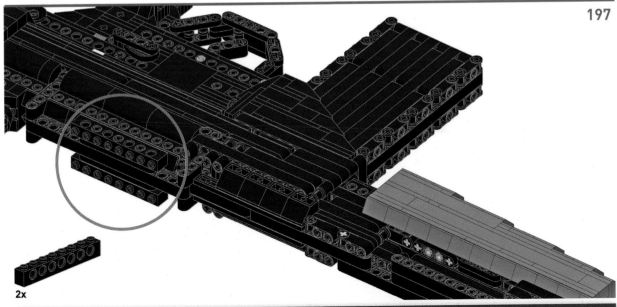

# RED DOT SIGHT

**1**

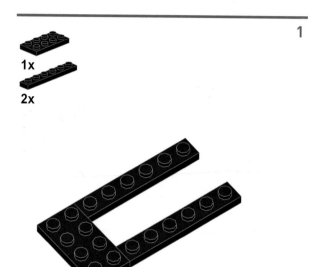

1x
2x

**2**

1x    3x    2x

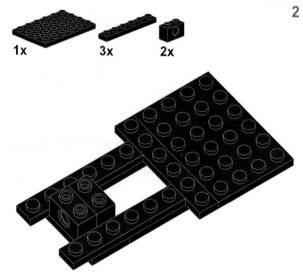

**3**

1x    5
1x

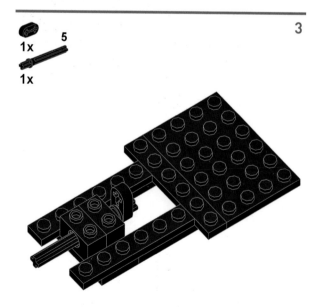

**4**

1x
2x    1x

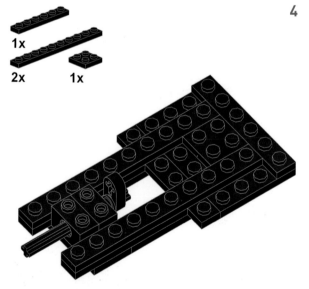

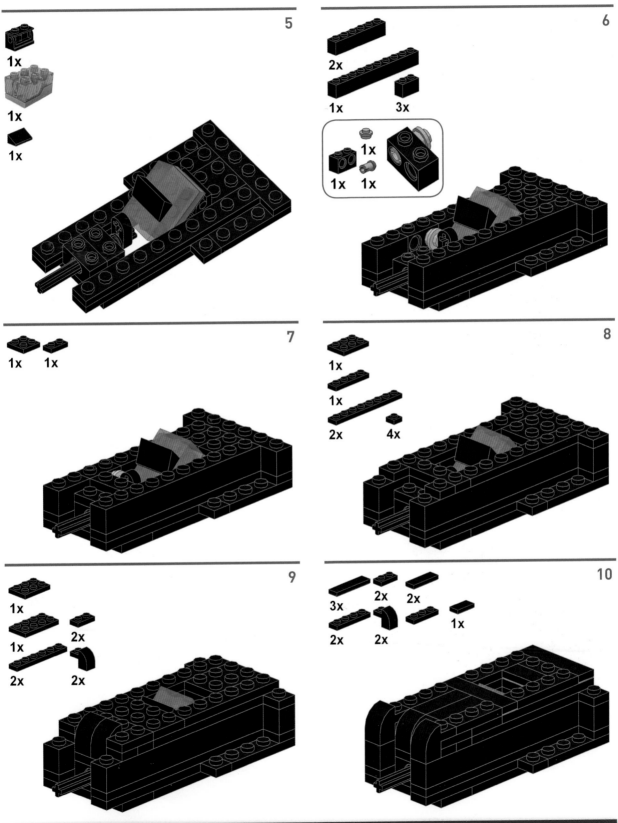

5

1x
1x
1x

6

2x
1x    3x

1x
1x    1x

7

1x    1x

8

1x
1x
2x    4x

9

1x
1x    2x
2x    2x

10

3x    2x    2x
2x    2x    1x

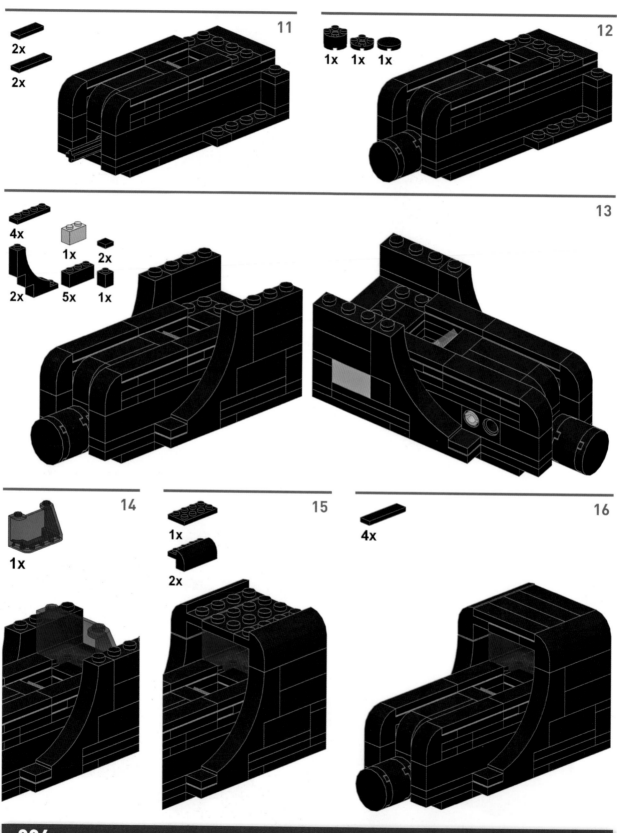

**11** 2x 2x

**12** 1x 1x 1x

**13** 4x 1x 2x 2x 5x 1x

**14** 1x

**15** 1x 2x

**16** 4x

# HOW IT'S LOADED

Fill the magazine with projectiles.

It's easier to insert the mag slightly angled.

Push the safety lever to firing position (red).

Pull the charging handle 90° to the side.

Pull the handle all the way back to
cock the launching mechanism.

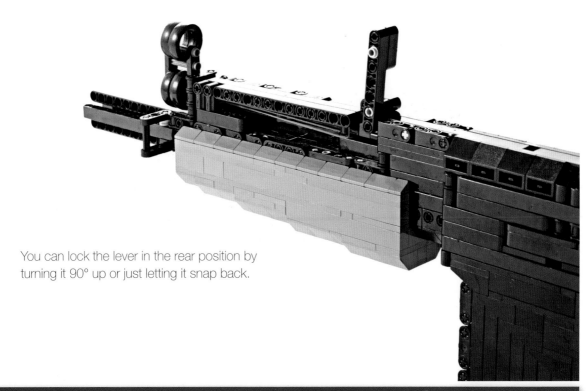

You can lock the lever in the rear position by
turning it 90° up or just letting it snap back.

Activate the reflex sight by turning it to the left while pushing it forward at the same time.

To extract the stock, push the locking lever.

Then pull the shaft all the way back.

To retract the stock, pull the locking lever and push the stock forward.

# TIPS

## Modding tip: fixed stock

# BRICKLINK

## How to Get Parts: BrickLink

Before you start reading, please note that shortly before this book was printed, BrickLink changed its ownership. The new guy in charge announced many improvements, so as of when you read this, a lot of things may have changed.

Getting the pieces is a hurdle to overcome. Since the year 2000, there has been only one acceptable place on the internet to buy LEGO parts: BrickLink.com. BrickLink offers every LEGO part ever created—in gigantic numbers. As I write this, BrickLink lists nearly 250 million LEGO items. It is a marketplace, which means that it is similar to eBay; BrickLink doesn't sell anything, but rather, the site provides the shopping platform for more than 7,000 different stores and charges them a 3% fee for each purchase. Because there are so many stores and they all offer more or less the same products, there is a hard price competition between them, which allows individuals to purchase LEGO parts for surprisingly low prices—it is much more expensive to buy a LEGO set than it is to order the respective parts from BrickLink. That's the reason why BrickLink sellers would rather sell a well-preserved LEGO set than rip it apart into individual parts. BrickLink not only offers LEGO parts, but also LEGO sets, LEGO instruction books, old LEGO catalogs, all kind of LEGO merchandising, and even empty LEGO set boxes.

The BrickLink sellers do a great and important job for the LEGO community. They are real idealists who have earned my highest respect. They comb the internet, classifieds, garage sales, flea markets, and attics for LEGO parts, clean them, sort them, store them, list them at BrickLink, and manage the orders. These are super time-consuming jobs and the sellers only get pocket change for them. In Germany, we have about 400 BrickLink stores—not even a handful of their workers can make a living off of it. Some of the more profitable BrickLink stores specialize in a particular sort of item, like Minifigs. Others even produce their own parts, like "chrome bricks," which are ordinary LEGO parts, but are chrome-plated by the seller.

The good news is that getting parts is possible and not too expensive. The bad news: It's not easy. BrickLink is an old-fashioned Web 1.0 page, created in 2000. The shop system has not been notably updated since 2003. At that time, the internet was still a place for idealists and pioneers, just like BrickLink founder Daniel Jezek. Being a computer genius, he programmed the site entirely on his own, and he implemented tons of features. The problem is that the unnecessary things have never been removed and the good things haven't been developed. Necessary features like a comfortable search function are missing. One of the reasons why BrickLink hasn't been modernized for so long is that Daniel Jezek died in 2010. With all that in mind, it's astonishing that this site, which is only kept alive by Jezek's family, is still growing and becoming more and more important. For example, as of April 2009 there were 167 BrickLink sellers in Germany, 20 of them with a stock of more than 100,000 parts. In summer 2013 there were 372 sellers, with 43 of them offering more than 100,000 parts. Also, the BrickLink parts catalog still gets updated regularly. The last I heard, BrickLink had been sold to a business man named Jung-Ju Kim, who will surely renew the page in the near future.

Using that ancient BrickLink front-end has sometimes brought me to the edge of despair. But we must not forget that BrickLink, because it is still the #1 LEGO parts shopping site, also features a big advantage: the lowest possible prices. Now imagine if BrickLink would, in a way similar to that of Amazon Marketplace, deal with encashment, have a state-of-the-art shop system, and take care of non-paying buyers, and so on. Then, with every purchase, you would not only be paying for the LEGO pieces, but also the accompanying lawyers, programmers, and credit institutes. . . . Do we really want that?

Trust me, the feeling of not being bound to LEGO sets anymore, the feeling that you can get every part you want, is just marvelous. So learn to use it, and BrickLink will provide you with unlimited possibilities!

## Registering

Registering is not only needed for placing orders; there are additional advantages to being logged in while browsing the site. That's because BrickLink's stock search settings are quite inconvenient and can only be permanently changed when logged in.

- Open http://www.BrickLink.com.
- Click on "Register" in the upper right screen corner.

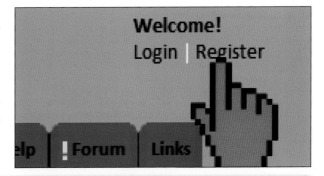

- Choose "New Member Registration."

- Select your country (it's important to choose the right one).
- Fill out the registration form correctly (it's pretty straightforward).

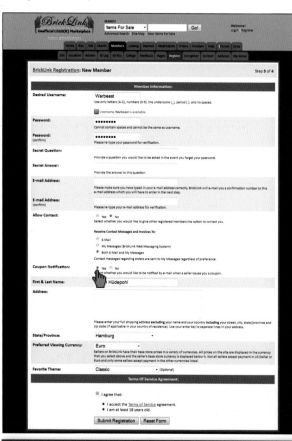

- Enter the registration code that has been sent to your email address.

# Customize Your Settings

It's incredible how significantly the shop system can be personalized. In my opinion, less would be more here. We only want to buy LEGO parts, not configure the background color! But it pays off to look through the settings. Some things can really be improved there.

- Click on the "MyBrickLink" tab.
- Click on "My Settings."

Here you will see 11 icons, linking to the several settings pages:

## My Action Items Settings

These settings relate to the page you see when you click on the "MyBrickLink" tab. There is a box headlined "My Action Items." That box notifies you when you have unread messages in your inbox, unpaid orders pending, sellers awaiting feedback, and so on. As a default, all notifications are activated. Leave that so.

## My Catalog Settings

What exactly is the "Catalog"? The BrickLink catalog is a cool thing, because every single LEGO part ever produced is listed there. I personally use the Catalog mainly to check in which colors a specific LEGO part is available. All parts in this book have colors, which they are actually available in.

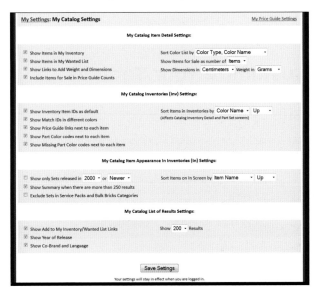

I recommend activating every checkbox, except for "Show only Sets released in . . ." and "Exclude Sets in Service Packs and Bulk Bricks Categories." Here, more information is better. The "Show Items for Sale as number of [. . .]" option should be "Items"—I think that's by far the most interesting information. Also, you should determine if you want your measurements in inches or centimeters and your weights in ounces or grams. Most importantly,

change "Show [. . .] Results" to the maximum number, which is 200. This delivers you the maximum amount of results and you don't have to extensively browse through the search results any more.

Don't forget to press "Save Settings" on the bottom of the page.

## My Chat Settings

This menu doesn't work anymore—forget it.

## My Contact Settings

The default settings are okay. I would just change the "Coupon Notification" to "Yes." You want to be notified when you receive a coupon, right?

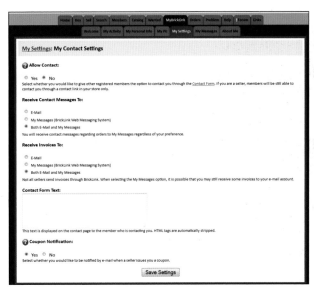

## My Discussion Forum Settings

Not interesting for somebody who just wants parts.

## My Feedback Settings

Only one checkbox is here: "Show Country Flags in Feedback Profiles." Nobody needs this and it doesn't work anyway.

# My Orders Settings

This relates to the page that you see when you click on the "Orders" tab. Every checkbox should be activated, including "Show 'Submit Changes' button also on top of page." Useful. Also, click on the "Orders Placed Columns" button on the upper right corner and activate all checkboxes here. Information is the key to everything.

## My Price Guide Settings

The Price Guide is a tool for price comparison. What is the highest and lowest price for an item? The Price Guide is more a tool for sellers, so leave the settings as they are.

# My Search Settings

Activate every checkbox here. All options are useful. Most importantly, change the "Show [. . .] Results Per Page" from 25 to 500. It's tedious to page through the search results, especially when there are only 25 results per page. Google knew that when they changed Google Images from "standard pagination" to "infinite scrolling" some years ago. The default number of only 25 search results per page was programmed in a time of slow internet connections. Don't forget to press "Save Settings"!

# My Store Shopping Settings

This affects the behavior of the site when you browse a store. Change "Lots Per Page" to 100 and activate "Show Weight in Shopping Cart." Press "Save Settings."

## My Wanted List Settings

The idea behind the Wanted List is this: You enter a LEGO product (part, set, book, gear, or catalog) and you get an email notification when this product gets listed. To be honest, you won't need that feature, except if you search for an extremely rare LEGO set. The Wanted List can also serve as a shopping list, but then you should urgently uncheck the "E-Mail Me Wanted Notifications [. . .]," unless you want to get 100 emails from BrickLink a day. Forget the option "Indicate My Favorite Stores." You won't have favorite stores. Your favorite store is the cheapest store that has the parts you need. A useful option is "Sort Stores in My Country on Top." Check that when you want to save shipping fees and prevent customs troubles. Also check the last two boxes regarding the coupons. Some sellers credit you with coupons as an excuse for delayed shipments or as reward for large orders—this seldom happens. Press "Save Settings," then click on "My Default Add Wanted Item Options" on the upper right corner.

Click "Not Checked," check "Default Item Type on Wanted Add screen to:", and choose "Parts" from the dropdown menu. Also check "If Save Form Values option is checked, keep option checked when page is reloaded." Press "Save Settings."

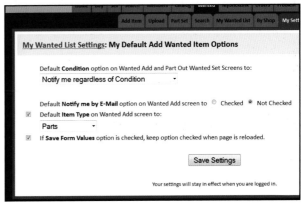

# How to Order Parts

- Write a list with all parts you need, with amounts, part numbers, and colors.
- Log in to BrickLink.
- Pick the item you will probably pay the most for (that means large parts in high numbers).
- Enter the color and part number in the search bar on top of the page. "Red 3001" will deliver results, "3001 red" won't. Also, "gray 3001" and "dark bluish gray" won't deliver results. I know what you're thinking: "WTF???" Right. As I write this, BrickLink is still full of these bugs. So if you are looking for a part in an extravagant color, such as "light gray" or "trans red," (that means in a color that consists of more than one word), do the following: In the dropdown menu left to the search bar (where "Items for Sale" is normally selected), select "Catalog Items." Then enter the parts number into the search bar, without color. Press enter and the next page will show a list with all colors this part is available in. Pick the color you want from the "Items For Sale" list on the left. Another method to find these parts is to click "Advanced Search."

Here you can enter the part number into the "Keyword" input field and choose the color from the " --- All Colors --- " dropdown menu.

- What you now will see is a list with sellers that offer this part, sorted by ascending price.

When you click on "Show More Filter Options," you can filter the search by country. This makes sense for saving customs and shipping costs. Only recommended when you're living in a big country with many BrickLink sellers, like the US, Netherlands, UK, France, Australia, and Germany.

- When you need a large amount of this part—for example, 68 pieces of part #32278 (TECHNIC beam 15, black) for the Dinosaur Superior—you can sort the search results by "Highest Qty."

- Pick the seller that offers the quantity you need for the best price and click "Go Buy It."
- Enter the number of parts you need at "Add to Cart."

- Click "Add Selected Items to Shopping Cart."

- On the left side of the screen you now see the text "Cart: [. . .] Items in one Lot, US$ [. . .]." Above this are the buttons "View Cart," "Empty Cart," and "Checkout." To place the order, click on "Checkout."

- But before you do this, first search the shop for other items you need. You can use the "Search Store:" search bar for this. Unlike the main search bar, this shop-specific search bar will even accept more elaborate search terms like "light gray 3001" or "blue technic brick."

Another method to search the shop for parts is to browse through the "Parts Categories" on the left side of the screen. I prefer this method because I always discover new and exciting LEGO parts there that I just must possess. There are 195 categories, but the models in this book just use parts from the categories found in this illustration:

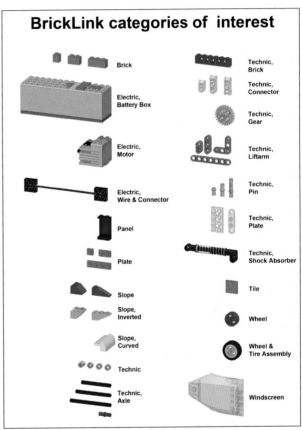

**BrickLink categories of interest**

Brick

Electric, Battery Box

Electric, Motor

Electric, Wire & Connector

Panel

Plate

Slope

Slope, Inverted

Slope, Curved

Technic

Technic, Axle

Technic, Brick

Technic, Connector

Technic, Gear

Technic, Liftarm

Technic, Pin

Technic, Plate

Technic, Shock Absorber

Tile

Wheel

Wheel & Tire Assembly

Windscreen

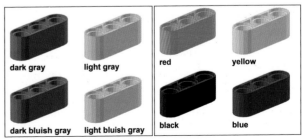

dark gray

light gray

red

yellow

dark bluish gray

light bluish gray

black

blue

- When you have placed your order, you will receive an order confirmation from the BrickLink system to your email address, and after a few days (sometimes weeks), the invoice follows. The invoice comes directly from the seller and contains all payment information you need. After the seller gets his money, he will assemble your order and ship it to you.

## Store Policies

And now begins the difficult chapter of the store policies. Store policies are left completely to the sellers. That means every store's policies are different. . . .

### Shipment fees

Some ship worldwide; some ship only within their state; some sellers don't ship to one or two specific countries. The shipment costs differ greatly from one other. And of course, every seller ships with the package service of his choice.

### Shipping time

Varies extremely. Dealing with BrickLink orders is a time-consuming job. Most BrickLink sellers are hobbyists; many of them only have time on the weekends. Sometimes it takes 3 days after payment to get your parts, sometimes it takes 6 weeks. And sometimes, you never get your order. That can happen when you order from very small shops (that offer only 200 items or so), which have already been forgotten by their owners. Only use safe payment methods, such as PayPal, when the shop seems less than reputable. To Hong Kong, as many BrickLink sellers point out, shipments will always take 2–3 months to arrive. The Chinese customs there seem to cause many delays.

### Payment methods

Again, something that's different for every seller. Some sellers offer a dozen payment methods, others only one. Some charge no markup for PayPal usage, others charge 5%, others $1, and some don't offer any PayPal option at all.

### Minimum order values

Most shops, not all, have a minimum order value, typically of US $5, $10, or $20. You will be warned when you go to check out and your shopping cart is not filled enough.

### Exchange rates

Assume you live in the Unites States and you just heard that the Euro crashed. Yes, that's the right time to buy cheap LEGO parts from the EU! When I wrote my last book, *Badass Lego Guns*, the BrickLink sellers usually used a fixed exchange rate, like €1 = US$1.2, which preferred the dollar. This resulted in EU citizens also wanting to pay in dollars, thinking that would save them money. But of course, the European BrickLink sellers ignored that and billed them in Euros anyways. That again frustrated the buyers and led to many disputes. Today, the sellers use the real exchange rate, so luckily, these disputes are avoided. Just use the currency you're used to.

### Lot minimum

One day, I received a BrickLink Invoice of €120 for a €90 order. The €30 difference was listed as "additional costs." What the heck?! What happened was that this seller offered hundreds of beautiful cockpit elements that I wanted to have, and I ordered only one of each part. The problem: I bought from one of the few sellers that charge a "lot fee." The idea behind this: It takes a seller much more time to pick out 1,000 items from 1,000 different boxes than to pick 1,000 of the same item from just one box (e.g., TECHNIC pins). For this extra work, the seller wants extra money. This is what he says about it in his "Store Terms":

*Your order should have an average lot value of at least €2.00. You derive the number by dividing your order total by the number of positions you have. (100 black 1 x 1 bricks are merely one lot).*

*Otherwise you still place the order for free!*

*If not, a small fee of €0.59 per surplus lot is added. Example 1: an order with an order total of €20 and 10 lots does not include ANY FEE. Example 2: an order with an order total of €20 and 20 lots effects an additional fee of €5.90. Thank you very much for your appreciation.*

So checking the store policy before ordering is never a bad idea!

## Customs

For BrickLink buyers within the EU and the USA, customs are not such a big problem. The Euro and US dollar currency zones have enough BrickLink sellers, so most stuff can be bought locally there. Also, customs and import sales taxes are no problems for small orders. Germany, for example, doesn't charge customs and import sales taxes for private-to-private shipments up to €45. The limit for commercial-to-private shipments is still at €22. (Some BrickLink sellers are private, others are commercial. Commercial sellers will always display their tax number on their shop site.) In Germany, if customs actually retains your order, you need to personally fetch the shipment from the customs station and pay import sales taxes in cash, which are 19% of the value of shipment. If we actually get the EU-USA free trade agreement in the next few years, things will hopefully be a lot easier.

# The Wanted List—A Cool Idea, Poorly Executed

The Wanted List was introduced at a time when BrickLink was still small and not all LEGO products were available in acceptable numbers. So they created a "Wanted List," where you can write down all your LEGO wishes. When they become available, BrickLink sends you an email: "Seller X now offers LEGO product Y from your Wanted List." Now, in 2015, BrickLink has a gigantic stock of nearly 250 million items. You need a part? You get it. This Wanted List email notification has become pretty useless. If you forget to deactivate it and still make an entry into your Wanted List, it will only result in spam.

But there is another purpose for the Wanted List: Imagine you search BrickLink for "Dinosaur Superior," then click on "buy parts." The system seeks the cheapest sellers, places the orders, and deals with the payments, and the next week, you get LEGO shipments from all over the world—all that's left for you to do is to unpack the stuff and assemble the model.

That's exactly what the Wanted List does—not. But if it had been developed in the last 10 years, it would surely work like this. What it *can* do is find sellers whose goods best match your Wanted List. For small models like the Hitman, you will even find sellers that offer all the parts. But for big models like the Dinosaur, you have to buy from many different stores. This is something the Wanted List doesn't support. After placing the first order, you would have to manually delete every position already bought from the Wanted List, and then let the system find the next best matching seller, and so on. Trust me, that process is nasty for somebody who expects BrickLink to be a LEGO-Amazon. But nevertheless, here follows a little Wanted List manual for you:

## Adding items

There are several ways of adding items to your Wanted List. The most common one is to regulary search for an item as described in the section "How to Order Parts" on page 312, and then click on "Add to Wanted List."

The second one is to use the "Add Item" form.

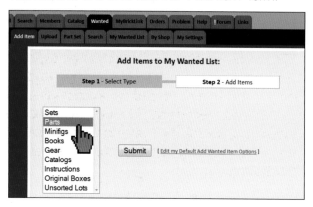

For this, click on the "Wanted" tab, choose "Parts," and click "Submit."

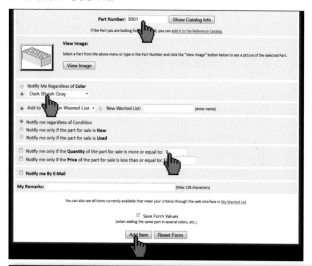

At "Part Number:" enter the part number. At "--- Select Color ---" select a color. Into the input field next to "Notify me only if the Quantity of the part for sale is more or equal to:" enter the number of parts you need. Ignore the irritating "notify" stuff; nobody needs that. The next step is to click "Add Item." Repeat this with all parts you need.

## Finding the right shop

When you're done, click on the tab "By Shop."

This page displays the sellers that match your Wanted List the best. In the "Lots (Unique)" column, the number in brackets is what you want to focus on. It indicates the number of lots on your Wanted List that the shop has actually in stock.

## Ordering

Click on one of the sellers with the highest numbers in brackets. The page will display a list with all the items from your Wanted List the seller can offer you. Clicking on "Auto-Fill Cart Min" will automatically fill out the "Add to Cart" input fields.

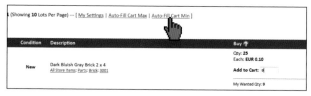

Then click "Add Selected Items to Shopping Cart" and proceed with your order as already described.

If the seller did not have all parts on your Wanted List available:

- Click on the BrickLink Logo on the upper left of the screen.
- Click on the "Wanted" tab.
- Click on "My Wanted List." Here you need to click on the categories, where you should delete all items that you've just ordered.
- Now click on the "By Shop" tab again and repeat the process until you have ordered all parts you needed.

# BrickLink FAQ

## What is a "lot"?

A lot is a group of items of the same shape and same color. If you have 100 red 3001 bricks in your cart, you have 100 positions in one lot. If you have 50 red 3001s and 50 blue 3001s in your cart, you have 100 positions in two lots.

## What is a bulk lot?

You recognize a bulk lot by the marker "(x50)" or "(x100)" or another "(x . . . )" next to its "Qty:.." "Qty: 1,000 (x250)" means the seller has a thousand pieces of this item in stock and wants you to buy it in multiples of 250. In other words, you can only order this part in quantities of 250, 500, 750 or 1,000.

| | |
|---|---|
| **chnic, Pin Long with Friction Ridges Lengthwise**<br>r Sale: Parts: Technic, Pin: 6558<br>nd, Min Buy: ~EUR 7.00 | 🔲 🖥 BRICKLAND.PL (1945) 🔲<br>Qty: **5,111** (x10)<br>Each: **~EUR 0.03**<br>(PLN 0.14)<br>**Go Buy It**<br><br>Catalog Entry \| Add to My Wanted List |

## What is a super lot?

There are LEGO parts that just don't make sense without a specific other LEGO part: e.g., window frame and window glass, the two sides of a hinge, or tire and wheel. These pairs of parts can sometimes be found grouped together in super lots.

| | | |
|---|---|---|
| 3830c01 (Inv) | **Hinge Brick 1 x 4 Swivel - Complete Assembly**<br>Catalog: Parts: Hinge |  |

## What is tiered pricing?

This item is on sale. The original price is crossed out and shown in grey color. The seller has also offered additional discounts to be applied to the cost of the item, depending on the quantity you buy.

🔲 🖥 All CZECH SHOP 70% SALE (547) 🔲
Qty: **18,319**
Each: **~EUR 0.03**
(CZK 0.8316)
Original Price: ~~CZK 0.99~~

Buy **200** or more for **~EUR 0.03** each
(CZK 0.7476)
Buy **500** or more for **~EUR 0.03** each
(CZK 0.6636)
Buy **1,200** or more for **~EUR 0.02** each
(CZK 0.4956)
**Go Buy It**

## What is a liftarm?

There is a disagreement about the correct name for these studless TECHNIC bricks that were first introduced in 1999 and became so important. LDraw.org calls them "Technic Beams," and BrickLink calls them "Liftarms." Ulrik Pilegaard, a former LEGO employee and LEGO book author, explains, "The liftarms are the smaller ones, i.e., a 3-stud-liftarm or a 3x3 lift-arm. I would call all bricks that are 5 [studs] and over beams." However, since we are discussing BrickLink, I will refer to them as liftarms here. Lift arm—funny name for such an extremely versatile part.

## What does "bush" mean?

This is the name for the little gray shims that you can put onto a TECHNIC axle.

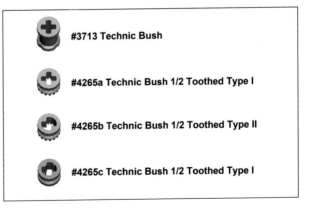

#3713 Technic Bush

#4265a Technic Bush 1/2 Toothed Type I

#4265b Technic Bush 1/2 Toothed Type II

#4265c Technic Bush 1/2 Toothed Type I

## What do the numbers next to a store name mean?

The number that appears next to each store name is how many parts that particular seller has in stock. The higher the number, the higher your chance of getting all the parts you need there. Also, large stores seem to be more reliable and ship faster than small ones. On the other hand, smaller stores often have better prices.

| | |
|---|---|
| KeeZor's shelf | 14 |
| Kerteminde | 2 |
| Klodsbutikken | 1 |
| klodsland.dk | 7,434 |
| KLODSMAJOR | 50 |
| Larsen Bricks | 5,131 |
| legetoys.dk | 814 |
| LeigoLars | 2,579 |
| Lerskov | 5,509 |
| Mini Part Store | 667 |
| Mix Your Bricks | 3,435 |
| MY OWN STORE | 26 |
| Nick's Toy Box | 14 |
| Nico´s Bricks and Sets | 444 |

## What is a pin with "friction ridges"?

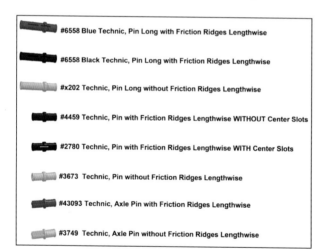

Friction ridges are little bumps on the surface of a TECHNIC pin, which make it sit tight inside an axle hole. There are three main types of pins: normal pins, axle pins, and long pins. The gray variants of these pins are the ones without friction ridges. When put into a pinhole, the pin can be turned easily and hence be used as an axle. Pins of colors other than gray (blue, black, etc.) have friction ridges. They are not as useful as axles, but they make much stiffer connections than the gray ones.

## Why is the black long TECHNIC pin so extremely expensive?

The part I use the most is #6558, the 3-studs-long TECHNIC pin, preferably in black. That's because:
- LEGO guns have often widths of 3 studs, because they typically frame a one-stud-wide barrel along their longitudal axis.
- Stability is important, especially for working LEGO TECHNIC models, so I always use as many pins as possible.
- These pins are only available in blue and black. While blue is a color with a certain tone only suitable to some designs, black is neutral, super versatile, and can be used for anything.

Now about the dilemma of the high price: Not only do I need the black long pin a lot . . . many people do! So the prices for this part increased in the last few years to what you would never expect 0.31 grams of plastic could be worth. Unfortunately, the LEGO company doesn't release very many sets with the black long pin anymore. They now prefer to produce the *blue* long TECHNIC pin. Why? The blue long TECHNIC pin is part of the color scheme of their extremely successful MINDSTORMS NXT series:

- Applications in orange
- Angled liftarms in dark bluish gray
- Connectors in light bluish gray
- Straight liftarms in very light bluish gray
- Pins in blue

These are the reasons why BrickLink currently offers 490,739 blue ones and only 63,791 black ones—an 8:1 ratio. As a result, a new blue 6558 costs US$0.05 on average, while a new black 6558 costs US$0.29 on average. The Dinosaur model needs 400 long pins. If you buy them for 29 cents per piece, you will be poor soon. So, here is my suggestion: If you buy parts, always look for the cheapest black 6558s first. I once ordered 1,000 pieces from a country that I had never heard of before, just because the seller was the cheapest. Or, if color doesn't matter to you, always use the blue variant.

## The part number seems incorrect. Why?

Sometimes, part numbers change. For example, the TECHNIC bushes once had the numbers 32123a, 32123b, 32123c, and now have the numbers 4265a, 4265b, 4265c. I don't know the exact reason for that, but the main problems seem to be:

1.      Small LEGO parts don't have their official number printed on them. LEGO doesn't publish those numbers, so the community has to find numbers themselves.

2.      There are not one, but two communities that classify LEGO parts: the BrickLink people, who photograph new parts and upload them to their catalog, and the LDRAW people, who make 3D models of new LEGO parts and integrate them into their database.

## Why does BrickLink look so weird?

Some browsers have problems displaying BrickLink correctly. Google Chrome, for example, hides important parts of the page when you zoom in slightly. BrickLink was made before browsers had the ability to zoom. So far, I've had the best experiences with Firefox.

# DESIGN EVOLUTION

## Hammerhead Sr

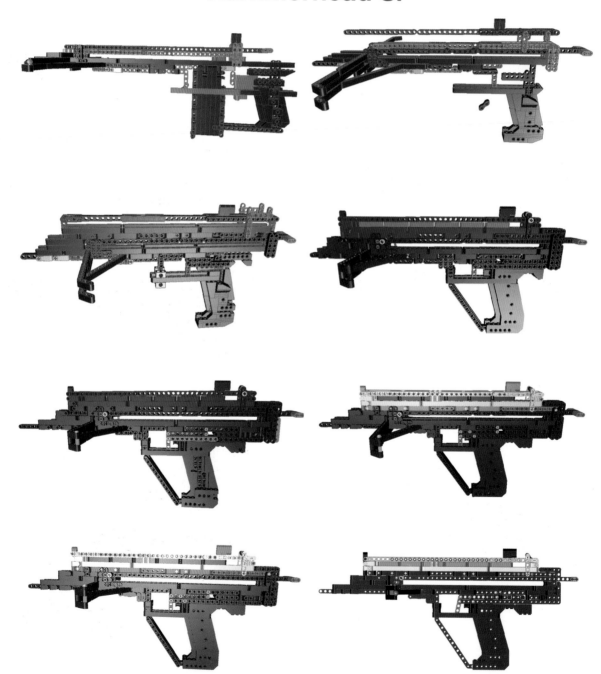

# Hammerhead Jr

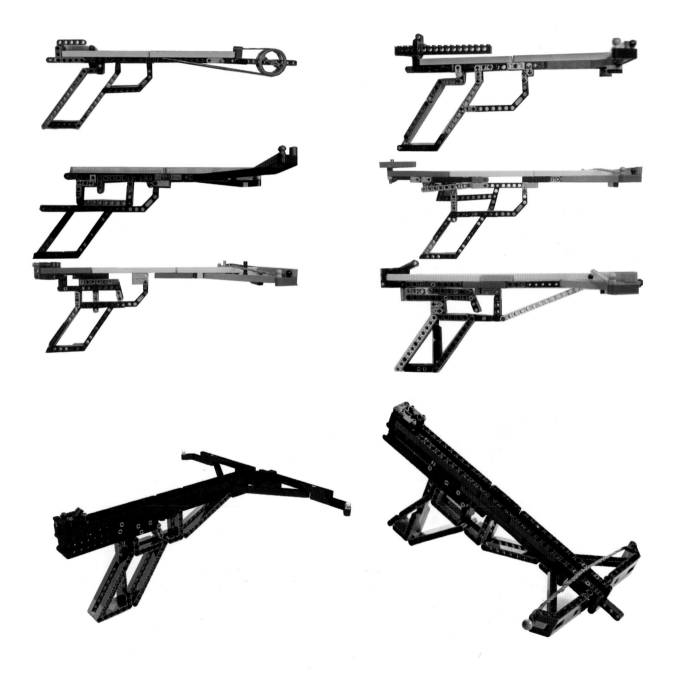

# Dinosaur Superior

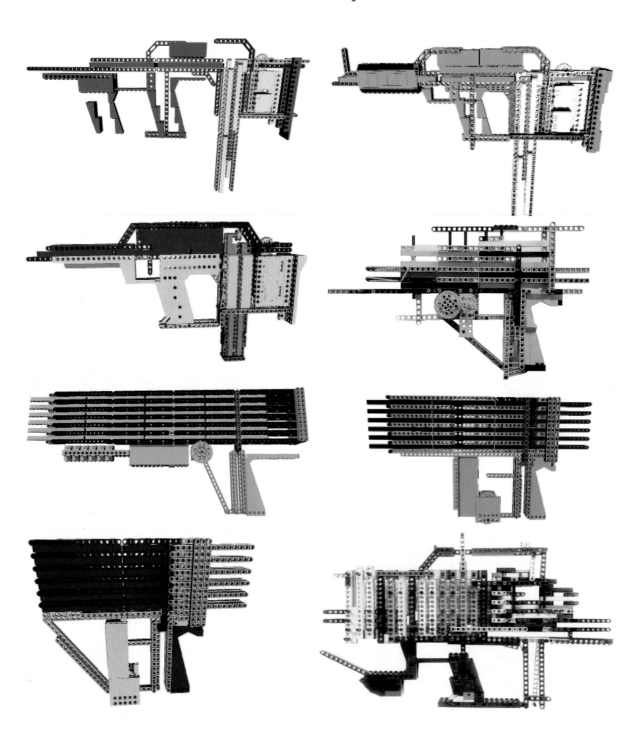

# Dinosaur Superior

# Dinosaur Superior

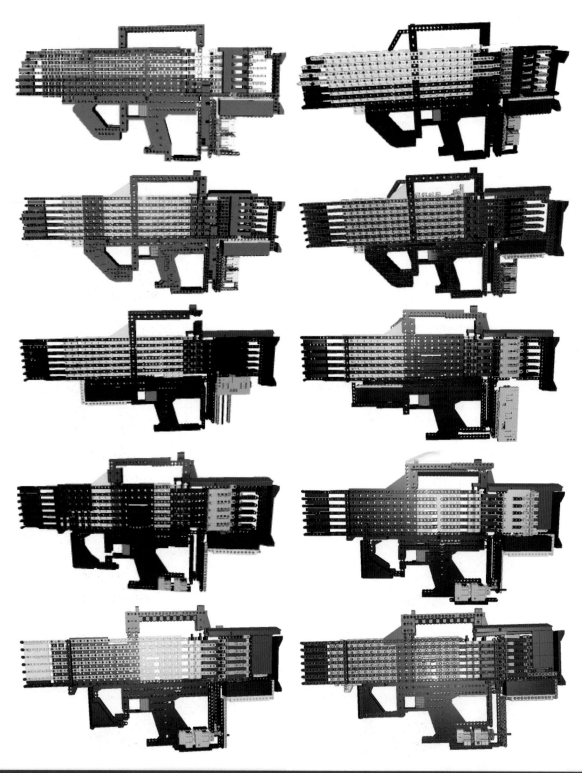

# Dinosaur Superior

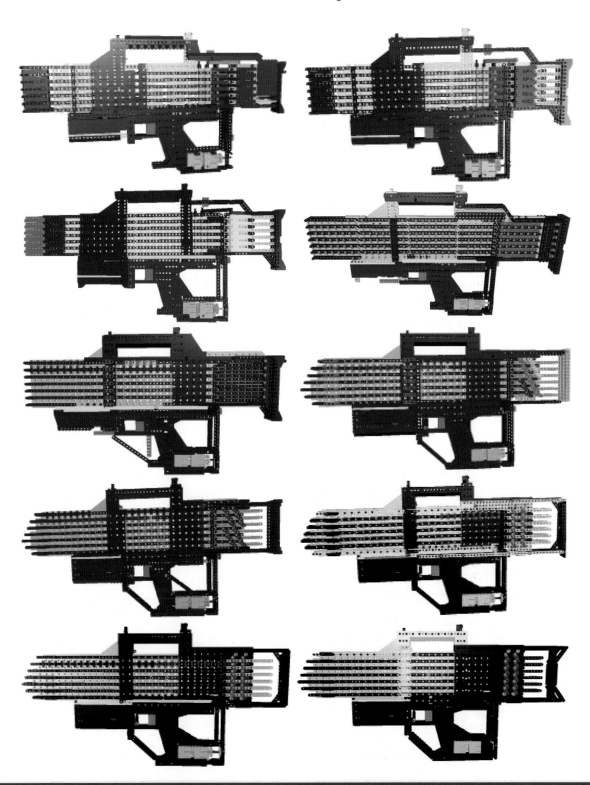

# Chinahook

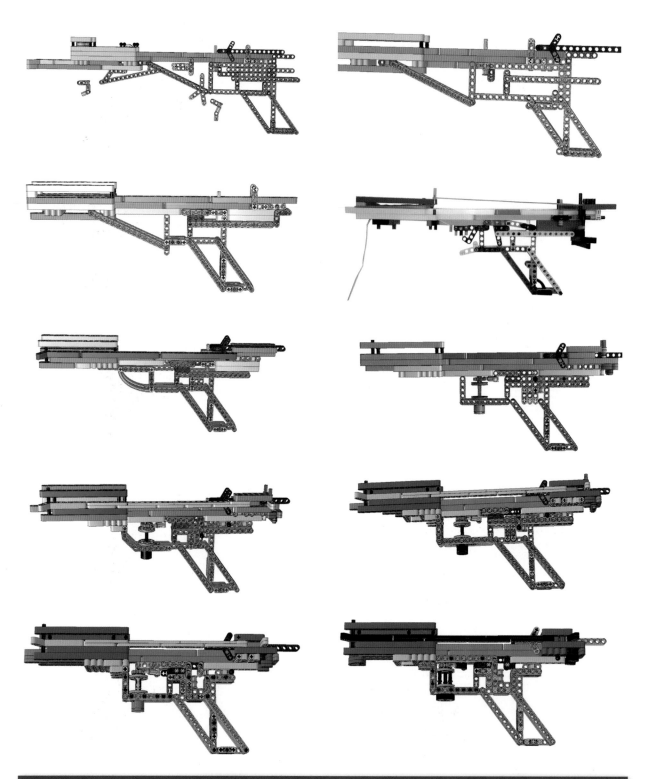

# Chinahook

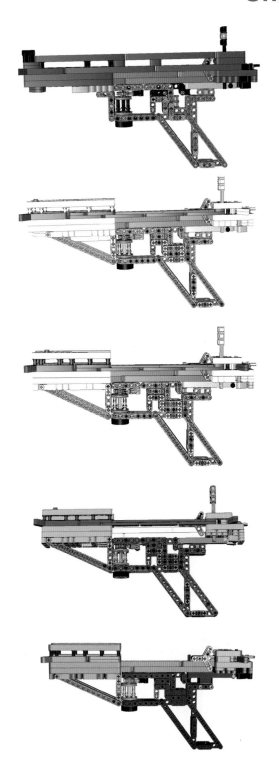
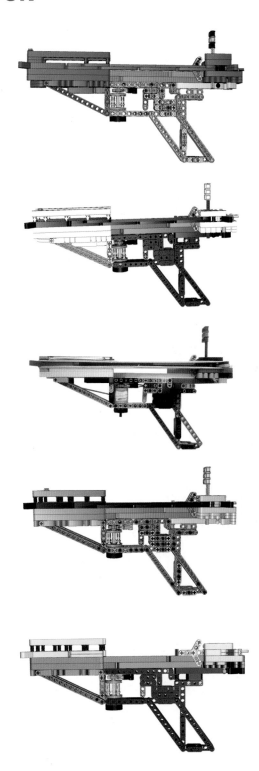

# Panzer Pod

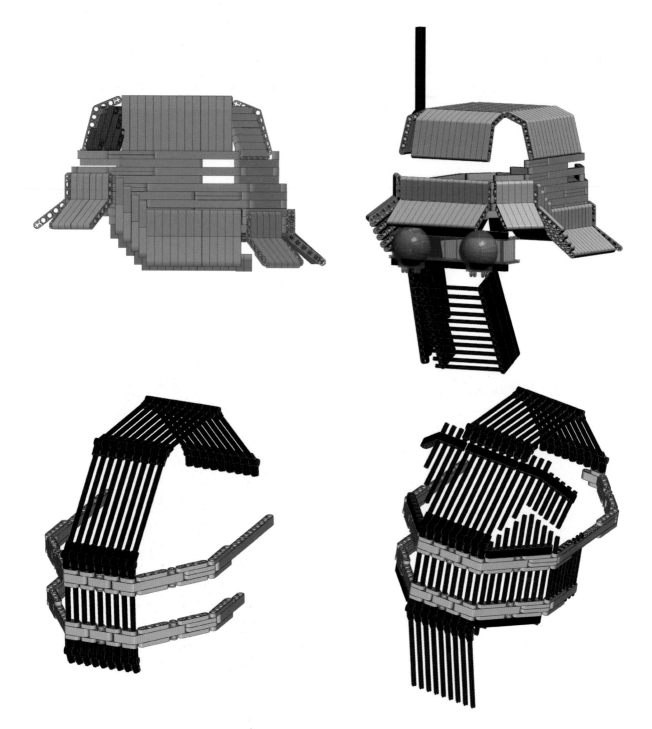

# Panzer Pod

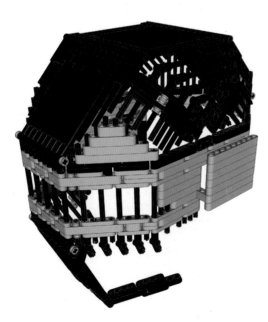

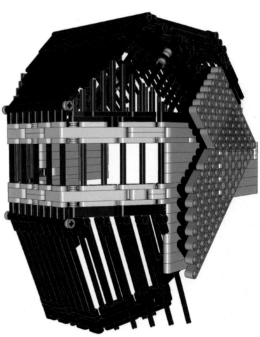

# Panzer Pod

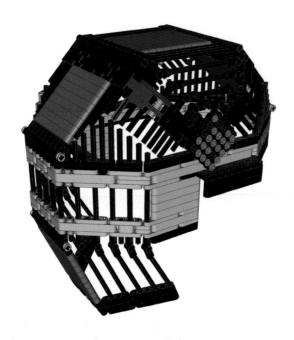
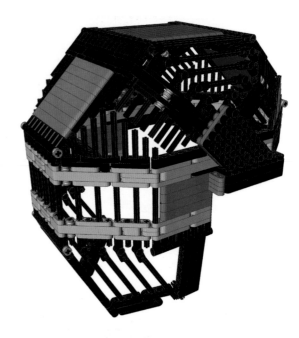
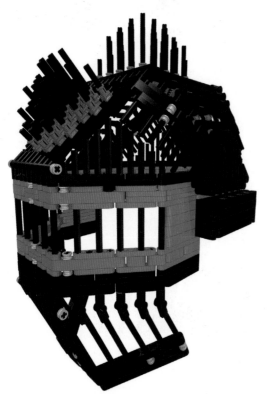
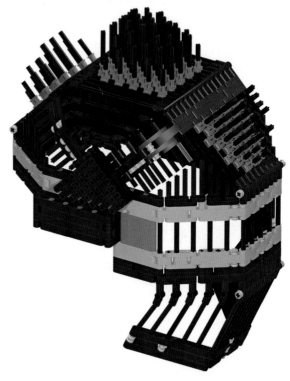

# Melody

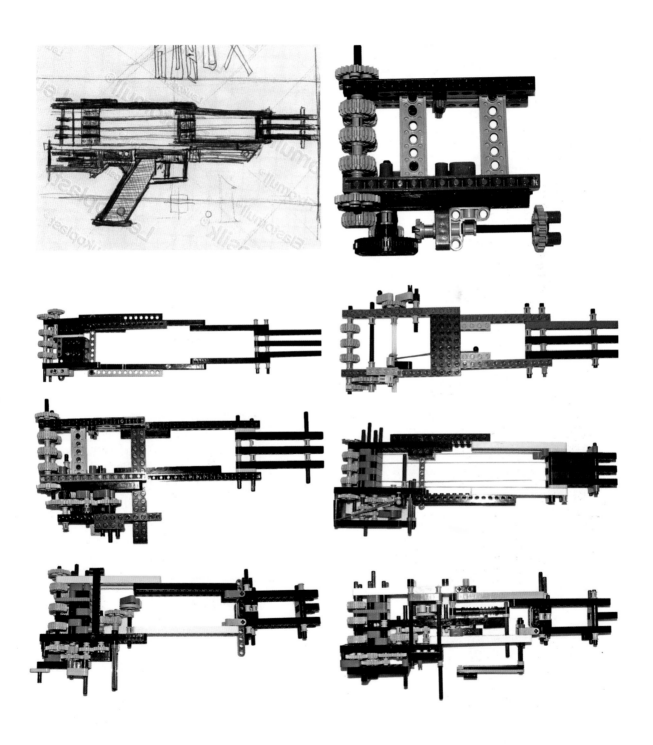

# Melody

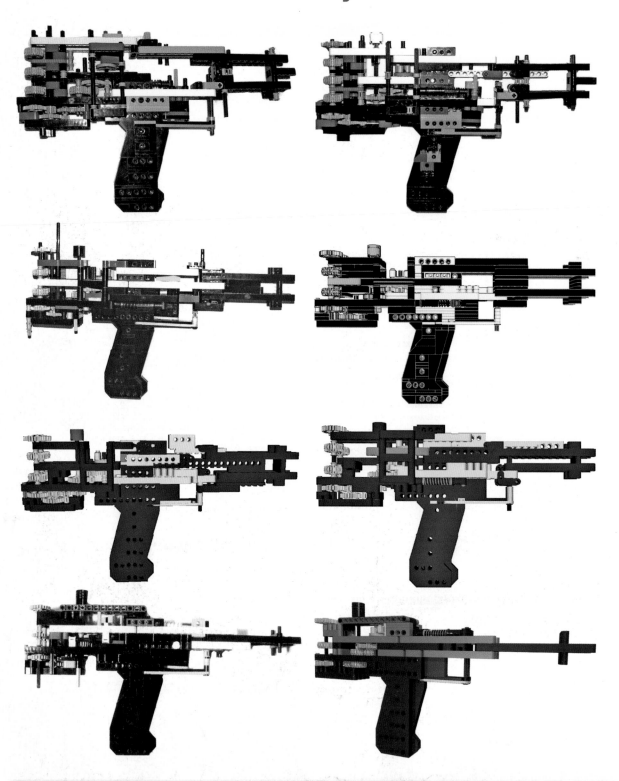